CW00403260

MasterClass in
English Education

Also available in the MasterClass Series

MasterClass in Drama Education, Michael Anderson

MasterClass in Music Education, edited by John Finney and Felicity Laurence

MasterClass in Religious Education, Liam Gearon

MasterClass in Mathematics Education, edited by Paul Andrews and Tim Rowland

Also available from Bloomsbury

Effective Teaching and Learning in Practice, Don Skinner

Conducting Research in Educational Contexts, Tehmina N. Basit

Inquiring in the Classroom: Asking the Questions that Matter about Teaching and Learning, edited by Nick Mitchell and Joanne Pearson

Educational Research and Inquiry: Qualitative and Quantitative Approaches, Dimitra Hartas

MasterClass in English Education

Transforming Teaching and Learning

Edited by Sue Brindley
and Bethan Marshall

MasterClass series
Series Editor – Sue Brindley

Bloomsbury Academic
An imprint of Bloomsbury Publishing Plc

B L O O M S B U R Y
LONDON • NEW DELHI • NEW YORK • SYDNEY

Bloomsbury Academic

An imprint of Bloomsbury Publishing Plc

50 Bedford Square
London
WC1B 3DP
UK

175 Fifth Avenue
New York
NY 10010
USA

www.bloomsbury.com

BLOOMSBURY and the Diana logo are trademarks of Bloomsbury Publishing Plc

First published 2015

© Sue Brindley, Bethan Marshall and Contributors, 2015

All rights reserved. No part of this publication may be reproduced or transmitted in any form or by any means, electronic or mechanical, including photocopying, recording, or any information storage or retrieval system, without prior permission in writing from the publishers.

Bethan Marshall (et al.) has asserted her right under the Copyright, Designs and Patents Act, 1988, to be identified as Author of this work.

No responsibility for loss caused to any individual or organization acting on or refraining from action as a result of the material in this publication can be accepted by Bloomsbury Academic or the author.

British Library Cataloguing-in-Publication Data
A catalogue record for this book is available from the British Library.

ISBN: HB: 978-1-4411-2906-2
PB: 978-1-4411-2996-3
ePub: 978-1-4411-9615-6
ePDF: 978-1-4411-5397-5

Library of Congress Cataloging-in-Publication Data
Masterclass in English Education : transforming teaching and learning / edited by Sue Brindley and Bethan Marshall.
pages cm. -- (MasterClass series.)
Includes bibliographical references and index.
ISBN 978-1-4411-2906-2 (hardback) -- ISBN 978-1-4411-2996-3 (paperback) 1. English language--Study and teaching.
2. Language arts. I. Brindley, Susan, 1951-
PE1065.M36 2015
428.0071--dc23
2014009297

Typeset by Fakenham Prepress Solutions, Fakenham, Norfolk NR21 8NN
Printed and bound in Great Britain

Contents

Notes on Contributors

Sue Brindley is Senior Lecturer in the Faculty of Education, University of Cambridge, UK, where she coordinates a blended learning Masters, Researching Practice, which focuses on developing teacher knowledge through teacher research, and which includes jointly taught modules with Shakespeare's Globe. She teaches and researches in English and in constructions of teacher knowledge, and coordinates a national teacher research network, CamStar. She taught English in north and east London, and has developed English teaching in both government policy and academic contexts.

Jane Coles is currently Lecturer at the Institute of Education, University of London, UK. Before moving into Higher Education, she taught English in London comprehensive schools for over 15 years. Her doctoral research explored ways in which Shakespeare has been constructed historically, culturally and pedagogically in the secondary school curriculum. She has written a number of articles about the teaching of Shakespeare and has edited three titles in the Cambridge Schools Shakespeare series.

Brenton Doecke is Professor in the School of Education at Deakin University, Australia. He has written extensively on English curriculum and pedagogy, including a co-authored book with Douglas McClenaghan, *Confronting Practice: Classroom investigations into language and learning* (Putney, NSW: Phoenix Education, 2011), and an edited collection of essays with Piet-Hein van de Ven, entitled *Literary Praxis: A conversational inquiry into the teaching of literature* (Rotterdam: Sense, 2011). He has been involved in many research projects in the field of English literacy education, most notably the development of Standards for Teachers of English Language and Literacy in Australia (STELLA).

Anton Franks is Associate Professor in Creative Arts and Education at the University of Nottingham, UK. Previously, he was a teacher of English and drama in London schools and then a teacher educator in English and drama at the Institute of Education, University of London. His publications include 'School drama and representations of war and terror ...' in *Research in Drama Education*, (2008), 13(1); 'Drama in teaching and learning, language and literacy', in *Routledge International Handbook of English, Language and Literacy Teaching*, Wyse et al. (eds), and 'Drama, desire and schooling' in *Changing English* 4(1).

Simon Gibbons began his career as a teacher of English, media and drama in an East London comprehensive school. After ten years working in London schools, ultimately as the Head of English in a large comprehensive, he moved, via a role as a Local Authority Consultant, into teacher education. He has recently taken up the post of Head of Department of Teacher Education at the University of Bedfordshire, following six years as a lecturer in English education at King's College London. Simon was the Chair of the National Association for the Teaching of English from 2011 to 2013.

Christine Hall is Professor of Education and Head of the School of Education at the University of Nottingham, UK. She teaches, writes and researches about the arts and creativity, children's reading and literacy development in schools.

Carl Hendrick is an English teacher and head of research at Wellington College. He is also completing a PhD at King's College London. He has taught for several years in both the state and independent sectors, where he has worked on several cross-sectoral collaborations. His areas of interest are Bakhtin, and the dialogism and the impact of technology in English.

John Keen is Senior Lecturer in Education at the University of Manchester, UK, Subject Leader for PGCE English and Project Director for The Process Writing Project. He has taught English in schools and colleges in the Northeast, London and the Northwest. He has written books and articles on teacher education, language study and the teaching of writing.

Ben Knights, a graduate of the Universities of Oxford and Cambridge, has taught at the Universities of Cambridge, Durham and Teesside, where he was head of English and Cultural Studies. From 2003 to 2011 he was Director of the national (HE Academy) English Subject Center, based at Royal Holloway, University of London, UK. His current research interests include masculinities in narrative and pedagogy, and the history of English Studies. He is currently writing a book entitled *Pedagogic Criticism: Reconfiguring University English Studies*. A National Teaching Fellow since 2001, he has recently been appointed as a Visiting Professor at the Institute of Education, University of London, UK.

Terry Locke is Professor of English Language Education at the University of Waikato, New Zealand. His research interests include the teaching of literature, teaching writing, constructions of English as a subject, action research in classroom settings and the relationship of literacy and technology. Recent books include *Critical Discourse Analysis* (2004), *Beyond the Grammar Wars* (2010) and *Developing Writing Teachers* (2014). He is coordinating editor of the journal English Teaching: Practise and Critique.

Bethan Marshall taught in secondary schools for nine years before starting at King's College London, UK. She has researched extensively in the English curriculum and its assessment. She has published widely on both including *English Teachers – The Unofficial Guide* and *Testing English*.

Douglas McClenaghan is an English and Literature teacher in a state secondary school in Melbourne, Australia. He is co-author of secondary English textbooks, chapters in academic texts and numerous articles in professional journals. He is a life member of the Victorian Association for the Teaching of English (VATE) and has served on the organization's Council as well as Publications and Curriculum Committees. He has presented numerous workshops at state, national and international conferences. He was also a participant in the research project that developed the Standards for Teachers of English Language and Literacy in Australia (STELLA).

Mark Reid has been Head of Education at the British Film Institute, UK, since 2006, where he looks after a range of education programs for schools, young people, local communities and the general public based at BFI Southbank in London. Before that he trained teachers for the BFI, having originally trained and worked as an English, Drama and Media teacher in the 1990s. He has been an active member of both the National Association for the Teaching of English, and the London Association for the Teaching of English, the editor of the journal *English in Education,* and an active researcher and practitioner in the role the moving image can play in English and wider literacy.

Michael Rosen is Professor of Children's Literature in the Educational Studies Department at Goldsmiths, University of London, UK. He is a former Children's Laureate (2007–09). He has published many children's books, most notably *We're Going on a Bear Hunt* (pictures by Helen Oxenbury), but his most recent book is for adults, *Alphabetical: How every letter tells a story*. He visits many schools, colleges, theaters and libraries, performing his poems.

Series Editor's Foreword

English teaching is, it would seem, perennially 'under discussion' if not 'under construction'. In some areas, the debates that surround English teaching have a longevity that can be traced back to Sampson's *English for the English* (1921). Others, established but still live, include the place of oracy and writing as genre or process. More recent debates include the place of film in teaching English, the role of dialogic teaching and whether technology has a place in English teaching.

In this book, we have taken some of these debates and explored them through both national and international perspectives, as we try to locate debates about English outside of a national agenda, and indeed outside of the usual 'language modes' approach. We have organized the book using familiar headings, but in so doing, we have also attempted to demonstrate the interrelationship of the language modes. Considering reading outside of writing, or writing without speaking and listening, is to fracture and fragment the cohesion of English. We invite readers to create different pathways through the book, and to make links across instead of only within the categories of Reading, Writing and Oracy, which were after all simply organization features used by the national curriculum – their reification to anything other than that is a questionable activity.

In proposing that English should be understood as 'across' as well as 'within' language modes, we also wanted to demonstrate that English is a dynamic subject. Its energies are located within its ability to change and accommodate new purposes, both from those who teach it and external bodies. The section The Making of English has a rich international contribution in order to demonstrate priorities that have been established, and the ways in which the significance of English travels far beyond the boundaries of countries.

In inviting you thus to create new pathways in thinking about English, our intention is to challenge the usual, and profile the possible. We hope you enjoy the journeys.

Sue Brindley
Senior Lecturer in Education
University of Cambridge, UK

Introduction

Bethan Marshall and Sue Brindley

We live, in the West, in a world that is standards-based. The introduction of Program for International Student Assessment (PISA) and Progress in International Reading Literacy Study (PIRLS) has made the desire to gauge where pupils are in standardized tests a key to many educational initiatives. And these have had a curious effect on the subject of English. It has meant that English, once seen as a holistic subject, has become compartmentalized into a series of definable skills.

In some ways this book has acceded to that desire to carve up the subject into its definable parts – speaking and listening, reading and writing. In doing so it has taken a particularly English view of how these skills might be defined. If we were Scottish, for example, we might define Speaking and Listening as Listening and Talking; Reading would be subdivided into Reading for Pleasure, Reading for Information and Reading to Appreciate the Writer's Craft; Writing would remain the same. Yet if we were in Australia we might look at writing and language conventions including spelling, grammar and punctuation. In fact it looks as though, at the primary stage in England, we might be adding grammar to our list of things that pupils will have to do – the new curriculum for the primary schools has grammar as a key part of the skills children must acquire to do the tests for eleven-year-olds.

Our book, then, is divided into those three areas – reading, writing and speaking and listening. Two sections are added to these – a brief look at what English might be and a conclusion – how we might assess the subject and what we think we might know about it. At first these areas seem uncontroversial. The reading section has, for example, a chapter on Shakespeare, the writing on grammar, the speaking and listening on dialog. But ours is not a book that allows for such neat classifications. Ours cannot be neatly standards-based organized.

To begin with we could have organized the chapters differently. We could, for example, have looked at the influences of new technology on the subject. The chapter on Shakespeare is called 'Teaching Shakespeare with Film Adaptations' and in part it examines the way pupils might learn to interpret versions of Shakespeare plays through watching filmic adaptations. Then there is 'Film, Literacy and Cultural Participation'. Mark Reid argues that literacy can no longer be print-based. Carl Hendrick's chapter, which is about dialog, is actually entitled 'Dialogism and Technology'.

Hendrick's chapter might also have been included in the section on assessment. Dialogue in the classroom is one of the key ways, for example, that formative assessment takes place. Our chapter on assessment is actually called 'Progression', which implies something more organic than a testing regime.

In essence, then, we want to suggest that the definable categories, so loved by the party political, are distinctly porous not to say intertextual. To cite Brenton Doecke:

> The word 'intertextuality' names a sensitivity towards the way texts transform other texts (cf. Frow, 2006, p. 148), refusing to be contained within a pre-existing notion of what a particular text or genre 'is'. Rather, to write intertextually is to step into the unknown.

So two of the writing chapters include the notion of reading or talk in them. One is called 'Thinking, Talking and Writing: What Lies Beneath?' another 'Writing, Reading and Rhetoric'. Rosen in his commentary on writing makes it plain that reading and writing 'are inseparable'. The chapter on drama is called 'Seeing Voices' and starts with a look at a play, which is written text. Even the chapter on Shakespeare can be seen as intertextual with not only differing interpretations of the play but a transformation from stage to screen.

In this way the book echoes Myra Barrs' and Valerie Cook's 2002 text *The Reader in the Writer*, based on a research project that looked at how young children develop as writers, through what they read. It illustrates the complex way in which children borrow, adapt, imitate and explore books they have read in the ways they write. It also looks at how they talk and assess each other's work. The whole business of English is examined in what they do in the classroom in a manner that is so different from the standards-based environment in which everything is ticked off.

This then is how our book should be read. The chapters, the headings under which they come, as we have said before, could all be done differently. The chapter, by Ben Knights on English Studies, provides a 'Very Brief History' but it gives one perspective. Terry Locke's 'Writing, Reading and Rhetoric' takes another perspective. The chapter on grammar is also about reading non-fiction, and so it goes on.

Nor have sections of each chapter been labeled for questions to be asked or bits taken out and placed in a box. Our argument in this book is that English is holistic. Items do overlap and are intertextual. It is for the reader to make their own connections.

Part 1
THE MAKING OF ENGLISH

English Studies: A Very Brief History

Ben Knights

Chapter Outline

The object of this chapter is simply stated. It is to invite you to reflect on the meanings and histories attached to the idea of 'English' as an educational subject. Those meanings and histories have implications for what you as a teacher know and do. Educational subjects are packaged and labelled as elements of the school and university curriculum, marketed and assessed by examination boards, and give their names to the teaching and scholarly professions attached to them. But as those labels pass over into popular currency, the effect is to simplify and obscure some very complex stories. They tend to suggest static and agreed objects rather than bodies of knowledge and activity always in process of change. We shall start by taking a brief look at the implications of the fact that disciplines and subjects have histories: the forces that continue to shape subjects, and to drive change. We shall then move on to examine the particular case of 'English'. After reviewing briefly some of the components and practises that go to making up the subject, we shall take a particular example from the history of English as a university subject, and ask about its implications for its students and those who go on to become teachers.

The evolution of educational subjects

In any complex society what counts as knowledge, and the status of different kinds of knowledge, is likely to be contested. Some knowledge is seen as being more the job of parents and families, some as needing to be acquired through formal education. Some kinds of knowledge will be less 'official' than others. Certain older but generally discredited forms of knowledge (e.g. Astrology) may go on leading a vigorous half-life within popular culture. Historically, religions have often played a major role in defining (and enforcing) what counted as proper knowledge, and who should know it. In advanced societies legitimacy is generally underpinned by the education system, which in turn is sanctioned by the state. Debates about validity and value surface in the making of curricula (e.g. the debate on whether it is legitimate to teach complementary and holistic medicine). Educational subjects themselves are not inevitable, nor do they simply reflect an objective, uncontentious parcelling up of knowledge. (Most systematic knowledge is deeply inter-disciplinary.) Historically, they emerge from, and are shaped and sustained within fields of social and political as well as intellectual forces. So some of those evolutionary forces are internal to the organism, some of them are environmental. Let us try to get hold of what this might mean. Here is a tentative list of some of the basic forces whose interaction and relative valency creates a dynamic.

- Widely held beliefs about what children or young people should know, or be able to do;
- A body of knowledge and practise, based on scholarship or research;
- A set of skills widely regarded as socially or economically valuable;
- An organized profession of teachers or scholars;
- Institutional interests: schools, universities, hospitals, awarding bodies, professional associations;
- The choices made by students themselves;
- The beliefs of influential members of the public – employers, politicians, journalists;
- The policies of governments;
- What other forces could you think of that might be at work?

You might want to reflect a minute about which of these forces you see as most likely to be influential, and the forms in which that influence might be exerted. Do these dynamics work in different ways in different subjects? How, for example, might student preferences influence the direction taken by a subject? Are governments and politicians more likely to want to shape or even control some subjects than others? The recurrent public argument about so-called 'Mickey Mouse subjects' provides a reminder of how rhetorical strategies can be used to discredit some subjects and legitimize others. For academics and teachers there is always a pressing need to persuade students, parents and the public of the value of what they do.

An educational subject usually emerges in tandem with a professional group dedicated to its advance, enhancement and transmission. Like any professional group it will have vested interests of its own (though the fact that human groups have vested interests in what they do does not rule out its validity: doctors have professional interests to maintain, but most of us do not want a society without them). What we see in the field of education is the formation of what Becher and Trowler (2001) call 'academic tribes', with their own social habits and learning styles, and their own ways of controlling entry into knowledge. School teachers may find themselves in the uncomfortable position of being pulled between tribes. Their university teachers will have tried to induct them into one, educationalists into another, schools into another. Each tribe will have its own take on what counts as knowledge, what being good at it looks like, and how and in what stages newcomers (children, students) can be inducted into that knowledge.

The rise of English

The debates surrounding the subject 'English' and who 'owns' it have been unusually fierce. Strongly defended beliefs are involved. 'English' has never been simply derived from bodies of knowledge generated by experts. Given that the word names simultaneously a nation, a language and an educational subject, the number of people who feel they 'own' the subject is more or less infinite. Politicians, media people, journalists, the Queen's English Society, industrialists and parents feel they have a right to pronounce on reading, spelling, grammar, dialect, pronunciation, the necessity of teaching Shakespeare – and the ways in which teachers (or university English departments) are letting down the nation's children or the economy. While you may detect a note of professional peevishness here, the openness of the subject to a myriad readers and speakers is in fact one of its glories. As a 'soft' subject, we have permeable boundaries with what readers and speakers do all the time. But it doesn't make life easy for those who propose to teach English. Nor is there much agreement among the professionals, either. English typically exhibits 'low paradigm consensus'. What that means is that there is a very low level of agreement about what counts as knowledge in the subject, or in what order its concepts and terms should be introduced to learners (or for that matter what those concepts and terms really are). This is of course what makes it such a rich and fascinating subject – and one endlessly open to influences not only from new creations in literature, media, and film, but from the concepts and working habits of other subjects. (You will have noticed during your degree course how English has consistently adopted or colonized elements of other subjects or disciplines: Philosophy, Anthropology, History, Psycho-Analysis, and so on. This process speeded up enormously in the 'Theory' era from the 1970s). But again, that is both difficult to explain, and does not help with deciding what children or students should learn or be tested on. Yet the problem has been around for a long time.

A subject called 'English' started to emerge in schools and in public debates in the years on either side of the First World War. It didn't, as yet, feature prominently in university curricula. While both English language and literary studies emerged on islands in the London Colleges and the Scottish universities, university English was very much an early twentieth-century phenomenon. This new subject represented a number of converging streams, and after the war the debate started to take on a particular urgency. A number of concerned people – poets and teachers, politicians and professors – started to speak publicly about *The Teaching of English in England* and *English for the English*. Many ingredients went into this new educational stew. Some of these drew on the rise of universal elementary education during the nineteenth century: the gravitational tug of reading and writing as functional skills has remained steady throughout the hundred-year history of English teaching. (The pre-history of English was widely known simply as 'reading and writing'.) The Newbolt Committee (this Committee, chaired by the patriotic poet Henry Newbolt, was set up in 1919 by the Board of Education to 'inquire into the position of English in the educational system of England') asked employers 'Have you found difficulty in obtaining employees who can speak and write English clearly and correctly?' This question, they reported was 'answered by an emphatic affirmative by all but a few firms' (*The Teaching of English in England*, Newbolt Report, 1924, § 137). The ensuing paragraph may sound familiar to prospective English teachers:

> All complained, often bitterly, of defects in spelling, punctuation, vocabulary, and sentence-structure. Spelling, in particular received adverse comment. Many firms ... insisted that the most serious defect was the total inability of their employees to express themselves readily and correctly on simple matters ...

But the emerging subject went well beyond what now might be called employability skills to encompass a growing attention to poetry and the literary heritage. Internalizing literary models through learning poetry by heart had been widely practised in late nineteenth-century schools, many contemporary educationists agreeing with the poet, critic and HMI (Inspector of Schools) Matthew Arnold that the

> acquisition of good poetry is a discipline which works deeper than any other discipline in the range of work of our schools. I find that of the specific subjects English literature, as it is too ambitiously called – in plain truth the learning by heart and reciting of a hundred lines or so of standard English poetry – continues to be by far the most popular. I rejoice to find it so; there is no fact coming under my observation in the working of our elementary schools which gives me so much satisfaction.
>
> (General report for the year 1880. Arnold 1910: 200)

The related idea that a literary heritage comprising Chaucer, Shakespeare, Milton, Wordsworth, or one of the increasingly popular poetry anthologies like Palgrave's *Golden Treasury*, should be propagated by schools became widespread in the years after the First World War, as the debate over the nature of 'Englishness' and the English heritage gathered momentum. There were implications and questions that were to become acute later. Suppose, for example, that you were not actually *English* – Irish, say, Scottish, Welsh, or a subject of that British Empire where English Literature was already being widely taught as a means of bonding colonial elites with the 'mother' culture and language? Who possessed the authority to lay down the rules of correct grammar, pronunciation or spelling? Who was to choose and according to what criteria, what counted as literature worth studying? Did that literature in actuality speak for and about a coherent heritage of national or even human wisdom? How did you decide if it even counted as English? (Many of the authors who emerged as canonical as the subject developed were, like W. B. Yeats or James Joyce, actually Irish – or US Americans like Henry James, Ezra Pound and T. S. Eliot.) What status had English writing compared to the classical (Latin and Greek) curriculum in which governing-class boys and young men had traditionally been educated? There were those who asked why, since any educated person could read books on English, anyone need be taught to study them. Or perhaps, said others, English was suitable as a substitute curriculum for women and working men (if the latter could be persuaded to read fiction and poetry at all). The Newbolt Committee had its doubts:

> We were told that the working classes, especially those belonging to organized labour movements, were antagonistic to, and contemptuous of, literature, that they regarded it "merely as an ornament, a polite accomplishment, a subject to be despised by really virile men." Literature in fact seems to be classed by a large number of thinking working men with antimacassars, fish-knives and other unintelligible and futile trivialities of "middle-class culture" … .
>
> (Newbolt Report, § 233)

A radical suspicion that literature was an ideological tool of the bourgeoisie set in early.

This short chapter cannot hope to review all the elements that composed the emerging subject. These included: philology and the history of the language (more recently, linguistics and English language); the study of early texts and their languages (Anglo-Saxon, Old Norse, Middle English); literary history (movements and biographies); and textual editing. What we shall do here is take as our case study a particular version of 'English' which was highly influential in the middle decades of the last century, and which carries on a trace existence in the DNA of the subject (especially at A-level) even now. This is 'literary criticism', a set of beliefs and practises that spread outwards from Cambridge during the 1930s and 1940s, until in many universities and sixth forms it became the predominant (though never undisputed) mode of performing the subject. (Literary Criticism had some similarities to, and is sometimes confused with, 'New Criticism', a corresponding movement that emerged, to some extent also under the influence of I. A. Richards, in the United States during the 1930s and 1940s and is associated with the names of Allen Tate, Cleanth Brooks, Robert Penn Warren, R. P. Blackmur, W. K. Wimsatt and others.)

Literary criticism

As we shall see, literary criticism and its core activity 'practical criticism' were conceived not as a body of scholarly knowledge, but as an oppositional activity: in opposition both to what was happening in universities and schools and – more importantly – to what was believed to be happening in the culture at large. Literary criticism also grew up in a close, almost symbiotic, relationship with contemporary modernism in poetry and fiction. To a considerable extent it used allusive modernist texts as the ground of its activity, or treated earlier texts as though they were dense modernist texts: while looking back from our own moment the key writers and texts may seem to be deeply frozen in time, but we should not underestimate the excitement of being in dialog with new works by Eliot, Pound, Yeats, Lawrence, Woolf and others as they were being published. The critics felt themselves to be on the side of the vigorously new. And in fact their view of literary history was to a considerable extent derived from that which Eliot had been promoting since the end of the war. At risk of crude generalization, it is possible to say that both modernism and literary criticism saw their task as challenging lazy reading and writing, and undermining the comfortable self-satisfaction of educational and cultural habits. Where modernism sought to disrupt or subvert conventional codes of representation, literary criticism aimed to subvert or disrupt conventional ways of reading. Both to greater or lesser extent exhibit the arrogance characteristic of avant garde movements. This history is somewhat obscured by the account of it that became commonplace in the 1980s (an example would be Terry Eagleton's influential 1983 *Literary Theory: An Introduction*) in which literary criticism and the so-called 'liberal humanism' with which it became associated were portrayed as essentially conservative and anti-political movements. Yet whatever became of it as time went on, we shall only understand the role of literary criticism if we grasp the oppositional, even subversive nature of its founders' intentions. The critics were 'angry young men' (they were mostly men) on an educational mission.

The narrative that the new literary criticism told about literature was as much or more a contribution to education and learning as a contribution to scholarship. (In fact, the critics tended to deplore and look down on scholarship, which they saw as a dusty escape from the real issues.) Its campaigning spirit was underpinned by what were effectively cultural and psychological theories – beliefs both about society and culture and about the process of growing up. The two domains are interconnected because, after all, people do their growing up in given social and cultural circumstances. If, as the critics argued, people were increasingly being infantilized by the commercial culture of the newspapers, publishing and the new technologies of wireless and film, drastic cultural intervention was needed to avert the danger of a society made up of passive, daydreaming, over-grown children. In her formative work *Fiction and the Reading Public*, Q. D. (Queenie) Leavis outlined what became the movement's theory of cultural decline, and gave currency to the Lawrentian idea of what she called 'substitute [or vicarious] living': the idea that film and the 'drug addiction to fiction' (1932, p. 152) were escapist phenomena, resulting in audiences that, lacking the will for mental effort, became passive consumers of fantasy. While, historically, it is perhaps not surprising if many people in the late 1920s and 1930s felt they were living in the end times of civilization, from our own vantage point, what we might not realize is how much of the energy of the new, rigorous approach to literature sits alongside the widespread narratives of decline mapped by Richard Overy in *The Morbid Age; Britain and Crisis of Civilization 1919–1939* (2009). In the face of the foreseen cultural disaster, the critics' program was much more than another way of studying English. As I. A. Richards, whose *Principles of Literary Criticism* (1924), together with his *Practical Criticism* (1929), was one of the formative texts of the movement, explained, the 'critic … is as much concerned with the health of the mind as any doctor with the health of the body' (1960, p. 46).

How does a program with reading at its core grow out of a narrative of cultural decline? One of our keys is the way in which 'maturity' became a buzzword in the movement. A preoccupation with how to grow up was never far away. To put it in terms of a more recent metaphor, where people were becoming habituated to junk food, a regime of difficult reading was prescribed as a necessary high-fiber diet. The argument articulated by Richards and subsequently adopted by the literary critics rested on a psychological theory about the management of impulse. In this theory there is powerful analogy between the operation of a good poem and the operation of the mature mind. Both work their way through opposed voices and impulses to a 'mature' point of equilibrium. The reader was required to unlearn their sloppy habits of thought – what Richards and his followers called 'stock responses' – in the presence of significant words. As their associate, the schoolteacher Denys Thompson, put it, 'The quality of a man's life [sic] nowadays depends largely on the quality of what he reads' (*Reading and Discrimination*, 1934, p. 3). Both poem and integrated mind worked through listening to and balancing opposed positions and impulses:

> The equilibrium of opposed impulses, which we suspect to be the ground-plan of the most valuable aesthetic responses, brings into play far more of our personality than is possible in experiences of a more definite emotion. We cease to be oriented in one definite direction; more facets of the mind are exposed and … more aspects of things are able to affect us. (I. A. Richards, 1960, p. 197)

That mature self is prepared to resist the seductions of the culture, and abjures self-indulgence. Tackling a complex, poem, play or novel becomes an exercise in that integration from which the mature self can emerge. This is very close to being a version of the modernist doctrine of estrangement: a text is valuable in so far as it refuses easy identification, or emotional wallowing. The eighteenth-century novelist, said Q. D. Leavis approvingly,

> is continually pulling up the reader, disappointing his expectations or refusing him the luxury of day-dreaming and not infrequently douching him with cold water. (*Fiction and the Reading Public*, p. 128)

The quality of reading turned into the quality of adult sensibility (another key word). The program evolved for schools and universities involved the exposure, under controlled conditions, to such difficult texts, above all to texts characterized by what William Empson had identified as 'ambiguity': texts that revel in the thick connotations of language and metaphor, and in dialog with which the critical reader's verbal and mental ingenuity unfolds (1930).

Criticism in the classroom

The cultural intervention that was literary criticism expended much of its energy on polemic, and, increasingly, on publishing critical essays about texts and authors. The printed output was increasingly addressed to a growing community of students and sympathetic readers. But with a movement grounded in education and an educational practise, we need to ask the classroom question: what did they actually do? Enough was written about it, and there are still enough people around who experienced the process for us to be able to provide a partial answer to that question. We saw earlier that the idea of the formative value of difficulty was central to the literary critical mindset. So too was the exorcism of slovenly and careless habits of reading. We're back to modernism and its drive to combat sloppiness of thought and expression. Writing on one of the movement's poetic heroes, F. R. Leavis noted:

> [Gerard Manley] Hopkins is really difficult, and the difficulty is essential … . If … we were allowed to slip easily over the page, the extremely complex process called for would not be allowed to develop. (*New Bearings in English Poetry*, pp. 134–5)

The point about the poems or passages literary critical teachers chose was their multi-layered symbolic density: un-pin-down-ability was their gift to readers. Poem and critic united in seeking to obstruct the tendency to 'slip easily over the page'. What the teacher did therefore was to put students in close contact with the words on the page – and, metaphorically, to try to prevent their escape into the temptations of easy generalization, or chat about characters or authors. The central practise was 'practical criticism' or 'close reading'. Alongside the tutorial class of the adult education movement, English criticism pioneered what by the 1940s had become recognizably the 'seminar' (see for example, F. R. Leavis's *Education and the University: A Sketch for an English School*: 'There was in the years before the war, a persistent undergraduate voicing of dissatisfaction with lectures, and an accompanying demand … for organized discussion-work' (1943, p. 47). A group of students sit with the text or texts in front of them, and with the guidance of a tutor, slowly and reflectively unpicks their meanings. Since, as we have seen, criticism held that every element of a text was integrated with every other element, the prospect held out to the student was one of grasping underlying connections and patterns of significance, often by following through the significance of patterns of imagery. This concentration on a poem or short passage was the characteristic method and has probably reinforced the mistaken belief that literary critics were not concerned with history or context. What they did assert was that before they set off on large-scale generalizations about history and meanings students should first go through the discipline of scrupulously weighing and thinking about the words in front of them. And that was very far from being a process of simple free association. While generally uninterested in (even hostile to) the technical study of language, the critics demanded close attention to the formal properties and linguistic nuance of the poem or passage. As in any formalist approach, form and content were held to be inseparable, how the poem *works* part and parcel of what it was saying. Although it was to be US New Critics who spoke of the 'heresy of paraphrase', the English critics, too, were averse to the idea that you could simply state what a poem said or generalize about the message of a novel. They taught a resistance to summary. For them, the linguistic complexity of the text represented the complexity of the thinking (conscious or unconscious) that created that text. 'These words in this order' provided a necessary resistance to jumping to conclusions. Even when not discussing Shakespearean drama, the critics tended to be interested in ambivalence (to become another key term), texts that are arguing with themselves, where potential meanings are held in suspension, or being hammered out in the very structure and balance of the clauses. (The same principle applied to their own written work, typically a fairly short reflective essay.) The key terms here – imagery, symbol, ambiguity, irony, feeling, response, tone – all rest upon an engagement with something more than labelling and generalizing. It's an attempt to get at and peel away the layers of writing to come to what D. W. Harding was to call 'the hinterland of thought' (1963, chapter 10).

Students practised in class the kinds of analysis that they subsequently performed in writing essays. Teaching, said F. R. Leavis's colleague Morris Shapira, was a matter of 'trying to eradicate conventionalities and clichés of thought to allow the growth of a vigorous, fresh, individual idea of literature' (MacKillop, 1995, p. 347). In a disenchanted, post-theory age, we might feel there is something naive about this conception of facilitating the emergence of the student's individual voice. We are perhaps too well aware of how easily students can imitate or learn to do what they think their teachers expect of them. But the idea that with a little help you might be able to unlearn the stereotypes and clichés you have internalized from your culture remains nevertheless educationally attractive – as is the idea that returning repeatedly to a powerful text is in itself a transformative experience. One of the living legacies of this form of study has been something that we might think of in Jerome Bruner's terms as a 'spiral curriculum'. The emerging subject was not cumulative, not just a matter of assembling the building blocks of knowledge in a prescribed order. The same text could be (should be) studied over and over, but each time you came to it a reader would be coming from a more sophisticated level of understanding, and see new things in it. *King Lear* or 'Ode to Autumn' read by a third-year undergraduate would conjure up different and more complex intellectual and emotional processes from *King Lear* read by a sixth former, but the second or third time of reading would recall the earlier reading as its pre-condition.

Above all, this was an evaluative, not simply descriptive process. As they engaged in the analytic process, students were called upon to practise 'discrimination' (another key word): to be able to show, by precise reference to the text, why and in what way this was a good (or as the case might be, bad) poem or passage. A typical procedure for both teaching and assessment was to set alongside each other two poems or passages (the author's name would be suppressed in an attempt to avoid assumptions springing into place) and to ask students to work out on the basis of close and argued analysis which one was the 'good' one. This fierce commitment to evaluation underpinned another phenomenon for which many of the literary critics became famous: an insistence on the pre-eminent value of a small canon of texts and authors; hence the notorious opening of F. R. Leavis's collection of essays on the novel, *The Great Tradition* (1948). 'The great English novelists are Jane Austen, George Eliot,

Henry James, and Joseph Conrad … .' (Leavis, 1962, p. 9). In all fairness, the Leavises could change their minds. Thus they later recanted their judgment that Dickens was merely 'an entertainer'.

Conclusion: English embattled

While it tended to promote a relatively small number of authors and texts, the movement we have been exploring was far from being simply a scholarly movement within English. It was a campaign to raise the national level of sophisticated reading by producing a 'vanguard' of strenuous and committed activists. Those activists were envisaged as applying their critical faculties to a huge variety of texts – not just to literature. If you were to look at the early issues of the Leavis circle's periodical journal *Scrutiny* (1932–53), you would find essays and reviews on politics, economics, science, religion, history and music. Above all, the group was passionately committed to the reform of education. Numerous articles were devoted to schools and educational matters, not least two major critical surveys on the teacher training colleges, and on public examinations. The former concluded that in our current crisis the agencies of teacher training were letting society down badly:

> The educational machine works in a round – School, University, Training College, School – and a study of the Training College in artificial isolation is only valuable if we remember that it gears on to the other two. The machine image comes naturally to mind, for the Training College, bent on justifying itself to the Board of Education, like the school which adopts the business man's conception of 'efficiency' … is a machine. So many compulsory lectures, so many notes assiduously taken, so many formulae repeated on examination papers, so many Diplomas and Certificates, and the 'efficient' teacher is produced … . (*Scrutiny*, 1.3, 1932)

The partisans of the *Scrutiny* group were committed to bringing about change in schools. Two of the first book-length publications of the movement were F. R. Leavis's and Denys Thompson's *Culture and Environment: The Training of Critical Awareness* (1933) and Thompson's own *Reading and Discrimination* (1934), both designed as textbooks for teaching the new practical criticism in schools. While their benchmark was drawn from an already recognizable canon of important writers, in directing critical attention to advertising, journalism and popular fiction these are both in effect early contributions to what in the 1970s would become 'Cultural Studies'. In the 1930s and on into the 1960s and 1970s, the movement that was literary criticism spread through the sixth forms, through teacher training and the education departments, through a stream of anthologies (for example the work of Raymond O'Malley, or David Holbrook) to a form of English that sought not only to provide its students with access to serious reading but also the verbal and intellectual skills necessary to see through the manipulations of advertising and the capitalist media. And as in 1951 Higher School Certificate gave birth to the more specialized A-level, the norms and procedures of literary criticism were there ready to be embedded in A-level English.

Since 1989 when the Education Reform Act introduced the National Curriculum we have all become accustomed to an historically unprecedented level of state prescription and control not just of the curriculum but of the detailed processes of the classroom. In these circumstances it can be difficult to hold on to the possibilities of subversion, and alternative cultural practise. English has had to keep its head down. (The story of the formation of the National Curriculum for English is vividly recounted by one of its key participants, Brian Cox (1991)). It is therefore all the more important to recall to historical memory the fact that on repeated occasions the subject we call 'English' has been inspired by a radical commitment to change, to cultural intervention, and (in a word that the critics would probably have deplored) cultural and linguistic empowerment. The movement discussed in this chapter is but one example of a dynamic in the broader subject which has over time given rise (for example) to: the 'Growth through English' movement in the late 1960s (see http://www.english.wisc.edu/comprhet/pdfs/Dixon.pdf); the work of James Britton and his era at the London Institute which persists as an underground current in the work of the National Association for the Teaching of English; and the daily work of numerous teachers and teacher educators. The history of literary criticism reminds us that 'English' has never been just about the acquisition of listable skills and business-friendly attributes. The negotiation between teachers and learners over language and the written word has always been grounded in the values of transformation and empowerment, and a belief (however shadowy or residual) in equipping learners with tools for living.

References

Arnold, Matthew (1910). *Reports on Elementary Schools 1852–1882*. London: HMSO.

Becher, Tony and Trowler, Paul (2001). *Academic Tribes and Territories: Intellectual Enquiry and the Culture of Disciplines*, rev. edn. Buckingham: Open University Press.

Cox, Brian (1991). *Cox on Cox: An English Curriculum for the 1990s*. London: Hodder and Stoughton.

Empson, William (1930). *Seven Types of Ambiguity: A Study of its Effects on English Verse*. London: Chatto and Windus.

Harding, D. W. (1963). *Experience into Words*. London: Chatto and Windus.

Leavis, F. R. (1963 [1932]). *New Bearings in English Poetry*. Harmondsworth: Penguin.

—(1943). *Education and the University: A Sketch for an English School*. London: Chatto and Windus.

—(1962 [1948]). *The Great Tradition*. Harmondsworth: Penguin.

Leavis, F. R. and Thompson, Denys (1933). *Culture and Environment: The Training of Critical Awareness*. London: Chatto and Windus.

Leavis, Q. D. (1932). *Fiction and the Reading Public*. London: Chatto and Windus.

MacKillop, Ian (1995). *F. R. Leavis: A Life in Criticism*. London: Allen Lane.

Overy, Richard (2009). *The Morbid Age; Britain and Crisis of Civilization 1919-1939*. London: Allen Lane.

Richards, I. A. (1929) *Pratical Criticism: A Study of Literary Judgment*. London: Kegan Paul.

—(1960 [1924]). *Principles of Literary Criticism*. London: Routledge & Kegan Paul.

Scrutiny: A Quarterly Review (1963). Leavis F. R. Re-issued. Cambridge: Cambridge University Press.

The Teaching of English in England (1924 [1921]). [The Newbolt Report] London: HMSO.

Thompson, Denys (1934). *Reading and Discrimination*. London: Chatto and Windus.

Paradigms of English

Terry Locke

Chapter Outline

'Paradigm' is not the only word we can use in relation to the realization that there is not just one 'version' of subject English. We can talk about *approaches* to English, or *discourses* of English. Fairclough, drawing on the work of Foucault, described a discourse as 'a practice not just of representing the world, but of signifying the world, constituting and constructing the world in meaning' (1992, p. 64). Different discourses of English tell different *stories* about what it means to be an English teacher. In the context of the classroom, these discourses are *instantiated* in a range of pedagogical practises.

While I will be referring to a range of paradigms of English, I need to make a number of things clear from the outset. First, my mapping of the subject should be seen as an heuristic, a way of making sense of the subject. Others have mapped the subject differently (for example, Ball, Kenny and Gardiner, 1990; Andrews, 1994; Green, 1997; Morgan, 1997). Secondly, I want to emphasize that discourses of English are unlikely to found in a 'pure' form in a particular teacher's practise. On the contrary, the practises of most teachers are generally shaped by more than one discourse of the subject. Thirdly, while I will be suggesting that the four discourses I refer to emerged at different times – and like any discourse need to be seen as historically and socially situated – they are likely to coexist in most educational settings today.

The potential for English or literacy to be multiply constructed makes sense when one identifies the elements that have a (potential) role to play in the construction itself. How one theorizes about the subject and how it might be taught depends on how one conceptualizes such entities as:

- writer (more generally the maker of the text)
- reader (viewer, listener)
- text (including oral texts)
- meaning-making mind
- meaning
- language (and other sign systems)
- technological mediation
- social context.

As we will see, different discourses of English conceptualize these entities and the relationships between them differently.

A person studying English at university between 1930 and 1980 in all likelihood would have been exposed to a paradigm of English that I will label 'Cultural Heritage'. This approach asserted that there was a traditional body of knowledge (including a canon of precious texts and specialist literary knowledge) which was to be valued and inculcated as a means of 'rounding out' learners so that they became fully participating and discriminating members of a society or culture. Literary study was seen as the heart of English. In their classic 'New Critical' text, *Understanding Poetry*, Cleanth Brooks and Robert Penn Warren asserted that 'literature is the most sophisticated example of the process by which we come to grasp our own environment, especially our human environment, with its complex and ambiguous values … ' (1976, p. 9). In simple terms, this approach suggested that imaginative and moral genius put meanings into literary texts, which well-trained readers would then explicate. There was no suggestion that the ordinary reader herself might produce literature, or that non-literary texts were particularly worthy of study in the English classroom.

Another paradigm for English began to emerge in the 1960s, stimulated in part by a growing interest in what individual readers brought to the act of reading and a desire to see English play a democratizing role in the development – cognitive, aesthetic and social – of individuals, especially those on the margins of society. Sometimes termed the 'Personal Growth' approach or 'progressive' English, this model argued that it was valuable to engage in literary and language-centered enterprises because this facilitated the personal, individual growth of learners, for whom the acquisition of certain linguistic competencies would play a central role in their ongoing task of making sense of their world. As mentioned, the model had an affinity with reader-response criticism, whose key theorists included Louise Rosenblatt (1978) and Wolfgang Iser (1978). There was a strong emphasis on individual creativity. In a telling phrase in *Growth through English* (1975, p. 55), John Dixon referred to 'the acceptance of pupils' work as embryonic literature'. This paradigm widened the range of genres considered appropriate for the English classroom (admitting popular culture texts, for example) and was linked with process approaches to writing, propounded by Donald Graves (1983) and others.

These two paradigms provided a backdrop for the emergence of a rhetorical/textual competence model of English.

A focus on textual or rhetorical competence

At its worst, the paradigm of English I am labelling 'rhetorical or textual competence' promotes decontextualized skills acquisition. You can see it operating in this way in tables of achievement objectives in some curriculum statements or as descriptions of competencies in various qualifications and assessment regimes. At its best, however, the model puts a value on the mastery of the forms and conventions of a range of textual practises or genres. A rhetorical model of English puts a focus on pragmatic competence – using texts to do things or get things done. In this section, I discuss two manifestations of this paradigm – the Australian Genre School and the New Rhetoric – and indicate the implications of both for classroom practise.

The Australian Genre School

The Australian approach to genre emerged in the mid-1980s (Christie, 2010) and is well represented by a key text edited by Bill Cope and Mary Kalantzis (1993) entitled *The Powers of Literacy: A Genre Approach to Teaching Writing*. The approach was strongly influenced by the functional view of literacy represented in the sociolinguistic theroizing of Michael Halliday and Ruqaiya Hasan (1985). For Halliday and Hasan, developers of systemic functional linguistic (SFL), literacy was viewed as a social practise. The meaning of a text or an element within a text was rendered meaningful by the relationship of the text to its social context, either the immediate context of production ('context of situation') or the broader cultural milieu ('context of culture'). As can be seen from the title of the Cope and Kalantzis book, there is a focus here on writing (text production) and the propounding of an explicit connection between literacy and empowerment. Indeed, one of the arguments these authors make for the explicit teaching of grammar is that the 'how' of language needs to 'be brought to the fore' because of 'schooling's unique social mission to provide historically marginalized groups equitable access to as broad a range of social options as possible' (1993, p. 8).

The Australian 'Genre' theorists saw themselves as reacting to earlier traditions of English, including the Progressive or Personal Growth model. For Cope and Kalantzis, the Progressive model had a number of shortcomings including that:

- It is 'culture-bound'. 'The progressivist mold with its prescriptions for individual control, student-centerd learning, student motivation, purposeful writing, individual ownership, the power of voice matches the moral temper and cultural aspirations of middle-class households';
- Its 'pedagogy of immersion' favors the children of society's elite groups and it simply reproduces educational inequity;
- It is not particularly motivating;
- It deprofessionalizes teachers by turning them into managers or facilitators (1993, p. 6).

Cope and Kalantzis (1993) described a genre-based approach to writing as involving:

- an explicit use of metalanguage in showing how language operates in texts to make meaning;
- the adoption of an apprenticeship model of English, with the teacher 'restored' to the role of language expert and the pupil now in the role of apprentice or novice;
- a systematic inculcation of the typical content that a pupil would need to acquire to become literate in formal school settings as related to the structures and linguistics features of particular textual categories. In previous research, Jim Martin had already identified these as: report, explanation, procedure, discussion, recount and narrative, and had defined a genre as a 'staged, goal-oriented social process' (Christie, 2010, p. 62);
- the return of the textbook;
- a return to the explicit teaching of grammar, but in a way that was markedly different from grammar-teaching practises associated with the cultural heritage model of English.

The term 'genre' is a slippery concept, as Cope and Kalantzis themselves conceded that there was more than one view on the matter. In the following discussion, for example, the term shifts from a focus on process, to an attribute of texts in general, to a way of categorizing texts by type:

> Genres are social processes. Texts are patterned in reasonably predictable ways according to patterns of social interaction in a particular culture. Social patterning and textual patterning meet as genres. Genres are textual interventions in society; and society itself would be nothing without language in all its patterned predictability. It follows that genres are not simply created by individuals in the moment of their utterance; to have meaning, they must be social. Individual speakers and writers act within a cultural context and with a knowledge of the different social effects of different types of oral and written text. (1993, p. 7)

The decision to select Martin's approach to genre on the basis of its 'educational influence' (1993, p. 9) has proved right in hindsight. In my current position as a teacher educator, I have just read (in 2010) two unit plans prepared by students for Year 8 (12-year-old) students in New Zealand. They are both underpinned by an approach derived from Martin's system of categorization and genre description as outlined by Cope and Kalantzis. In this system, we:

- begin with a broad definition ('reports are factual texts ... ');
- identify textual purpose and function
- describe the typical structure in terms of sequence ('they usually start with general classification which locates the phenomena, followed by successive elements contributing to a description, such a types, parts and their functions, qualities, uses or habits and so on');
- identify a participant focus ('the focus ... is on generic participants');
- and note typical lexico-grammatical features (' ... without temporal sequence and mostly using the simple present tense [with] considerable use ... made of 'being' and 'having' clauses". (1993, p. 9)

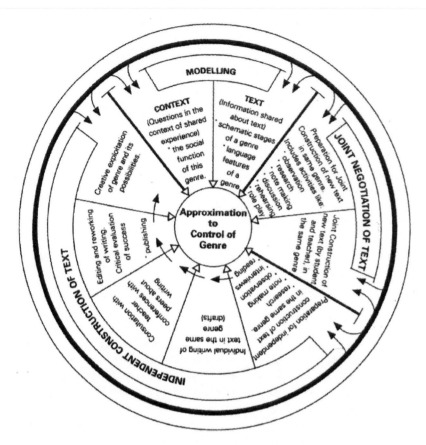

Figure 2.1 The "genre wheel" (Macken et al., 1989 in Cope & Kalantzis, 1993, p. 11).

Figure 2.1, the 'genre wheel', has attained iconic status as representing the approach to pedagogy developed by members of the Australian Genre School engaged in the LERN (Literacy and Education Research Network) Project which took place in New South Wales in the late 1980s. The approach was reflected in a range of textbooks, such as Wing Jan, where the chapter on 'Reports' begins with a description ('Reports are used to present factual information in a concise, accurate manner without any irrelevant details' [1991, p. 29] and so on) and proceeds to offer teachers a range of specific activities aimed at helping them model and jointly construct/negotiate a report text with their students.

The traditional grammar I was introduced to in my schooling was 'bottom up'. It began with words and parts of words (for example, prefixes) and moved to an examination and analysis (usually decontextualized) of phrases, clauses and sentences. Occasionally, it dealt with issues of text structure. The appeal of systemic function grammar to genre theorists was its 'top down' orientation, which viewed the text/context relationship as the prime determinant of linguistic function. As Cope and Kalantzis put it, 'Sentence and clause analysis is only performed in order to explain the workings of the whole text and how it realizes its social purpose' (1993, p. 10). Writing about reports in her text for teachers Wing Jan asserts that:

- Most reports use very economical speech;
- The language is not flowery and does not employ unnecessary descriptive devices, for example irrelevant adjectives, adverbs, similes, metaphors etc.;
- The use of personal pronouns is limited as reports aren't written in a personal manner;
- Most reports are written in the present tense;
- Some reports use technical or scientific terms in the information. (1991, p. 30)

What is being modelled here, in a friendly and accessible way, is the use of a metalanguage, aimed, I feel, not just at pupils but at developing the metalinguistic expertise of teachers themselves.

The new rhetoric

The genre-based approach to writing as developed in Australia was not without its critics (see particularly Richardson, 1994; Sawyer, 1995). In Sawyer's book (1995), there is an essay by Dixon and Stratta, archdeacons of the church of Personal Growth English, relishing the opportunity to take issue with the genre theorists who had maligned their particular brand. They make a number of points:

1. That genre theorists were confused in terms of how many genres there are and what genres actually are. There are issues with a simple connection between text type and purpose/function, since most texts and text-types are multifunctional. A lyric poem, for example, describes, argues and can also explain, instruct and narrate. A film review narrates, describes and argues.
2. That their short-list of written genres is arbitrary and untheorized and there are shortcomings in the ways these 'typical' school-based genres are defined.
3. That the notion of a 'staged structure' is problematic. 'Why this structure [for a report] is selected rather than others is ... neither explained nor theoretically justified' (Dixon and Stratta, 1995, p. 86). This point is supported by research conducted by Andrews which found that of 300 student compositions analyzed (half with arguments and half with narratives), only two had the same structure, the same arrangement (both were narratives). He writes: 'I now see ... that structure is a much more variable and flexible phenomenon that I had assumed' (1992, p. 278).
4. That these 'staged structures' may be having the adverse effect of producing 'normative' definitions. 'Who does that empower, we wonder, apart from the textbook writer?' (Dixon and Stratta, 1995, p. 87).
5. That the practise actually sets up a disjunction with the 'real' world. 'Is this the way we use language socially in the real world? Or is it simply another example, alas, of classroom practises cut off from the complexity of real life?' (Dixon and Stratta, 1995, p. 87).

A more flexible view of genres, but equally socially situated, can be found in the new rhetoric, and is represented by Freedman and Medway's definition as 'typical ways of engaging rhetorically with recurring situations' (1994, p. 2). When I was a high-school English teacher,

I used to tell my students that *rhetoric* is the art of making language work for you and that *function* was the *work* that the language in a text was doing moment by moment. In his introduction to the collection, *Rebirth of Rhetoric*, Richard Andrews attempts to get at the essence of rhetoric in the following way:

> Underneath the pockmarked skin, as it were, we see a frame that is alive and strong. The cardinal points of the frame are the speaker(s) or writer(s) or maker(s) (e.g. film-makers, fashion designers); the audience (a term that describes theatre-goers, television-watchers and so on, but whose etymology is aural) or reader; and the subject-matter, the 'world' that is to be communicated, however 'real' or fictional or selective that 'world' is. Mediated by these three agencies and central to the whole business is the 'text', however tightly or loosely that is defined. (1992, p. 2)

The new rhetoric was powerfully influenced by the thought of Russian literary theorist Mikhail Bakhtin (1986), who viewed genres as eclectic, prone to hybridity and dynamic. As Andrews put it, 'A rhetorical view of genre would accept this flexibility rather than wanting to categorize distinct and rigid forms' (1992, p. 9).

It needs to be remembered that the rhetorical is not the enemy of the literary. As Terry Eagleton points out: 'A poem … is a rhetorical performance, but (unlike most rhetorical exercises) not typically an instrumental one. It does things to us, though not usually so that we can get something done' (2007, p. 89). Traditionally, a text was viewed as effective if its formal qualities were consistent with its message and appropriate to its audience, that is, if it entertained or pleasured the audience. It is arguable that this Bakhtinian aspect of the rhetorical approach, with its focus on the literary, got lost in the work of the Australian genre theorists, who brought to their pragmatic competence agenda a focus on academic literacy and the adoption of Hallidayan or systemic functional grammar. In this instance of the 'linguistic' turn, subject English underwent a huge shift in its disciplinary base, away from literary criticism towards linguistics.

A rhetorical approach to text can be summed up in the following points:

- People construct texts with a view to achieving a desired result with a particular audience.
- Text is a product of function (form follows function).
- Texts are generated by contexts. Social/cultural contexts call forth texts.
- All texts assume a kind of social complicity between maker and reader.
- The expectations of people participating in such acts of complicity become formalized in the conventions of genre.
- These conventions can apply to such language features as layout, structure, punctuation, syntax and diction in the case of print texts, with other configurations of features operating for other modes and modal combinations.
- In a rhetorical approach, literature is not devalued but revalued.

Rather than discussing the pedagogical shape this approach might take in an English classroom, I will defer this topic and treat it in my chapter 'Writing, Reading and Rhetoric'.

Critical literacy

The seeds of a critique of the rhetorical competence model of the Australian genre theorists can be found in the very Cope and Kalantzis chapter that summarizes the approach and its rationale. If genres are socially constructed and particular genres reinforce the power and privilege of certain privileged groups, is it a good idea to teach these genres uncritically, even if they do offer access to social power? Isn't there a danger here of 'transmission pedagogy' and a cultural assimilationist model of education (Cope and Kalantzis, 1993, p. 16). Though originally associated with the Australian Genre School, Gunther Kress is already distancing himself from it in *The Powers of Literacy*, calling for an approach to English that would emphasize 'the whole set of connections of culture, society and language, codings of value systems, structuring and realizations of systems of power, and to the possibilities of making meanings in language as such, and in the languages of a specific plurilingual society in particular' – an approach that would allow for the analysis and critique of the status of various languages in terms of 'existing particular configurations of power' (Kress, 1993, p. 29).

Critical literacy fits Kress's prescription. Critical literacy as pedagogy also has its origins in a socio-cultural view of language (see Gee, 1996), critical theory (poststructuralist and feminist criticism, for example) and has links with critical language awareness (see Janks and Ivanic, 1992; Gee, 1996; Davies 1997; Morgan, 1997; Janks, 2010). As an approach, it has found a place in both mainstream English/literacy classrooms and increasingly in EAL/EFL settings (Wallace, 1995). Of central importance is the concept of discourse, discussed previously. In poststructuralist theory, the concept of discourse replaces the unitary self with the notion of multiple selves or subjectivities, each the product of discourse (Misson, 1998). The originary self as maker of meanings – the meaning-making mind – is replaced by human subjectivity/ies as produced by culture. We no longer tell stories; stories tell us. Human beings are thought of as *inscribed* by various discourses, not always consistent with one another or *subscribing*, consciously or unconsciously, to various discourses.

Critical literacy puts a value on encouraging language-users to see themselves as engaged in textual acts which are part of a wider set of discursive practises that actively produce and sustain patterns of dominance and subordination in the wider society and offer members of society prescribed ways of being particular sorts of people. In this model, a literary text can be thought of as a space within which a play of meaning might be enacted by the deconstructive, 'writerly' reader. Meaning becomes a function of discourse and individual texts lose their discreteness and become meaningful only in an infinitely complex network of intertextual relationships among utterances. The cultural context has become pre-eminent. No text, then, is innocent. All texts, using a range of linguistic devices, seek to position readers to view the world in a particular way. No reader is innocent either. Each brings to the act of reading a set of discursive lenses, each of which will interact with the discursive designs of a text in a particular way, ranging from submission to resistance.

A deconstructive reading of a text is one that reveals its underpinning discourse(s). Such deconstructive acts might be viewed as a first step in resisting the reading position or positions a text offers. Typically, a critical literacy reading of a text invites students to interrogate it via a set of questions, of which the following is a generic example:

- What kind of text is this?
- What social functions does this text serve?
- How does this text construct a version of reality and knowledge? And what is left out of this story?
- How does the text represent the reader (or viewer or listener) and set up a position for reading? And what other positions might there be for reading?
- How does this text set up its authority and encourage your belief? And how might its authority be deconstructed and challenged, where its ethical stance is at odds with yours? (Morgan, 2004, p. 107)

A potentially powerful complement to deconstructive reading is deconstructive writing. Such a strategy involves the production of a text that *disrupts* (Yeoman, 1999) or *contaminates* (Chou, 2007) one or more discourses in the text to be resisted by producing versions framed by alternative, sometimes marginalized discourses (of race, gender and class, for example). To do this, writers need to be aware that the language they use *is not* a transparent medium of communication, but rather an opaque instrument that inevitably constructs its 'object' in a particular way. What Allan Luke says about the relationship between reading and metalanguage (or grammar) for critical readers, applies equally to critical writers.

> By 'critical competence' … I refer to the development of a critical metalanguage for talking about how texts code cultural ideologies, and how they position readers in subtle and often quite exploitative ways. My argument is that in order to contest or rewrite a cultural text, one has to be able to recognize and talk about the various textual, literary and linguistic, devices at work. (Luke, 1992:10)

So, 'grammar' retains its place in the critical literacy classroom, but with a different kind of justification, not so much to support pragmatic writing competence as to serve the purpose of linguistic analysis in the service of a critical awareness of the job all texts do in positioning readers to see the world in particular ways.

There is no one way of doing 'crit lit' in the classroom (Morgan, 1996). However, the following example, based on the classroom-based research of a project teacher and friend, is reasonably typical (Sturgess and Locke, 2009). Janet taught an eager Year 9 (13-year-olds) class in a multicultural school in Auckland, and her repertoire of practises included critical literacy. Having completed a novel-based unit on the theme of bullying, her students expressed an interest in stereotypes. Janet decided to implement a 'critical literacy' unit with them, which began by their drawing on their own cultural knowledges to construct a set of descriptors of the typical fairytale prince and princess (see Table 2.1). They then viewed the movie *Shrek* (Adamson, 2001), in order to ascertain analytically the ways in which the movie broke with the stereotypes they had established. They then moved to a research phase of the unit where they investigated, explored and shared fairytales from their own cultural background(s). The unit ended with their writing their *own* fairytales in ways that contested or deviated from the stereotypical characterization and plot structuring they had identified earlier in the unit (for examples, see Sturgess and Locke, 2009, pp. 398–402).

Table 2.1 Prince and princess stereotypes (Sturgess and Locke, 2009)

Princes	Princesses
Are always good looking	Are always slim and beautiful
Usually tall, dark, handsome and have a deep clear voice	Usually have long hair with fair or tanned skin
Are always clean	Also always clean
Have accessories (horse)	Own nothing of their own
Are always charming	Know how to behave (demure)
Generally come from somewhere else	Are often victims in their own land
Have plenty of money	Money is never mentioned or she is poor, or has been disinherited
Eat roasts and/or other foods that cost heaps	Are never seen to eat anything
Always save the princess	Always need saving
Have to fight something terrible to prove bravery or worth	Fall in love with his bravery and him as a result
Easily runs to mum/dad or someone with money	Loves and worships their husband and lets them be the boss
He usually has to kiss the princess	The kiss is the magical moment

Critical eclecticism

While it is possible to envisage classrooms whose practises might reflect in some 'pure' way, one or other of the paradigms of English discussed here, the reality is generally far more complex. A range of factors contribute to the formation of an English teacher's professional knowledge and classroom practise. These include the critical orientation of their various degree courses, emphases in their initial teacher education, the history of their professional development, the theoretical underpinnings of official curriculum and assessment documentation, the modelling of other teachers and the pedagogies embedded in text books and other resources, and last, but not least, understandings related to the production, consumption and dissemination of texts developed in the wider social context.

In terms of the English teacher's professional content knowledge (Shulman, 1986), what I would argue for is a kind of informed and critical eclecticism. Such eclecticism would not privilege any particular version of English *per se*, but would be aware of the extent to which each is characterized by a particular ideological underpinning. Teachers thus oriented would be aware of the way in which different reading and writing traditions effectively construct different kinds of reading and writing practise and, to some extent, different readers and writers.

It needs to be emphasized that such knowledge is not going to be developed in teachers' heads out of books. It will only be developed by teachers performing acts of interpretation and self-reflexivity as integral to their own reading and practises. To the extent that these acts are cognitively based, teachers will benefit from metacognitive reflective tools. To the extent that these acts are social practises, teachers will benefit from a critical awareness of ways in which these are discursively constructed. As I see it, this is not an either/or situation.

Moving from the practitioner to the practise, Table 2.2 indicates ways in which different versions of English might lead to different reader/writer orientations, that is, the goals and dispositions readers might be encouraged to bring to the act of textual engagement. Hopefully, critically reflective English teachers would see a place for each of these orientations at different times in their classroom programs.

Table 2.2 Versions of English and textual orientation

Cultural heritage	Personal growth
Textual orientation:	Textual orientation:
Appreciation and emulation	Self-realization through meaning-making
Deference	Creative exploration
Acculturation	Personal integration
Rhetorical competence	**Critical literacy**
Textual orientation:	Textual orientation:
Formal mastery of textual practises	Critical linguistic analysis
Pragmatic competence	Detachment
Social adeptness	Social transformation

The potential for the development of this eclecticism in terms of professional content knowledge and practise can be thwarted in a number of ways. It will be undermined should instrumentalist approaches to teacher education become widespread. I'm referring to simplistic, 'how to' approaches to teacher training coupled in classrooms with curriculum and assessment regimes, which train students to jump through hoops constructed via the mechanism of behavioral and predetermined learning outcomes. Such approaches are antithetical to theory and problematization. It can also be undermined in situations where one particular approach to reading or writing, or where there is only a particular version of English becomes entrenched as an orthodoxy.

There are dangers when statements such as 'Literacy is a social practice' are transformed from insights into slogans and even mantras. When such a statement becomes read as asserting that 'Literacy is *exclusively* a social practice', then the ground has been established for marginalizing traditions that focus on the relationship between language/text and mind/cognition (Pinker, 1995; Sadoski, 1998; Damasio, 2000). Likewise, a privileging of critical theories of literature based in cultural studies and views of the text as socially constructed, has the potential to marginalize, for example, views of the literary text as rooted in competing epistemologies and aesthetics – views such as those represented by evolutionary-based literary theories (Carroll, 1995; Boyd, 2009).

Conclusion

In conclusion, my argument here is for a kind of openness as opposed to closure – an appreciation of the fact that there is a potential richness in the range of reading and writing approaches and versions of English available. Like critique, problematization is not a bad thing. On the contrary, it can be seen as characterizing detachment, the opposite pole to engagement. Effective learning requires both: passionate (dare I say) engagement with a task (say, reading) or issue at hand, followed by detachment for reflection, questioning, and so on. And then a return to engagement. Without problematization and critique, the range of possibilities for textual engagement are never canvassed. And classrooms can only be the worse for it.

References

Adamson, A. (dir., 2001). *Shrek*. Glendale, CA: Dream Works Animation.

Andrews, R. (ed.) (1992). *Rebirth of Rhetoric: Essays in Language, Culture and Education*. London: Routledge.

—(1993). 'Argument in schools: the value of a generic approach'. *Cambridge Journal of Education, 23* (3), 277–85.

—(1994). 'The future of English: Reclaiming the territory'. *English in Aotearoa, 22*, 34–45.

Bakhtin, M. (1986). 'The problem with speech genres' (V. McGee, trans.). In C. Emerson and M. Holquist (eds), *Speech Genres and Other Late Essays: M. M. Bakhtin*. Austin, TX: University of Texas Press, pp. 60–101).

Ball, S., Kenny, A., and Gardiner, D. (1990). 'Literacy, politics and the teaching of English'. In I. Goodson and B. Medway (eds), *Bringing English to Order: The History and Politics of a School Subject*. Lewes: Falmer Press, pp. 47–86.

Boyd, B. (2009). *On the Origin of Stories*. Cambridge, MA: Harvard University Press.

Brooks, C. and Warren, R. P. (1976). *Understanding Poetry*, 4th edn. New York: Holt, Rinehart and Winston.

Carroll, J. (1995). *Evolution and Literary Theory*. Columbia, MO: University of Missouri Press.

Christie, F. (2010). 'The "Grammar Wars" in Australia'. In T. Locke (ed.), *Beyond the Grammar Wars: A Resource for Teachers and Students on Developing Language Knowledge in the English/literacy Classroom*. New York: Routledge, pp. 55–72.

Chou, W.-H. (2007). 'Contaminations of childhood fairy tale: pre-service teachers explore gender and race constructions'. *Journal of Social Theory in Art Education, 27*, 55–73.

Cope, W. and Kalantzis, M. (1993). *The Powers of Literacy: A Genre Approach to Teaching Writing*. Pittsburgh: University of Pittsburgh Press.

Damasio, A. (2000). *The Feeling of What Happens: Body, Emotion and the Making of Consciousness*. London: Vintage.

Davies, B. (1997). 'Constructing and deconstructing masculinities through critical literacy'. *Gender and Education, 9*(1), 9–30.

Dixon, J. (1975). *Growth Through English (Set in the Perspective of the Seventies)*. Edgerton: NATE (Oxford University Press).

Dixon, J. and Stratta, L. (1995). 'New Demands on the Model for Writing in Education: What does Genre Theory Offer?' In W. Sawyer (ed.), *Teaching Writing: Is Genre the Answer?*. Springwood, NSW: Australian Education Network, pp. 77–91.

Eagleton, T. (2007). *How to Read a Poem*. Malden, MA: Blackwell Publishing.

Fairclough, N. (1992). *Discourse and Social Change*. Cambridge: Polity Press.

Freedman, A. and Medway, P. (1994). 'Introduction: New Views of Genre and Their Implications for Education'. In A. Freedman and P. Medway (eds), *Learning and Teaching Genre*. Portsmouth, NH: Boynton/Cook, pp. 1–24.

Gee, J. (1996). *Social Linguistics and Literacies: Ideology in Discourses*, 2nd edn. London: Taylor & Francis.

Graves, D. (1983). *Writing: Teachers and Children at Work*. Exeter: Heinemann.

Green, B. (1997). 'Rhetorics of meaning or renovating the subject of English teaching?' *Changing English, 4*(1), 7–30.

Halliday, M. and Hasan, R. (1985). *Language, Context, and Text: Aspects of Language in a Social = Semiotic Perspective*. Geelong, VIC: Deakin University.

Iser, W. (1978). *The Act of Reading: A Theory of Aesthetic Response*. Baltimore: John Hopkins University Press.

Janks, H. (2010). *Literacy and Power*. New York/London: Routledge.

Janks, H. and Ivanic, R. (1992). 'CLA and Emancipatory Discourse'. In N. Fairclough (ed.), *Critical Language Awareness*. London: Longman, pp. 305–31.

Kress, G. (1993). 'Genre as Social Process'. In B. Cope and M. Kalantzis (eds), *The Powers of Literacy: A Genre Approach to Teaching Writing*. Pittsburgh: University of Pittsburgh Press, pp. 22–37.

Luke, A. (1992). 'Reading and critical literacy: redefining the "Great Debate"'. *Reading Forum New Zealand, 2*, 3–12.

Misson, R. (1998). 'Poststructuralism'. In W. Sawyer, K. Watson and E. Gold (eds), *Re-Viewing English*. Sydney, NSW: St Clair Press, pp. 144–53.

Morgan, W. (1996). 'Critical Literacy: More than Sceptical Distrust of Political Correctness?' In W. Morgan, P. Gilbert, C. Lankshear, S. Werner and L.Williams (eds), *Critical Literacy: Readings and Resources*. Norwood, SA: AATE, pp. 35–46.

—(1997). *Critical Literacy in the Classroom: The Art of the Possible*. London: Routledge.

—(2004). 'Critical Literacy'. In W. Sawyer and E. Gold (eds), *Reviewing English in the 21ˢᵗ Century*. Melbourne, VIC: Phoenix Education, pp. 103–114.

Pinker, S. (1995). *The Language Instinct: The New Science of Language and Mind*. London: Penguin.

Richardson, P. (1994). 'Language as Personal Resource and as Social Construct: Competing Views of Literacy Pedagogy in Australia'. In A. Freedman and P. Medway (eds), *Learning and Teaching Genre*. Portsmouth, NH: Boynton/Cook, pp. 117–42.

Rosenblatt, L. (1978). *The Reader, the Text, the Poem: The Transactional Theory of the Literary Work*. Carbondale, IL: Southern Illinois University Press.

Sadoski, M. (1998). *Mental Imagery in Reading: A Sampler of Some Significant Studies*. http://www.readingonline.org/research/Sadoski.html [accessed 31 March 2003].

Sawyer, W. (ed.) (1995). *Teaching Writing: Is Genre the Answer?* Springwood, NSW: Australian Education Work.

Shulman, L. (1986). 'Those who understand: knowledge growth in teaching'. *Educational Researcher, 15*(2), 4–14.

Sturgess, J. and Locke, T. (2009). 'Beyond *Shrek*: fairy tale magic in the multicultural classroom'. *Cambridge Journal of Education, 39*(3), 379–402.

Wallace, C. (1995). ' "Reading with a Suspicious Eye": Critical Reading in the Foreign Language Classroom'. In G. Cook and B. Seidlhofer (eds), *Principle & Practice in Applied Linguistics: Studies in Honour of H. G. Widdowson*. Oxford: Oxford University Press, pp. 335–47.

Wing Jan, L. (1991). *Write Ways: Modelling Writing Forms*. Melbourne, VIC: Oxford University Press.

Yeoman, E. (1999). ' "How does it get into my imagination?": elementary school children's intertextual knowledge and gendered storylines'. *Gender and Education, 11*(4), 427–40.

Intertextuality and Subversion 3

Brenton Doecke and Douglas McClenaghan

Chapter Outline

Intertextuality. The elaboration of a text in relation to other texts. The radical import of the concept in contemporary criticism has to do with its implication that, rather than being self-contained and self-present structures, texts are traces and tracings of otherness, shaped by the repetition and transformation of other texts. (Frow, 2006, p. 148)

Words like 'intertextuality' bring to mind the moment of 'theory'. Especially significant for our own professional learning were journals like *The English and Media Magazine*, including resonantly titled essays such as 'The Post-Structuralist Always Reads Twice' (Exton, 1982). These essays advocated new understandings of texts and textuality that challenged the interpretive practises that had traditionally held sway in English classrooms. In Australia, the moment of 'theory' prompted some remarkably innovative work in the area of English curriculum and pedagogy, as Bill Corcoran's time as the editor of *English in Australia* shows (see Corcoran, 1998).

During Corcoran's editorship, *English in Australia* published a raft of articles exploring the potential of post-structuralist insights for opening up new readings of texts (see, e.g. Moon, 1990; Mellor and Patterson, 1991, 1994).

The moment of 'theory' also saw the advent of Chalkface Press, which produced an engagingly provocative set of resources that modelled new approaches to reading (see, e.g. Mellor, O'Neill and Patterson, 1987; Mellor, 1989), including Brian Moon's *Literary Terms: A Practical Glossary* (1993/99). As the title of Moon's book suggests, for many English teachers the challenge of 'theory' was experienced as one involving the acquisition of a new lexicon, a new way of thinking and talking about their work. We ourselves remember making the transition from 'work to text' (to borrow the title of one of Roland Barthes's essays), tentatively stepping beyond notions of the unity of the literary work that had been a feature of our own undergraduate education, and affirming the heterogeneous character of literary texts, in which (to borrow again from Barthes) 'a variety of writings, none of them original, blend and clash' (Barthes, 1978, p. 146; cf. also Reid, 1984/88, pp. 53–74).

We are self-consciously revisiting 'theory' as a moment in our professional lives. Truly worthwhile learning is something you experience, an event that might be said to transcend time because it remains with you, an ineradicable part of your identity, shaping your engagement with the present. This is in contradistinction to claims that have recently been made by theorists that we are somehow now living in a moment that is 'post-theory' (see, e.g. Eagleton, 2003; Culler, 2007). 'Literary theory has been rather out of fashion for the last couple of decades', so Terry Eagleton opines at the beginning of his most recent book (Eagleton, 2012, p. ix), thus conceding to a pervasive tendency to treat ideas simply as intellectual fads. The complex relationship between our experiences as educators and the reading that we have done in an effort to understand our work is not captured by this notion of intellectual 'fashion'.

Yet we are also obliged to confront the fact that the history of English teaching has featured a series of 'fashions'. 'Growth' pedagogy, 'genre' theory, 'critical' literacy, 'multi-literacies' – these pedagogical bandwagons have typically been heralded as 'revolutions' overturning everything that has gone before them. We might instance the way that the process writing 'revolution' was featured in *English in Australia* (Walshe, 1982), or the claim that 'genre teaching represents a fundamental new educational paradigm' (Cope and Kalantzis, 1993, p. 1), or, more recently, the assertion that 'multiliteracies' is 'a radical new way of thinking about education' vis-à-vis 'the emerging cultural, institutional and global order' (Cope and Kalantzis, 2000, p. 5; cf. Doecke and McClenaghan, 2011b). The moment of 'theory' obviously lends itself to caricature in precisely the same way, as Harry Ballis and Paul Richardson suggest, when they liken Annette Patterson's 1992 account of her 'odyssey from "personal growth" to "post-structuralism"' as a 'conversion story' (see Patterson, 1992). As Ballis and Richardson observe wryly, not only of the impact of post-structuralism but of other pedagogical bandwagons such as 'whole language': 'Each innovation in literacy instruction generates its own round of stories of conversion which prompt new, more exciting and better ways of learning and teaching' (Ballis and Richardson, 1997, p. 115).

Our aim in this essay is to inquire into the way 'theory' has figured in our professional practise as English teachers and the role that it continues to play in our attempts to understand our work better. We shall be focusing specifically on the word 'intertextuality' and reflecting on what it can mean when applied to the meaning-making practises in which young people engage in classroom settings. But this is to do more than use 'intertextuality' as a small window on how theory might inform the work of English teachers. We shall also be arguing that intertextuality as it is practised by young people provides a significant counterpoint to attempts by governments in Australia and elsewhere to regulate teaching and learning – hence the ambition reflected in the title of this essay, namely to show the 'subversive' potential of 'intertextuality' vis-à-vis neo-liberal reforms.

The claims and counterclaims that have been made about each new educational paradigm appear in an ironical light when they are placed against the backdrop of a changing policy environment that over the past two or three decades has involved ever-increasing regulation of teaching and learning. Australia has witnessed wave after wave of standards-based reforms (Darling-Hammond, 2004) that are beginning to have the same destructive effect on English teachers' work that they have had in the US and the UK. These reforms have involved the implementation of nation-wide standardized literacy testing and a new English curriculum that emphasizes the importance of Literature teaching (with a capital 'L') that is conceived in decidedly traditional terms (see the Australian Curriculum, Assessment and Reporting Authority (ACARA), 2011; Doecke, McClenaghan and Petris, 2011). The language of theory echoes strangely within a policy setting where teachers are now obliged to teach texts 'that are recognized as having enduring social and artistic value' (ACARA, 2010). What has become of the anti-essentialist emphasis with which theory once confronted the privileging of any corpus of writing as somehow embodying 'enduring social and artistic value'? Was Tony Bennett's statement that 'in history, nothing is intrinsically "literary", intrinsically "progressive" or, indeed, intrinsically anything' (Bennett, 1979, p. 136), simply a bit of intellectual posturing? Rather than simply falling 'out of fashion', the rich insights into texts and textuality that were part and parcel of the moment of 'theory' are being legislated out of existence. That, at least, appears to be the aim of the neo-liberal policy agenda that holds sway at the moment.

Yet the regressive nature of these reforms only lends more point to revisiting 'theory' and re-evaluating the insights that it provides into the nature of texts and textuality. The traditional understandings of literature's value that have proliferated in the preliminary papers and final version of the recently published *Australian Curriculum: English* are part of a blueprint for education designed to equip 'young people with the knowledge, understanding, skills and values' to take their place in a twenty-first-century economy. We are borrowing from the language of the *Melbourne Declaration on Educational Goals for Young Australians* (MCEETYA, 2008, p. 4), a document that is full of rhetoric about the requisite skills and dispositions for young people to be 'successful learners', 'confident and creative individuals', and 'active and informed citizens', but devoid of any recognition of the way young people are actually experiencing the world that adults have created for them.

Perhaps we should breathe a sigh of relief that the social engineering proposed by the 'Melbourne Declaration' eschews overtly nationalist rhetoric, such as the language used in recently published professional standards in the UK about the need for teachers to propagate 'fundamental British values' (DfE, 2011, p. 9). The years prior to the establishment of the Australian Curriculum, Assessment and Reporting Authority (ACARA) and the writing of the national curriculum witnessed a sustained media campaign on the part of the Murdoch

Press to restore so-called Australian values, including a valuing of 'our' national heritage, to the school curriculum, and it is indisputable that this campaign had an impact on the writing of the national curriculum, most notably with respect to the way it restores the study of capital-L Literature to pride of place in English teaching. However, the rhetoric of both the Declaration and the new curriculum still involves privileging a set of norms, a certain construction of 'young Australians' that undermines any attempt on the part of teachers and their students to dialogically engage with values and beliefs that might not be comprehended by this vision of educational goals that will take Australia into the twenty-first century. This includes the language that the English Curriculum uses to justify the study of literary texts that 'are recognized as having enduring social and artistic value', which 'are chosen because they are judged to have potential for enriching the lives of students', and expand 'the scope of their experience'. These passive constructions elide the question of who is actually making these judgements, echoing a traditional understanding of English teachers as custodians of 'the best that has been thought and said in the world'.

But it is obviously necessary to distinguish between what the curriculum dictates and what happens in classrooms as teachers go about implementing it, even though the forms of regulation being imposed on schools (largely in the form of standardized literacy testing) are designed to enforce an unprecedented level of surveillance. There is, however, good reason to suppose that the potential of young people cannot be contained by such regulatory mechanisms, that the work they are capable of creating exceeds the proscriptions that any government might try to impose on them. All the examples of students' work that we are about to consider show young people engaging in far more interesting meaning-making practises than those specified in the outcomes set down in the official curriculum, reflecting the rich, communicative life of the classroom in which they were participating (Barnes, 1975/92, p. 14), and thus providing cause for hope that the creativity of young people will continue to exceed the 'educational goals for young Australians' imposed by the *Melbourne Declaration*. The challenge for teachers consists in how to continue to scaffold such creativity, and maintain a capacity to respond to the work that students produce, rather than simply classifying it according to the learning outcomes dictated by the official curriculum (cf. Sawyer, 2005; Doecke and McClenaghan, 2011a).

It would be difficult to overestimate how much we have learned from young people over the years, when we have observed their capacity to draw intertextually on other writing, as well as other semiotic resources that are at their disposal, in order to engage in authentic meaning-making practises. We have written about this many times. 'Crime stories' (Doecke and McClenaghan, 2011b, pp. 73–82), 'fantasy adventures' (Doecke and McClenaghan, 2011, pp. 42–9), 'science fiction' (McClenaghan, Doecke and Parr, 1995, pp. 37–54), 'gothic' stories (McClenaghan, Doecke and Parr, 1995, pp. 55–66) – students' forays into 'intertextuality' typically take the form of an exploration of the potentialities of a literary genre.

Mention the word 'genre', and you find yourself up against the sterile schemata propagated by the so-called 'genre' school: each genre supposedly embodies a set of rules, and each has its place in a reified taxonomy of text types ('recounts', 'instructions', 'narratives', 'explanations', 'arguments') that amounts to little more than a crude caricature of the ways in which texts actually mediate social relationships and provide a means of representing human experience (see Derewianka, 1990). 'Genre' pedagogy promotes school writing as an exercise in compliance, positioning young people as hapless apprentices who must learn to follow the rules, and completely discounting the repertoire of meaning-making practises they have developed as active participants in the world around them. (It is little wonder that so-called 'genre' theory has been recruited to serve the socially alienating purposes of system-wide, standardized literacy testing in Australia.)

To promote intertextuality as a meaning-making practise is to step beyond any under-standing of genres as somehow discrete and self-contained (cf. Frow, 2006, p. 148). It is to foreground the intertextual work by which a genre 'shapes and re-shapes itself in an ongoing and open-ended process' (Frow, 2006, p. 136). Crucially, it is to see young people as being at the center of this process, appropriating and transforming the semiotic resources available to them, as part of a continuing inquiry into language and meaning.

We shall first revisit a set of resources that we developed a few years ago, when Douglas's students engaged in an inquiry into the potential of gothic fiction, or 'teenage gothic', as we put it, as there is no doubt that for young people gothic fiction provides a powerful means for them to grapple with questions and issues that are of concern to them. The prompt for this investigation was several stories pitched at young adults by talented Australian writers, including Judith Clarke and Caroline MacDonald, which arguably display features of gothic fiction. However, the point of such an inquiry was not to develop a list of characteristics that are supposedly peculiar to gothic fiction, as though a short story or other literary work might be said to 'belong' to this category. Students were encouraged to talk about gothic in terms of its effects on them as readers, their expectations of a gothic story, what makes this a suitable term to use with respect to a particular story (in comparison with, say, calling it a thriller or a mystery), as well recognizing that a gothic story might combine other genres. This embraced stories that might be said to be 'classic' instances of the genre, such as Mary Shelley's *Frankenstein*, Bram Stoker's *Dracula*, and Edgar Allan Poe's 'The Tell-Tale Heart', as well as the 'distress and delight' (Buckingham, 1995) that teenagers experience when watching horror movies. However, the very mention of the word 'horror', as distinct from the connotations associated with the word 'gothic', reveals both the provisional nature of such categories when readers attempt to explain their tastes and enthusiasms, and the transformations that can occur when writers borrow from or rewrite a story in order to give representation to contemporary experience. We chose, indeed, to deliberately muddy the waters with respect to the range of resources that we used in order to scaffold this inquiry, bringing some famous examples of 'urban myths' into class (most notably 'The Hook'), reflecting on the ways in which these combined gothic elements, and yet still appeared to warrant another generic label (see McClenaghan, Doecke and Parr, 1995, p. 63).

What did we learn from this particular inquiry into texts and textuality? As always, the compositions that the students produced offer the best stimulus for thinking critically about our intentions and what we actually accomplished by scaffolding these young people's efforts to write gothic fiction. John Frow argues that texts do not 'belong' to a genre, as though a genre somehow exists in a realm apart, as a set of 'rules' that writers should follow. The short stories the students produced might be said to be a 'performance' of a genre, a 'transformation' of existing textual structures, rather than simply the 'reproduction of a class to which they belong' (Frow, 2006, p. 3). This becomes apparent from the form their writing assumes, as distinct from its content. Here is how Lorrelle Fortune, Erin Oliver, Samantha Kelley, Kate Hargreaves and Abbie Sharps begin their co-authored gothic story:

> It all began on a dark and stormy night when a young woman called Ella was driving home from a friend's place, along a stretch of deserted road. She was singing along with the radio when she noticed a semi-trailer driving closely behind her. She thought nothing of it until she saw the semi's lights flashing higher and lower every few minutes. (Fortune, et al., 1996, p. 62)

The opening line works intertextually to evoke all those stories that begin with 'a dark and stormy night', which is exactly the right time to begin reading a frightening story of this kind. Yet we also sense the ordinariness of Ella's circumstances, something that is underlined when, having eventually stopped her car, with the truck coming to a halt behind her, 'she breathed a sigh of relief', when the truck driver walked towards her', smiling 'in a friendly way, reminding her of Tim Shaw, the Demtel man'. Tim Shaw became famous on Australian television as a salesman who was always offering bargains, typically throwing in steak knives as a bonus to the other specials on offer (http://www.timshaw.com.au/aboutus.html). In this case, Ella realizes that the truck driver is indeed clutching 'a glittering knife', which she cannot escape:

> The truck driver grabbed her around the neck and forced her to the ground. Ella struggled but the man was too strong. He plunged the knife into her and blood flowed through her clothes onto the ground. Blackness enveloped Ella and she knew no more. (Fortune et al., 1996, p. 62)

The story, however, does not stop at this point, but its authors leave a space, and then begin the narrative again. Here is the final paragraph of the story:

> Ella opened her eyes again. Her surroundings came into focus. She was sitting in the driver's seat of a large truck, the steering wheel in her hands. The truck was thundering down a dark stretch of road. She saw, far ahead in the blackness, the rear lights of a car. Out of the corner of her eye she noticed the silvery glint of a long knife. She laughed maniacally, flipped the lights on high and pressed the accelerator to the floor.

Without changing the point of view from which the story is told, the authors succeed in the final paragraph in radically recasting the story from the perspective of the victim to that of the perpetrator of the crime. The reversal remains mysterious, and as a textual effect it can be traced in both 'The Cuckoo Bird' and 'The Thief in the Rocks', stories written respectively by Judith Clarke and Caroline MacDonald, which involve transformation of this kind. As with these stories by published writers, 'Ella's story also raises questions about her identity, who she is, her relationships with those around her, and her potential for both good and evil.

These questions are explored in other 'gothic' stories written by Douglas's students. We shall, however, limit ourselves to mentioning briefly one more example, namely Chas Pagon's 'The Phone Box', which again has an open-ended character that will not allow it to be pinned down in the form of simplistic schema, such as the requirement for a story to have a beginning, a middle and an end (yet another simplistic tenet of genre-theory). The distinctive feature of this story, when compared with other gothic fiction that students produced, is that it is cast in the first person, with the point of view changing from section to section, beginning with the daughter, then the mother, and then the father. The father's section is very short: 'I came home from a hard day's work on that blasted bus over that blasted road in the blasted rain and my tea wasn't even on the table' (Pagon, 1996, p. 61), providing a stark contrast to the points of view of the daughter and the mother, both of whom have fallen victim to an evil force associated with a phone box. Here is what the daughter says:

> I walked up to the phone box and opened the door. Immediately a cold rush of air blew up into my face. I picked up the dangling receiver and spoke into it. The world went black and then light again, but the world looked evil – no, I was looking at it through evil eyes. I dropped the receiver and I saw that it was a monster, a big evil monster … . (Pagon, 1996, p. 61)

We then switch to the mother's point of view, again cast in the first person, when we see her approaching the same phone box, and exactly the same words are used: 'The world went black and then light again, but the world looked evil – no, I was looking at it through evil eyes … ' (etc.).

We can again seek the sources of this repetition and parallelism in the stories by Judith Clarke and Caroline McDonald that the students read prior to writing their own gothic fiction. Clarke's story, for example, revolves around the sentence 'I can cheat strangers with never a word', which is repeated several times in the story, prompting the narrator to find its source, but too late to prevent the mysterious presence replacing her sister. There is no doubt that Chas Pagon, Lorelle Fortune and the other student writers whose stories we have been considering have made these techniques their own, writing out of their situations as young people and using characteristic features of gothic fiction to give representation to their own experiences. The mention of Tim Shaw, the Demtel man, in the story that Lorelle produced with her co-authors also shows how these young people are not shy in making use of whatever semiotic resources are available to them, that they are not bound by conventional distinctions between 'literary' work (as represented by the range of texts they read, from Edgar Allan Poe to contemporary YA writers such Judith Clarke) and popular culture. Tim Shaw, the Demtel man, still has a reputation in Australia for his phrase – 'But wait there's more!' – which he would use several times in the course of promoting Demtel knives on day-time TV ('But wait, there's more! Not only will I give you the steak knives for $39.95, but I'm also prepared to throw in a couple of carving knives!'). So it is possible that this reference to him when describing the way the truck driver approached Ella is doubly ironical, in that the repetition embedded in the narrative (when the victim becomes the perpetrator of the crime) echoes the way Shaw obsessively repeated the phrase: 'But wait, there's more!' The story also conveys a macabre sense of humor in the fact that a television personality famous for his sales pitch when advertising knives should appear before Ella in this story as a homicidal maniac who 'plunged the knife into her and blood flowed through her clothes onto the ground', thus defusing the realism of the horror of Ella's situation. The story is not real. It is a textual artifact. It is a text combining other texts. It is made up of words.

Yet the examples of students' writing that we have just been examining show that their creativity is about more than 'words' or 'text'. One of the most problematical aspects of post-structuralist theory has always been the way literary critics have bracketed out the referent, imagining that Derrida's famous statement – 'there is nothing outside the text' (Derrida, 1974/76, p. 158) – somehow gave them a license to engage in semiotic analysis without getting bogged down in the grubby business of considering the social and political uses that texts actually serve (cf. Eagleton, 1983, p. 206). Classroom settings never allow such bracketing out. The reading and writing that we have been considering is grounded in the social relationships that comprise an English classroom, and crucially bound up with the way these young people negotiate their identities from day to day. 'Intertextuality', indeed, is about more than the relations between texts. Those relations can only be realized through the activities of reading and writing – activities that must be located in the social relationships of the classroom, when young people are given the opportunity to engage in authentic forms of communication in order to make sense of themselves and the world around them.

To highlight this dimension of the way young people read and write intertextually, borrowing from the texts around them in order to create new texts, we shall take a slightly different tack from that which we have followed thus far. The following comprises two classroom narratives by Douglas McClenaghan, in which he enquires into how the reading and writing that students do are inextricably bound up with their attempts to negotiate the social relationships in which they find themselves. These stories highlight the nature of intertextuality as an ongoing activity, as a ceaseless proliferation of meanings, as texts fold into other texts, and each generation attempts anew to make sense of life as it presents itself to them. Our aim is to illustrate how literary theory and specifically 'intertextuality' can sensitize us to the life-worlds and meaning-making practises that young people bring with them into class each day.

Reading and writing intertextually (Two narratives by Douglas McClenaghan)

Tobias Wolff's *This Boy's Life*

When she was in my year 10 English class a couple of years ago, Hannah's anger at the slow break up of her family exploded unexpectedly during our discussion of 'We Remember Your Childhood Well' by Carol Ann Duffy. The poem depicts parents who have abused their child, rationalizing their behavior with euphemisms and platitudes that serve to undermine their message rather than reinforce it. Hannah's contempt for her father, whom she saw as the main culprit in the breakup, was persistent and withering. To her he was a 'try-hard', a 'loser' who pretended to the world that he was a great father while indulging himself in a pathetic mid-life crisis borne of nothing more than dissatisfaction with his life.

Hannah is the second of three sisters, each of whom I have taught. The girls are all tall, blonde and athletic and they share a tough, sardonic view of the world. Hannah combines these traits with blunt outspokenness. It is not surprising that when she eventually found herself in my year 12 Literature class her favorite text was Tobias Wolff's *This Boy's Life*.

Year 12 Literature students are required to write a creative response to one of their set texts. The parameters for this task are fairly broad. Students must write a piece that in some way(s) links to the original text studied and they must write a commentary on how they have drawn on this text or been inspired by particular stylistic features of it. This is a tough task, many students find it daunting, but they come away from having completed it feeling gratitude for the scope that the task has given them to explore and articulate experiences, thoughts and emotions. It is noteworthy that a considerable number of their pieces deal with issues very darkly: violence, madness, incest, death, sexuality, brutal dysfunctional relationships, cruelty. Unsurprisingly, family breakdown is a common focus. Their world hardly matches the bright new projections into the future to be found in government policy documents, such as *The Melbourne Declaration on Educational Goals for Young Australians*.

By the time she was in year 12, Hannah's parents' marriage was over. She decided to write about this in her creative response to *This Boy's Life*. In conversation with Hannah I noted that her contempt for her father that she had so forcefully articulated back in year 10, and now in discussion with me about her piece as it evolved, was much less evident in her writing. Hannah admitted that he was an easy target. Her scornful laughter when describing his purchase of a Harley-Davidson motorbike, when he rode around the local suburban streets 'like a dickhead', contrasted with the brevity, the almost dismissive paragraph she allocated him in her writing. There, her focus was on herself and her response to the breakup, in particular her struggle to understand how she was 'supposed to feel' and 'the expectations of others of who I should be'.

Hannah's understanding of Wolff's memoir gave her the capacity to write her own memoir with far greater nuance and subtlety than might otherwise have been possible. This school task, quite circumscribed in that she must draw explicitly from Wolff, provided a context, as well as supporting ideas and strategies for her to confront the question of how she has dealt with her parents' separation. In her commentary she wrote:

> I feel I succeeded in my memoir, encompassing many Wolff tropes and stylistic techniques, e.g. inserting someone's voice into first person prose or using rushed and heavy sentences to convey urgency. I included reference to identity, failed parents, appearance versus reality, chaos of the universe, and finished off in typical Wolff style – unfinished and unresolved.

I mentioned that family breakup is a common theme of these memoirs. Before Hannah's class embarked on their writing I read to them examples of other students' work that I have collected over the years, knowing that students usually find the work of other students inspiring. I do not hand out copies of these texts but read them aloud, and I then read the self-reflective commentary for each. At times I stop and discuss what the writer is doing, both in the memoir and in the commentary, and ask students to note down ideas that they might find interesting. It might, perhaps, be an observation about the structure of the piece, or a link to the original text.

One piece that I read to Hannah's class was written by a student who had done exactly the same task based on *This Boy's Life* a few years previously. Looking at both Hannah and Michelle's pieces, it is interesting to note how the earlier piece has influenced the latter. Both begin with a contextualizing introduction about the family crisis, then immediately begin to explore the complexities of each writer's response to this crisis. Each piece looks at how the writer sees her position and identity in the world differently to her life before the breakup. Both girls explore, with ruthless honesty, their sense of self and their efforts to reconstruct their identities against the ways in which others attempted to position them and the existential crisis that ensued. Michelle writes, 'My made-up life began to have more of an impact than my real life', as she turns away from the hurt of the breakup and tries to pretend that her family is still normal – an idea taken from Wolff and used to give meaning to her own behavior. Hannah writes: 'As I lay in bed that night I wondered if I'd broken down because I actually cared, or because I wanted to pretend like I did' – echoing Wolff in its ambiguity and sense of conflictedness and irresolution.

Judith Clarke's *The Cuckoo Bird* revisited

I sometimes read a blog about so-called e-learning written by a primary school assistant principal here in Melbourne. This is a fancy name for computer-mediated learning that typically highlights the significance of electronic communication. The language he uses is replete with the usual technophile clichés about how e-learning and technology are revolutionizing classrooms. It reflects disdain for those of us who are benightedly working within outmoded paradigms. Unsurprisingly, his focus is narrowly on the technology itself and what it will do, with only a gesture in the direction of the young people who will be forced to use it in the ways dictated by experts like him. Typically of educational 'leadership' in Victoria at the moment, he fulsomely enthuses about the potential of e-learning for teaching and learning, jumping on board this pedagogical bandwagon without any regard to the way young people might meaningfully appropriate the technologies named by this buzz term and use it in ways that are personally meaningful to them.

1:1 technology refers to classrooms where each student is working with a computing device, such as a netbook computer or iPad. Netbook computers are considered passé by the e-learning cognoscenti and 1:1 computing is similarly dismissed as positively Jurassic. However, I want to look at an alternative interpretation with my observations of a class of year 9 students who were using 1:1 technology writing stories. The school in which I work has purchased class sets of netbook computers and strategically positioned these in different parts of the school to give as many classes as possible access to computers. They provide internet access and a suite of approved software, including the ubiquitous Microsoft Office. Funding has not extended to providing professional development for using the netbooks with classes or specific professional development on the programs provided. However, teachers seem happy with the current setup and the netbooks are used regularly, albeit for a limited range of applications, such as writing, which is what I used them for with my group.

My year 9 Literature class had been reading a range of short stories. One story that shocked and impressed them was a gothic tale, *The Cuckoo Bird*, by Judith Clarke, a story that I have used with my classes many times before (as in the account that we have given of working with 'teenage gothic'). Before reading the story, I always ask the class to think about what kind of story this is as I read it aloud, and to think about how they could justify their decision by referring to specific aspects of the story. When I finish reading, this is the first task I set them, to write responses to these questions without discussing their opinions with each other. At the end of the story on this particular occasion some students gasped or murmured feelings of shock, as the horror of what had happened enveloped them. Then we began to examine everyone's responses by discussing textual features that they thought made the story a gothic story or horror tale.

I was intrigued by the range of comments they made that instanced other horror stories, mainly films, which they invoked in order to explain or elaborate their responses to *The Cuckoo Bird*. They drew analogies between what they had seen in films and what we had read in the story. Some students shared my enthusiasm for Stanley Kubrick's film version of *The Shining*, and they were keen to talk about how this film built up suspense, as our story had. 'You know there's something wrong but they don't show what it is, you just have to get it slowly' was one student's observation. Some students simply wanted to discuss gothic films and books in general. Recommendations for viewing and reading flew around the room. I was struck by the way their response to *The Cuckoo Bird* was shaped by their considerable knowledge of other books and films that might be read as examples of the gothic genre, and by the discriminations they were exercising in discussing the similarities and differences between these texts.

The Cuckoo Bird was the most popular of the stories we looked at and inspired some of the students to have a go at a gothic tale of their own. The writing process was interesting to observe and provides a riposte to those who see little value in 1:1 computing in schools. Each student had a netbook computer as part of a class set wheeled into the classroom in a massive trolley, and wrote their stories over two weeks. The e-learning blogger dismisses 1:1 working as simply entrenching 'traditional' ways of learning, with each student busy on his or her own work. He argues that this precludes 'interacting', 'collaborating' and 'cooperating', which are among the current modish vocabulary used to depict 'best practice' in schools. However, the year 9 students' work on their stories actually involved a lot of sharing of work and collaboration. Some students sat on the floor so that they could prop the netbooks on their knees or rest them on the floor because they were keen to keep up with what their friends were writing. The students in these groups wanted to share with just a couple of friends and this involved regular swapping of computers so that they could read each other's work, or reading aloud while the others in the group paused in their writing in order to listen. Occasionally part of a story was then shared with the rest of the class by the student who read it aloud to everyone who wanted to listen. Eventually netbooks were being passed from hand to hand, and from group to group, like pizzas being shared at a party. Any student's story might be passed along to a succession of readers who yelled approval to the writer. Sometimes they would call out, asking whose story they'd just read; at other times students called 'Where's my story?' or 'Who's got my computer?', as they lost track of where their work had gone while reading other students' work.

I required students to write a commentary on their story. Asking them for this reflection helps them to think about and learn from the way they have constructed their writing. The commentary gives them an opportunity to foreground literary elements of their story such as creating a certain kind of atmosphere. In particular I ask them to look at where they found ideas or inspiration in other texts and to look at this specifically. Here is an excerpt from Lara's commentary:

> I just felt like they were a figure of sadness, in a sense, a shadow of humanity itself, like a solid form of our faults, if that makes sense? Like they really emphasize how cruel society can be. There are a few times when I thought that the main character was a spirit, trapped on this earth really to serve their purpose before moving on, which makes the humans look innocent, but then there are more points in the story where the main character is real and living, so that's what I decided to stress. I created this character with a little help from the book *Hate List*, where the main character is an outcast. And so I exaggerated the loner aspect and came up with the whole view of the main character. Also, I got the idea for them to be wanting to sort of change, and fix people before themselves from the book *The Bone Doll's Twin* where the character doesn't really understand the world and is quite naïve and fragile, but caring.

Intertextuality appears to be at the heart of the way Lara conceives composition or creativity. Not only can she explain the influences from other texts on her writing, but she has a strong sense of the literary qualities she is striving for: '… a figure of sadness, in a sense, a shadow of humanity itself, like a solid form of our faults'. Lara's story contains such self-conscious literary effects in part because this is a Literature class and she sees herself as a 'Literature' student. Most of the students aimed to produce a 'literary' story. As Caroline, another girl in Lara's class, said, as I was reading her draft, she 'really wanted to include a romance scene but my story won't let me'. Her previous year's teacher had told her that all school stories had to be rated 'PG' or Parental Guidance, just as films are. The implication of the teacher's directive was that she must write something mild and innocuous. With this story she was determined that it be 'more mature and sophisticated'.

Conclusion

Lara's comments that the characters in her story presented 'a figure of sadness, in a sense, a shadow of humanity itself, like a solid form of our faults' is what you might expect from a student who enjoys reading stories and poems and experimenting with literary form. She might thus be said to be dialogically appropriating the language associated with literary discourse, using words that are 'half someone else's' (Bakhtin, 1981/87, p. 293) in an effort to write and talk her way into the ways of knowing and feeling that we value as literary educators. This may not seem very subversive, to pick up the theme we announced in the title of this essay. It might instead be read as an example of how English teachers are a 'self-perpetuating race' (cf. Doecke and McKnight, 2003), inducting their students into values and beliefs of their professional community, and thus maintaining the status quo.

And yet where, after all, would we expect Lara to begin in her efforts to make sense of her experiences than with the language that pre-exists her? As John Frow has observed, 'no text is unique; we could not recognize it if it were' (Frow, 2006, p. 48). Texts always invoke other texts; they 'are constituted as such by their relationships with other texts' (ibid.). And this is not simply a matter of a relationship between texts. A problematical aspect of literary theory has always been its tendency to fetishize the text, as though life can be bracketed out of any consideration of what texts do. This is most famously captured by Roland Barthes' pronouncement of the 'death' of the author (Barthes 1978, p. 143), as though any attention to the 'person' of the author, including the values and beliefs that he or she may have held as an active participant in society, hopelessly compromises a literary critic's attempt to tease out the significance of that author's writing. What classrooms show us is that the perpetual borrowing in which young people engage is mediated by the social relationships that they negotiate each day as they attempt to understand themselves and each other. Their writing is a crucial form of identity work, reflecting their struggle to make sense of the world around them. Lara's comments reveal more than an adolescent attempting to mime a discourse, as though her writing is not yet the 'real' thing. Her comments provide a compelling perspective on the social engineering in which neo-liberal governments are currently engaging in their efforts to produce a citizenry that serves the interests of corporate society. They speak back to the schemes of government, gesturing towards realms of thought and emotion that those schemes deny.

Where, in neo-liberal policy statements like *The Melbourne Declaration on Education Goals for Young Australians* is there space for words like 'sadness', or any recognition of our 'faults'? What, indeed, would the anonymous authors who wrote this document make of the notion of 'a shadow of humanity'? Where does the idea of 'humanity' fit within the futuristic scenarios in which this document traffics? Are the authors of this document capable of entertaining the idea, suggested by the word 'shadow', that we might not be behaving as humanely as we ought, that we might be not sufficiently mindful of our obligations to respond to others around us, or, indeed, to respond to the call of 'the other within' (cf. Howie, 2008)? What do we really make of our behavior when it is measured against this particular 'benchmark' or 'performance indicator'?

We remain struck by the contrast between the futuristic rhetoric of neo-liberal policy statements, such as *The Melbourne Declaration on Education Goals for Young Australians*, and the evocative accounts of human situations that we constantly encounter in the writing that students present to us. The language of the Melbourne Declaration comprises sweeping generalizations about young people and the global changes they face, presenting a vision of a citizenry that is monolithic. It constructs individuals as blank slates, defined primarily by an impulse to compete for a place within the economy. Young people, to use the words of the preamble to the Melbourne Declaration, who wish to participate in 'a high quality life' that will be produced through Australia's capacity 'to compete in the global economy', need to strive for 'the knowledge, understanding, skills and values to take advantage of opportunity and to face the challenges of this era with confidence' (p. 4). This is hardly a compelling vision of an Australian democracy, especially when it is set against the background of 40 percent youth unemployment in some regions of Australia that has led to severe social alienation and political disenfranchisement (http://www.abc.net.au/7.30/content/2012/s3564551.htm).

Needless to say, the ways in which young people compose intertextually hardly gives rise to an explicit critique of the complex ideological machinery underpinning policy statements like the *Melbourne Declaration*, such as nationwide standardized testing or the competitive academic curriculum that has recently been introduced in Australia. We could hardly expect young people to be fully aware in this way. Recent curriculum and policy documents comprise a world that they are obliged to negotiate, as they try to make their way through the Australian education system, just as their teachers have no choice but to implement the curriculum that the Australian government has imposed on them. Teachers face the prospect of not only teaching capital-L Literature but also drilling and skilling their students in the rules of basic grammar, all set out in the form of a multitude of outcomes specified by the new curriculum. Yet hope is not something that needs to be justified on the basis of rational calculation, if it really lends itself to rational calculation at all – that would be to remain locked in the modes of thought that typify standards-based reforms, where everything must be pinned down in advance, reflecting a deep-seated fear of the potential of people to imagine their lives differently. What people do is always more complex than what they think they are doing, and by trying to attend to what they do we can always gain a glimpse of other possibilities, other forms of thought and imagination to those that prevail at the moment. Young people, as we have observed earlier in this essay, are not necessarily able to explain fully the writing they produce. The subversive potential of what they do lies, rather, in a certain excess, a certain complexity of form and content that challenges the parameters that adults seek to impose on them.

The word 'intertextuality' names a sensitivity towards the way texts transform other texts (cf. Frow, 2006, p. 148), refusing to be contained within a pre-existing notion of what a particular text or genre 'is'. Rather, to write intertextually is to step into the unknown. This does not mean that anything goes (as Caroline remarked, her story wouldn't let her incorporate a romantic element, because it was taking her somewhere else) but engaging in an inquiry into the potential of the language available to us to give form to our experiences. The readiness of young people to appropriate and transform texts is a sign of their capacity to resist the essentialism of supposing that people and things are simply what they are, or indeed that the world is simply what it is (now and forever). When young people appropriate and transform texts they are thinking relationally, challenging traditional forms of classification and boundary protection.

References

Australian Curriculum, Assessment and Reporting Authority (ACARA) (2010). *The Australian Curriculum: English.* http://www.australiancurriculum.edu.au/English/Curriculum/F-10 [accessed July 2014].

Ballis, H. and Richardson, P. (1997). 'Roads to Damascus: conversion Stories and their implications for literacy educators'. *English in Australia*, 119–20, October, 110–17.

Bakhtin, M. M. (1981/87). *The Dialogic Imagination: Four Essays.* Austin: University of Texas Press.

Barnes, D. (1975/92). *From Communication to Curriculum*, 2nd edn. Portsmouth, NH: Boynton/Cook.

Barthes, R. (1978). *Image, Music, Text*, trans. S. Heath. New York: Hill and Wang.

Bennett, T. (1979). *Formalism and Marxism.* London: Methuen.

Buckingham, D. (1995). 'Distress and delight: children's horror talk'. *The English and Media Magazine*, No. 32, pp 18–32.

Cope, B. and Kalantzis, M. (eds) (1993). *The Powers of Literacy: A Genre Approach to Teaching Writing.* London: The Falmer Press.

Cope, B. and Kalantzis, M. (2000). *Multiliteracies: Literacy Learning and the Design of Social Futures.* South Yarra, Australia: Macmillan.

Corcoran, B. (1998). 'Facing up to Boomer's "Epic Challenge": The progressives under fire – *English in Australia*, 1990–1996'. *English in Australia*, 122, July, 104–17.

Culler, J. (2007). *The Literary in Theory.* Stanford: Stanford University Press.

Darling-Hammond, L. (2004). 'Standards, accountability, and school reform', *Teachers College Record, 106*(6), 1047–85.

Department for Education (DfE) (2011). *Teachers' Standards.* Available online at http://media.education.gov.uk/assets/files/pdf/t/teachers%20standards%20%20%20oct%202011.pdf [accessed April 2012].

Derewianka, B. (1990). *Exploring How Texts Work.* Newtown: PETA.

Derrida, J. (1974/76). *Of Grammatology*, trans. Gayatri Chakravorty Spivak. Baltimore and London: Johns Hopkins Press.

Doecke, B. and McClenaghan, D. (2011a). 'Classrooms, Creativity and Everyday Life: A Continuing Inquiry'. In B. Doecke, G. Parr and W. Sawyer (eds), *Creating an Australian Curriculum for English*, pp. 35–54. Putney, NSW: Phoenix Education.

— (2011b). *Confronting Practice: Classroom Investigations into Language and Learning*. Putney, NSW: Phoenix Education.

Doecke, B. and McKnight, L. (2003). 'Handling Irony: Forming a Professional Identity as an English Teacher'. In B. Doecke, D. Homer and H. Nixon (eds), *English Teachers at Work: Narratives, Counter Narratives and Arguments*, pp. 291–311. Kent Town: Wakefield Press/AATE.

Doecke, B., McClenaghan, D. and Petris, L. (2011). 'Teaching small 'l' literature: Lessons from *English in Australia*'. In B. Doecke, L. McLean Davis and P. Mead (eds), *Teaching Australian Literature: From Classroom Conversations to National imaginings*, pp. 266–92. Kent Town: Wakefield Press/AATE,

Eagleton, T. (1983). *Literary Theory: An Introduction*. Oxford: Basil Blackwell.

—(2003). *After Theory*. London: Allen Lane.

—(2012). *The Event of Literature*. New Haven and London: Yale University Press.

Exton, R. (1982). The Post-Structuralist Always Reads Twice', *The English and Media Magazine*, 10, 13–19.

Fortune, L., Oliver, E., Kelley, S., Hargreaves, K. and Sharpe, A. (1996). 'Takeover'. In D. McClenaghan, B. Doecke and H. Parr (eds), *Englishworks Collection 2*, p. 62. Oakleigh: Cambridge University Press.

Frow, J. (2006). *Genre*. Abingdon: Routledge.

Howie, M. (2008). 'Embracing the other within: dialogical ethics, resistance and professional advocacy in English teaching', *English Teaching: Practice and Critique*, May, 2008, 7, (1), 103–18. http://education.waikato.ac.nz/research/files/etpc/2008v7n1nar1.pdf [accessed April 2012].

McClenaghan, D., Doecke, B. and Parr, H. (1995). *Englishworks 2*. Oakleigh: Cambridge University Press.

Melbourne Declaration on Educational Goals for Young Australians (2008). Melbourne Australia: Ministerial Council on Education, Employment, Training and Youth Affairs (MCEETYA).

Mellor, B. (1989). *Reading Hamlet*. Scarborough: Chalkface Press.

Mellor, B. and Patterson, A. (1991). 'Reading character: reading genre', *English in Australia*, 95, 4–23.

—(1994). 'Producing readings: freedom versus normativity', *English in Australia*, 109, September, 57–75.

Mellor, B., O'Neill, M. and Patterson, A. (1987). *Reading Stories*. Scarborough: Chalkface Press.

Moon, B. (1990). 'What is post-structuralism?' *English in Australia*, 94, 8–22.

—(1993, rpt. 1999). *Literary Terms: A Practical Glossary*. Cottesloe, WA: Chalkface Press.

Pagon, C. (1996). 'The Phone Box'. In D. McClenaghan, B. Doecke and H. Parr (eds), *Englishworks Collection 2*, p. 61. Oakleigh: Cambridge University Press.

Patterson, A. (1992). 'Individualism in English: From personal growth to discursive construction'. *English Education*, 24, (3), 131–46.

Reid, I. (1984/88). *The Making of Literature: Texts, Contexts and Classroom Practices*. Norwood, SA: Australian Association for the Teaching of English.

Sawyer, W. (2005). 'Becoming a *New* New Critic: Assessing Student Writing'. In B. Doecke and G. Parr (eds), *Writing=Learning*, pp. 129–48. Kent Town: Wakefield Press/AATE.

Walshe, R. D. (1982). 'The writing revolution'. *English in Australia*, 62, October, 3–15.

Knowledge in English Teaching – The Naming of Parts?

4

Sue Brindley

Chapter Outline

Models of knowledge

In writing this chapter, I am going to reference two other chapters from this book: Locke's 'Paradigms of English', and Doecke and McClenaghan's 'Intertextuality and Subversion'. Both chapters refer to the ways in which knowledge about English and English teaching are developed:

> It needs to be emphasized that … [professional content] knowledge is not going to be developed in teachers' heads out of books. It will only be developed by teachers performing acts of … self-reflexivity. (Locke, 2014, p. 26)

> Truly worthwhile learning is something you experience, an event that might be said to transcend time because it remains with you, an ineradicable part of your identity, shaping your engagement with the present. (Doecke and McClenaghan, 2014, p. 30)

Knowledge as represented in these two quotes is generated through *self-reflexivity*, and is integrated into your 'self' as part of your identity. It is a highly personalized version of knowledge which English teachers are encouraged to consider as part of their professional development. To most English teachers, myself included, this is an entirely appropriate way to develop knowledge in English. However, in the UK at least, knowledge in English also falls under the remit of policymakers. The context of policy knowledge development is a centrally assessed and inspected national curriculum, and within this context, knowledge is not constructed through self-reflexivity, but by policy committees. As I have argued elsewhere (Brindley, 2013a), policy knowledge is not necessarily knowledge that becomes an 'ineradicable part of your identity', but may well instead represent a version of knowledge that does not shape your version (or vision) of yourself but with which you *have* to engage. In short then, I am contending that knowledge in English is constructed in at least two ways, which might be described as competing both in content and construct. I refer to this as the 'knowledge dichotomy'.

The 'knowledge dichotomy' that English teachers are likely to encounter throughout their careers is no abstract theoretical notion, but a reality which impinges on – indeed, shapes – day-to-day practise. Consider, for example, the following statements, taken from the UK Teachers' Standards (DfE, May 2012):

> 3 [Teachers must] Demonstrate good subject and curriculum knowledge:
>
> - demonstrate a critical understanding of developments in the subject and curriculum areas, and promote the value of scholarship
>
> - demonstrate an understanding of and take responsibility for promoting high standards of literacy, articulacy and the correct use of standard English, whatever the teacher's specialist subject.

Although not articulated as such, the knowledge dichotomy is clearly represented here. The first statement places the teacher as the *constructor* of knowledge. Importantly, English teachers are required to engage with a 'critical understanding of developments in the subject and curriculum areas'. *Critical* understanding is central – engagement with, and consideration of, differing interpretations is at the heart of English teaching: text is, for example, examined through a conceptual framework of possible *meanings* (plural) – the hermeneutic of the subject. Espousing intellectual engagement is reinforced through the additional clause '… and promote the value of scholarship', an activity that implies depth of investigation and opportunity to build new knowledge – or at least new understanding – from sustained engagement with the work of others in the field.

The second statement, however, has implicit in it a model of knowledge that *excludes* knowledge as a negotiated domain, and thereby also excludes the teacher (and indeed the student) as being active in the construction of knowledge. Rather, knowledge is a given, with 'correct' and incorrect versions extant. The teacher is *deliverer* of 'the knowledge', constructed and agreed elsewhere, and judged as accurately delivered ('effectively taught') against criteria developed by others, that is, examination boards, or inspection agencies such as Ofsted.

The second knowledge model is seen clearly in policy documents in the UK – the national curriculum, literacy strategies and associated assessments, SATs and GCSEs, and it is the model that dominates teachers' working lives in UK schools within a regime of accountability and league tables.

The conundrum that English teachers have placed before them is that these two models of knowledge are fundamentally in opposition one to another: is knowledge constructed, or given; and is the place of the teacher (and student) to debate and develop, or to 'acquire' knowledge? And yet, it is obligatory for English teachers to interact with both models.

The argument of this chapter is not whether these two versions of knowledge are both legitimate – that is an argument that can be found elsewhere (see for example Brindley, 2013a). The chapter concerns itself rather with the balance of emphasis given to these two types of knowledge, and to consider, given that both, in the UK at least, are *required* models of knowledge, how English teachers can continue to be constructors of knowledge in an environment dominated by accountability.

Ways of knowing: Policy and professional knowledge

Teacher education, at initial (pre-service) and continuing (in-service) level is currently preoccupied with 'getting it right' – that is, responding to the variety of policy demands that emanate from government. Teacher education, whatever the stage or route, is focused on ensuring familiarity with the demands of the national curriculum and syllabuses, and the how-to of ensuring students are successful in the assessment of these areas – where assessment formats inevitably can only deal with the outcome of acquired knowledge, since demonstrating sophisticated thinking and deep engagement with scholarship is not possible through a timed written examination – thus the PhD viva rather than written exam. Since assessment is such a high-stakes activity for schools, with success being measured almost entirely through the end-point public reporting of examination results rather than student progression over time statistics, time and energy become focused on ensuring high examination pass rates. Teacher professional development becomes increasingly fixated on ensuring, in the infamous words of one UK education minister, 'everyone performs above average' – the Lake Wobegon effect. Within this logically impossible demand, teachers are urged to solve the problem of the 'long tail of underperformance' or to address the 'catch up' agenda. As I write this chapter, I have little doubt that other, similar, demands will be made of teachers in the future, and all constructed within the imperative of international comparison charts of educational success (PISA – Program for International Student Assessment) – the Ministerial version of accountability. Education as defined by global statistics constructs the model of knowledge defined as a given, and in a bid to compete within this arena, the emphasis on control of teacher activity by policy makers is inevitable. We might refer to this version as *policy knowledge*. However, and as important as this type of knowledge might be argued to be, there is, as we have seen, another type of knowledge that is required – that of criticality and scholarship, which we might call *professional knowledge*. Professional knowledge reflects an understanding of the subject in terms of, for example, its own history, its social and historical context, its placement in key debates such as structuralism and post-structuralism, of the cultural shaping of text, of genre, of relationships between literature and art or music or philosophy, of issues in language that reflect power or historical narratives of use, of the very purposes and functions of teaching English – in short, the wider and deeper concerns of the subject. It is perhaps worth noting too that for English teachers, the value of professional knowledge lies not only in their own way of knowing, but also in the type of knowledge that will be required of English students at post 16, and particularly at University, where acquisition of the knowledge of others without intellectual engagement with those ideas is little-prized.

Knowledge and discourse

What I am arguing, that is, the existence of two types of knowledge in English teaching, draws on a respectable history of such constructions (Bernstein, 2000). That knowledge is shaped by specific discourse and is also rooted in compelling scholarship. In 1947 Durkheim developed the notion of 'sacred' and 'profane' knowledge, each with its particular discourse, representing respectively the discourse of the types of knowledge I am calling professional and policy. Sacred knowledge was to be found in the notion of the professional as autonomous, that is, self-governing. The discourse of sacred knowledge is marked out by its assumption of knowledge as in and of itself valuable, outside of any policy demands: 'the sacred … refers to knowledge for 'intrinsic' non-instrumental purposes, such knowledge being accorded a higher legitimacy and authority than that tied to … instrumental practices' (Beck, 1999: 225).

In contrast, profane knowledge is that which precisely deals with 'instrumental practices' – that is, in Beck's argument, the demands of policy makers. Beck links profane knowledge, and its associated discourse of managerialism, to the 'profane' sphere of economic production (2002, p. 620) with education as subject to the imperatives of the marketplace. We might think, for example, of the way in which English became linked, indeed synonymous in some cases, with literacy as a skills-based construct, and connected to the notion of the employable global citizen. In this instrumentalist version of English, the emphasis is on the acquisition of skills needed in the workplace, not to any idea that English should be about, for example, Cox's (1991) personal growth model or, in Locke's terms, that knowledge should be built through self-reflexivity. Instead, the discourse of the profane is about functionality, relevance and workplace success. The discourses of the sacred and the profane do not overlap, but are rooted in quite different versions of knowledge. The knowledge dichotomy is alive and well. The juxtaposition of purpose and outcome raises issues of some complexity. Do we teach English to provide literate workers for a global economy, or to develop self-realizing individuals within a democratic society? Do we teach Shakespeare because his plays are set within the national curriculum, or because he speaks to universal themes that shape our lives? If both, what takes priority in reality? And where is this discussed?

Discourse

Knowledge literally needs to be given a voice. Without a language to express key ideas, those ideas cease to exist. As Foucault points out: Discourse may seem of little account, but the prohibitions to which it is subject reveal soon enough its links with desire and power (1971, pp. 11–12).

For example, the emphasis given to policy knowledge has ensured that the discourse of policy is firmly embedded in teachers' working lives. In terms of English, where once the introduction of the national curriculum required explanation and courses to secure understanding about technical terminology such as level descriptors, SATs and so forth, and the curriculum itself required training to understand the demands of Standard English, and grammar requirements such as modal verbs, teachers are now more than familiar with such terms, and indeed, routinely deal with far more complex curriculum demands: the discourse of this type of knowledge is established and unquestioned. We all speak, as it were, policy.

English professional knowledge discourse though has experienced a concomitant dip. It is now an unusual event in an English department to hear talk about English *as a subject*, outside of the curriculum and syllabus demands. This is not a pejorative observation, but an acknowledgment that English teachers have had their working lives so dominated by the onslaught of policy knowledge demands (including those of Ofsted's inspection regime), and their commitments to their students have been so reliant on the delivery of that knowledge (indeed now with the unhappy situation of students themselves seeing knowledge defined by policy, demanding only to know 'what is needed to pass exams') that professional knowledge and its associated discourse have become marginalized, simply by virtue of survival within schools. This is a matter of professional regret and, ironically, simultaneously a neglect of the type of professional knowledge and access to a discourse that is required by the Teachers' Standards. It is, I would argue, possession of professional knowledge that actually distinguishes between the 'competent' and the 'outstanding' teacher: the competent teacher can teach about a text or a language theme, but an outstanding teacher uses that text or language theme to demonstrate English as an intellectual mapping of ideas through word and image. Understanding English in this way is the difference between standing in a room lit by a single (low-energy) light bulb and standing under a canopy of brilliant stars.

Teacher identity

Given that Doecke and McClenaghan claim that worthwhile learning shapes teacher identity, it is interesting to find that 'sacred and profane' knowledge and discourse are also to be found in research into teacher identity. In 2000, Bernstein applied the notions of sacred and profane knowledge to types of teacher identity. Specifically, Bernstein argued that professional knowledge, owned and legitimized through the teacher (the sacred discourse), was being replaced by that owned and legitimized through the state (the profane discourse) and that this relocation of knowledge to state control (the dimension of power) results in a dislocation of the professional values and beliefs held by the individual: '… knowledge is being separated from inwardness, from commitments, from personal dedication, from the deep structures of the self …' (Bernstein, 2000, p. 87).

The result, Bernstein claims, is the replacement of the moral positioning of the teacher as professional by a set of values tailored to state needs, which in turn teachers are required to internalize as their own – a 'policy' identity. The introduction of competences and standards are, Bernstein argues, mechanisms whereby state controls are exercised, but also a means of producing a generation of teachers whose working lives are defined by the boundaries of the 'profane' rather than the 'sacred' knowledge. In other words, the identity of the English teacher is shaped by knowledge through policy demands, and our identity is that of the 'good teacher' as effective deliverer of this type of knowledge.

Teachers as intellectuals

Developing professional knowledge requires an approach that does not respond to the types of short-term skills-based training courses normally associated with updating policy-demands knowledge, but rather requires an approach to the subject in ways that demonstrate critical engagement with a network of concepts, rather than discrete 'units' of knowledge. Professional knowledge constitutes the development of frames of reference that deal with relationships in literature and language – between texts, genres, authors, ideas in history, social themes, philosophical constructs – the list is as extensive as the knowledge is deep. Embedded within this is the notion of values and education as a political act – the shaping of the democratic citizen. This constitutes quite a shift from the policy idea of being a good teacher, that is, as compliant, to a professional version of the good teacher, that is, engaged with a complex of ideas, active in shaping knowledge, and with a moral imperative. Giroux (1988) refers to the teacher's role thus developed as 'teacher as intellectual', active and critical constructors of meaning. Developing this role can be through a number of routes: formalized through masters and doctoral courses, undertaken through sustained personal study over time, through reading widely, through discussion and debate – but what all routes have in common is that such knowledge is built cumulatively and over time, and involves active engagement with ideas. This is what Giroux means when he describes the need for teachers to be intellectuals.

It could be argued that a quite different framing of effective teaching must be developed if the role as intellectual is to be realized, one that locates teacher education within professional knowledge. One such way of achieving this mindset is through positioning teachers as researchers: 'In order to function as intellectuals, teachers must create the ... conditions necessary for them to write, research, and work with each other ...' (Giroux, 1988, p. xxxiv).

It might be said that the 'conditions necessary for [teachers] to write, research and work together' are already in place (Giroux, 1988, p. xxxiv). Certainly, teacher research (or as it is sometimes referred to, teacher enquiry) is already established as practise within many schools. The issue here is the *purpose* that such research is put to. For example, research is firmly on the agenda of government as a way of developing policy knowledge (see for example, Cordingley, 2008). However, in Giroux's terms, teacher research is much more than simply a way of implementing policy knowledge more effectively (though it is that too). It is an opportunity to critically explore and develop understanding and knowledge in a specialist field, in our case, English, with a view to professional knowledge as vision: 'Change is a fundamental goal of the teacher as a critical researcher.... Such teachers hold a vision and act through their research to achieve that vision ...' (Kincheloe, 2003, p. 47).

In my own research (Brindley, 2013a, b) the findings included the ways in which teachers find themselves both committed to ensuring student success through compliant observation of policy knowledge whilst simultaneously being aware that this type of teaching does not represent learning as they would have it – that is, exploratory and heuristic. Bringing about that vision is, as I have argued thus far, dependent on teachers as intellectuals reclaiming – indeed owning – professional knowledge with teacher research as a mechanism for achieving that.

Teacher knowledge, discourse and research

The area now to be explored then is how teacher research might support the generation of both professional knowledge and the discourse of professional knowledge. I am going to explore this through an examination of a research project on dialogic teaching, undertaken by two English teachers, David and Emma, from one department in a highly successful school on the outer reaches of London. The context for this research project was the CamStar (Cambridge, School teachers and research) project which I co-ordinate. David's school is a CamStar school and David is an experienced teacher with a clear commitment to teacher research. He was a founder member of CamStar, and his own enthusiasm for learning was made clear in one of a series of interviews I undertook with teachers in exploring teacher knowledge and learning:

> I've always wanted to ... always been hungry to keep learning about teaching and learning, you know to keep refining my own practice. And I feel a sense of responsibility that as English subject leader it's important that I show a lead, bring on others who are leaders in learning. And it really helps with the teaching. (David: Head of English)

The research into dialogic teaching I describe here was part of CamTalk: dialogic teaching and learning – one of the projects within CamStar. Originally the CamTalk project was designed to last one year. So powerful was it found to be by participating teachers that the project was extended to three years. In this project, David involved a colleague, Emma, who had recently completed her MEd (Researching Practise) at Cambridge following her PGCE at the Faculty. Her thesis for her MEd was on dialogic teaching and learning, and this thesis was used as part of the CamTalk research at the school. The reports from which I am going to quote in this section (Dialogic Teaching, and Still talking … Dialogic Teaching) describe and reflect on David and Emma's year two and year three outcomes. Their decision to research into dialogic teaching, an area of professional (rather than policy) knowledge, makes a claim for the significance of professional knowledge for teachers.

Briefly, dialogic teaching challenges the dominant form of classroom discourse (IRF – initiation, response, feedback) that is found in most classroom exchanges. It seeks to alter the classroom from a site of monologic teacher discourse to one that values learning through discussion between teacher and student, and student and student, developing a discourse shared by all participants. Robin Alexander (2004, p. 28) cites five major types of classroom exchange:

- *collectivity*: teachers and children address learning tasks together, whether as a group or as a class;
- *reciprocity*: teachers and children listen to each other, share ideas and consider alternative viewpoints;
- *support*: children articulate their ideas freely, without fear of embarrassment over 'wrong' answers; and they help each other to reach common understandings;
- *cumulation*: teachers and children build on their own and each other's ideas and chain them into coherent lines of thinking and enquiry;
- *purposefulness*: the dialog is planned and transacted with specific learning outcomes clearly in view.

Developing teacher awareness of these alternative ways of constructing dialog has, Alexander claims, substantial positive impact on student learning.

At the launch CamTalk conference, Alexander outlined his research and its importance for the classroom. David wrote that he found the conference:

> … inspiring. It led to focused reflection upon the way in which dialogue is used to enhance teaching and learning within English lessons, with specific consideration of Alexander's ideas of the importance of questioning as well as engaging with student response to extend learning.

However, what most interested David was a part of Alexander's presentation where he illustrated, through video taken in classrooms in Russia, an exciting approach to developing cumulative dialog that encouraged students to take part in individual extended dialog of seven/eight minutes with the teacher, much like a tutorial, while other students were trained to listen and analyze the exchange for their own learning. So powerful was this felt to be that David's English department decided to change classroom strategies to reflect this approach. David stated:

The decision was made that extended teacher–students dialogues were to be added to the department's teaching and learning repertoire which, as a consequence, would potentially reduce the number of strategies used during certain lessons, and possibly lead to less pace in general. It was important to concentrate upon the quality and the content of classroom talk, and to give space for increased opportunities for more dialogue to become 'cumulative' – the notion of teachers and students working together to build upon their own and each other's ideas – arguably the most important, and the most challenging, of Alexander's five 'principles' of Dialogic Teaching.

David and Emma's response was to design an action research project (identify a problem, develop a possible solution, implement that, evaluate the outcomes) to explore the use of extended dialogic teaching. The account that follows is edited from David and Emma's (Greenwood, D. and Barton, E. (2009/10) Dialogic Teaching), and gives an indication of the research focus, approach and outcomes:

Dialogic Teaching Extended teacher–student dialogs in the Secondary English classroom: An English department research project

The pilot of this new method of dialogue took place with a shared AS/A2 class of 14 students. Extended teacher–student dialogues occurred numerous times with the same class, choosing different students each time (Emma was completing AS work on Donne's Songs and Sonnets before moving to Shakespeare's *Measure for Measure* for A2, and David was finishing AS work on Miller's *Death of a Salesman* before turning to Coleridge's *The Rime of the Ancient Mariner*). Both teachers had several lessons filmed, using teacher–student dialogues alongside other strategies, enjoying the opportunity to engage in far more meaningful talk with students. The recordings were watched and evaluated together with specific focus upon questioning as well as on the students' responses and how successfully these were built upon during the extended dialogues in order to move students' learning forward. Typically the following types of 'open' prompts and questions were used:

- 'Talk to us about … '

- 'Why … ?'

- 'What do you think … ?'

- 'Help us to evaluate … '

- 'How is this shown … ?'

- Can you explain … ?

- What questions do you now have … ?

Data were collected though observations of each other's lessons, concentrating either on questioning or the development of student response. A total of seven of the students involved were interviewed, in two different focus groups, on different days, with recordings made – a total of 30–35 minutes' feedback. Several DVD recordings were also shared and discussed with the rest of the English department, as well as with teachers involved with a cross-school Dialogic Teaching Group (CamStar).

Interim conclusions were identified, notably, that extended dialogues:

- had to involve reasoning, hypothesizing and 'thinking aloud';

- needed to last for long enough to make a difference;

- had to include more 'wait time' (for both students and teachers);

- were perhaps best done with three to five students overall in the middle of a longer lesson, e.g. following pair or group discussions; presentations; prior to writing; prior to a whole class 'plenary' but that they

- Encourage 'deeper' learning and recall, particularly helpful for exams.

Clearly the project was felt by David and Emma to be successful. In a later commentary they wrote 'Our exploration of the benefits of extended dialog has been exciting'. To what extent though can we say, in terms of terms of this chapter's focus, that this example of teacher research has indeed generated professional knowledge and an associated discourse?

Certainly this research project illustrates one of the central principles of professional knowledge, that is to investigate an area that is not contained within policy demands. Dialogic teaching is not part of the English national curriculum, nor is it 'standards' focused. Instead David and Emma made a decision to explore an area of *intellectual* interest. The justification for this decision is based in a belief that professional knowledge is the foundation of excellent teaching. It contributes to a deeper understanding of the processes of teaching and learning, rather than just the procedures. The significance of teacher ownership of knowledge, another characteristic of professional knowledge, is clear in their observations of the impact of this research:

> As practitioners, engagement will continue during critical, reflective and active discussion, to explore both positive and negative experience in order for our own learning to be furthered.

The claim to 'critical[ity]' is, as discussed earlier, explicitly linked to professional rather than policy knowledge. David and Emma's measured statement, 'to explore both positive and negative experience' indicates the informed position that the research will allow them to bring to their data. That they talk about data, and both collection and analysis of that data, is indicative of a different stance towards knowledge – that it is *constructed* and open to interpretation of meaning. Such active positioning contrasts sharply with the 'given-ness' of policy knowledge, where ownership resides outside of teachers. With professional knowledge, the sense of ownership allows an intellectual confidence. Criticality becomes part and parcel of evaluating knowledge and professional judgment is both enhanced and developed through the act of evaluation. For David and Emma, evaluating the impact of dialogic teaching through interview data has enabled them to produce secure recommendations for practise based on their own findings. So convincing were they that dialogic teaching still informs practise in this English department some five years after the start of the project, and indeed, so persuasive their findings that the dissemination of their research and recommendations in the school has led to other departments also adopting dialogic teaching strategies. Such active positioning contrasts sharply with the 'given-ness' of policy knowledge, where ownership resides outside of teachers, and cross-departmental sharing of knowledge is rare.

David and Emma's claim to criticality through 'reflective and active discussion' also demonstrates that what has been generated is not only professional knowledge, but importantly a discourse that will allow that professional knowledge be explored and secured. If sacred knowledge has been marginalized as claimed, and research is the revivification of that knowledge, then concomitantly the associated discourse will be re-established. Most notable, however, is their claim that this discourse will allow their 'own learning to be furthered'. This statement demonstrates immediately how powerful professional knowledge and its associated discourse is for teachers. Research offers not a single 'acquisition of skills' but rather an ongoing engagement with ideas and findings which informs development in teaching and learning in quite different, and much more enduring, ways. Evidence for this can be found immediately in that the CamTalk project, originally planned for a year's duration, was extended, by request, for all participating schools into a three-year project, and many schools, including David and Emma's, are, as the title of their research suggests, 'still' talking. This is thus knowledge, that, to return to Doecke and McClenaghan 'remains with you'; Locke's act of 'self-reflexivity'.

Securing professional knowledge is not however simply a matter of applying interesting strategies. As David and Emma state, their research has also achieved 'An opening up of classroom theory and practise to reveal a potentially new and powerful teaching approach'. Research builds on scholarly knowledge. Without that, there can be no development of teacher knowledge; and critical engagement, without ideas and claims as intellectual history, becomes an impossibility. David and Emma's research was deliberately informed by theory. Their report shows that they read not only Alexander's (2004) research, but also that by Bakhtin (1984), Pinker (2000) and Mercer and Dawes (2009), thus developing awareness of research that had already been undertaken and informing their own developing knowledge of the area. However, reading existing research is not only about gaining knowledge in the field: it is also about being exposed to and thus developing a professional discourse within that area. To use a well-known parallel, medicine, doctors who did not have access to professional research discourse about a specific disease would be seen as inadequate. I do not have to paint a picture of how worrying it would be to be on the receiving end of treatment from such a doctor. Teachers equally need access to professional research discourse as integral to the development of a knowledge base.

This research, then, has generated professional knowledge and has developed a professional research discourse. These both serve to inform professional practise, not necessarily by directly impacting on the Standards' construction of the teacher, but instead contributing to the 'sacred' knowledge that underpins the excellent teacher. It is an example of Giroux's exhortation in action, that teachers must 'write, research, and work with each other … ' (Giroux, 1988, p. xxxiv).

It is, I would argue, the generation of that authentic knowledge which values the teacher, reinstates professionalism and speaks to teacher identity in ways that re-engage practise and knowledge in identities reflecting Bernstein's 'deep structures of the self'. Policy knowledge is acquired – skills based and responsive to the demands of others; professional knowledge is, however, not about acquisition of skills and facts. It is more demanding than that: it is a merging of self with the 'quicksilver' of English (Dixon, 1967).

Conclusion: Knowledge, discourse and research implications

This chapter has asked you to reflect on the ways in which knowledge is to be found in education, and the implications this might have for you as a teacher. I have put the case that teachers are being asked to deal with a knowledge dichotomy without acknowledgment of the tensions and dilemmas that raises. My argument has been that professional knowledge has been marginalized by policy, but that it is in fact central to good teaching. I have suggested too that the professional discourse that is integral to professional knowledge has also been marginalized and that this damages the professionalism of teachers. In illustrating professional knowledge and discourse generation through teacher research, it is my claim that teachers have to be active in developing professional knowledge and professional discourse and that research is the arena for this. A different approach to teacher education is thus called for, which positions teachers as constructors of professional knowledge, not merely recipients of policy knowledge, able to critique and evaluate claims about curriculum and pedagogy, and bring informed voices to the debates. Such a development would allow for a deeper and more profound engagement with English the subject, building a breadth and depth of understanding that truly effective teachers of English must possess if they are to demonstrate the ways in which English the subject is not the naming of parts, but a place of ideas linking across time and contexts.

References

Alexander, R. J. (2004). *Towards Dialogic Teaching: Rethinking Classroom Talk*. York: Dialogos UK.

Bakhtin, M. (1982). *The Dialogic Imagination: Four Essays*. Texas: University of Texas Press Slavic Series.

Beck, J. (1999). 'Makeover or takeover? The strange death of educational autonomy in neo-liberal England'. *British Journal of Sociology of Education*, 20(2), 223–38.

—(2002) 'The sacred and profane in recent struggles to promote official pedagogic identities'. *British Journal of Sociology of Education*, 23(4), 617–26.

Bernstein, B. (2000). *Pedagogy, Symbolic Control and Identity: Theory, Research, Critique,* Maryland: Rowman and Littlefield.

Brindley, S. (2013a). 'Teacher education futures: compliance, critique, or compromise? A UK perspective'. *Journal of Teacher Development,* Special Issue. Aubusson, P. and Schuck S. (eds), Vol. 17, No. 3, August 2013, 393–408.

—(2013b). 'An epistemic frame analysis of neoliberal culture and politics in the US, UK, and the UAE'. *Interchange,* Special Issue. Mullen, C. (ed.), Vol. 43, Issue 3, August 2013, pp. 187–228.

Cordingley, P. (2008). 'Research and evidence-informed practise: focusing on practise and practitioners'. *Cambridge Journal of Education*, 38(1), 37–52.

Cox, B. (1991). *Cox on Cox: An English Curriculum for the 1990s*. Abingdon: Hodder Education.

Department for Education and Skills Teachers' Standards (May 2012) (London, HMSO).

Dixon, J. (1967). *Growth through English Set in the Perspective of the Seventies*. Oxford: Oxford University Press/NATE.

Doecke, B. and McClenaghan, D. (2014). 'Intertextuality and Subversion'. In S. Brindley and B. Marshall, *MasterClass in English Education*. London: Bloomsbury, pp. 16–28.

Foucault, M. (1971). *L'ordre du discours*. Paris: Gallimard.

Giroux, H. A. (1988). *Teachers as Intellectuals: Toward a Critical Pedagogy of Learning*. Connecticut and London: Bergin and Garvey.

Greenwood, D and Barton, E. (2009/10). *Dialogic Teaching*. http://www.kegs.org.uk/leading-edge-and-learning-lessons/2628.html [accessed June 2013].

Kincheloe, J. L. (2003). *Teachers as Researchers: Qualitative Inquiry as a Path to Empowerment*. London: RoutledgeFalmer.

Locke, T. (2014). 'Paradigms of English'. In S. Brindley and B. Marshall, *MasterClass in English Education*. London: Bloomsbury, pp. 29–44.

Mercer, N. and Dawes, L. (March 2009). 'Making the most of classroom talk: dialog in the classroom'. *English Drama Media* (NATE), Issue 16, 19–25.

Pinker, S. (2000). *The Language Instinct*. Harmondsworth: Penguin Books.

Part 2
Reading

Understanding Reading 5

Christine Hall

Chapter Outline

Learning to read is not just something that most people do in primary school. We carry on learning to read all through our lives. On one level, this is obvious. On another level it seems difficult to grasp.

As adults, we are probably most aware of the need to continue to learn how to read when we try out new technologies or text forms that we have not encountered before. Sometimes it is a matter of finding out how to approach the text: how to turn the pages of an electronic book, where to begin reading if we are new to Arabic or Chinese texts. Sometimes we have to learn how to decode the text itself, in the case of some SMS messages on phones, for example, or a passage in Chaucerian English.

Despite the obviousness of these points, there is a widespread assumption, reflected in and fuelled by the media, that the business of learning to read should be concluded by the time children move on to secondary school (and preferably earlier). Learning to read, in this formulation, is conflated with learning to decode and to achieve a degree of fluency with the range of texts that are offered to young people in school. Because these achievements are to some extent measurable through tests and examinations, they allow comparisons to be made over time and between different countries, regions, schools and individuals. These comparisons are important in holding institutions and policy makers accountable for the services, frameworks and support they provide. Because of the judgments involved, there is a sharp focus on the aspects of reading that are easily measured, both in the political arena, through the media, and in the educational arena, in school. There is a sense of urgency about meeting targets and a corresponding sense of concern when identified standards and results have not been achieved.

These concerns are framed in the language of the measurements and assessments from which they were derived: in terms of failure and deviation from the norm. There is an easy slippage, linguistically and emotionally, between the child's failure to achieve the target set in the test and the perceived failure of the teacher/system/school to provide the child with the tools to be successful. Similarly, there is an easy assumption that what is normal is what you are entitled to, so that below-average attainment on the tests becomes equated with denying children their entitlement to a fair start in life. Parents' anxieties rise; politicians come under pressure to prove that their policies are improving standards; teachers feel blamed. Children absorb many of these pressures and risk seeing themselves as failures before they have even really got going on their reading careers. And 'learning to read' becomes something that should have happened in primary school, so energies are focused on remediation and catch-up, identifying problems and thinking up potential solutions.

This is, in my view, a dispiriting, poorly informed and counterproductive view of the immensely complex task of developing as a reader. It infantilizes the process of learning to read, associating it with the early stages of childhood rather than with processes that intelligent people continue to develop throughout their lives. It damages readers' self-confidence and often discourages their interest in reading; it deskills teachers and others who feel they lack the expertise to address the increasingly technical reading 'problems' they are presented with. Fundamentally, it leads to too narrow a view of what learning to read is about, reducing reading to a set of school-related, measurable competences at the very time when we need to think broadly and deeply about what it will mean to be literate in the future.

In this chapter, then, I aim to take a longer and broader view. I start with two assumptions: that school should lay the foundations for lifelong learning in reading, and that it is the duty of teachers, especially English teachers, to have in mind the literate adult who will be the eventual beneficiary of their teaching. With reference to relevant research, I discuss what learning to read means beyond decoding, and the implications of this for teachers of children and young people today. Inevitably, in one short chapter, I can offer only a very sketchy account, but I hope that a step back might offer a different view on systems that are often myopically focused on levels, grades and distinctions in performance at the expense of alternative priorities and values.

Reading, broadly

How then might we think more broadly about what it means to learn to read? In a book called *Literacy: Reading the Word and the World*, Paulo Freire, the radical educator and theorist, writes: 'The act of learning to read and write has to start from a very comprehensive understanding of the act of reading the world, something which human beings do before reading the words' (Freire, 1987, p. xiii).

The notion of 'reading the world' – reading facial expressions, reading situations and events – is commonplace in language. But is the use of 'reading' here more than just a metaphor for parallel processes of decoding and interpretation that take place in relation to verbal texts (actual reading) and to predominantly non-verbal contexts (metaphorical reading)? For Freire, it is. Learning literally to read and write comes after humans change and 'touch', or interact with, the world. Literacy is a means of engaging with the world, part of learning how the world works socially and culturally, and as such it is part of developing an understanding of how individuals and groups can 'take cultural action in the world' (Lankshear and Knobel, 2003, p. 6).

Gunther Kress, a linguist and semiotician, also sees reading in terms of engagement and transformative action: 'Reading is our means of engaging with the world. That engagement takes place in a multiplicity of ways, in a multiplicity of dimensions … . In 'taking in the world' we transform it' (Kress, 2000, p. 95).

In the current 'new media age', the means by which we 'take cultural action in the world' are, themselves, being transformed. As new technologies are developed and the screen replaces the book as the dominant medium, new kinds of text are produced. Screens, for example, require different page layouts to books, with more still images and, sometimes, moving images too. These layouts and forms in turn influence printed texts, so that, for example, modern textbooks set out information in very different ways to their counterparts in the past.

Kress makes the point that the process of reading a screen text is basically different to the process of reading a standard page of a traditional book, particularly in relation to the 'paths' they require the reader to take. A traditional page, written in English, guides the reader from top to bottom, left to right, whereas the reading path for the screen is more open – you can begin with image or text and move about between the different elements according to what interests you most. Kress argues that these basic changes in how the reading occurs point to profound differences in the act of reading that is taking place. On the traditional page, with its clear reading path that has to be followed, 'the task of reading lay in interpretation and transformation of that which was clearly there and clearly organised'. With the screen format, on the other hand:

> The new task is that of applying principles of relevance to a page which is (relatively) open in its organisation, and consequently offers a range of possible reading paths, perhaps infinitely many. The task of the reader in the first case is to observe and follow a given order, and within that order to engage in interpretation (where that too was more or less tightly policed). The task of the reader of the new page, and of the screens which are its models, is to establish the order through principles of relevance of the reader's making, and to construct meaning from that. (Kress, 2003, p. 162)

As the language of the quotation suggests with its emphasis on order and policing, Kress sees the reader as being in a very different relationship to the authority of the text in these two instances. For Kress, the two reading experiences embody 'utterly different principles' which relate to wider forms of social and cultural organization and different eras in the development of literacy. The tightly controlled reading experience of the traditional page 'fits into the social forms and orders of the preceding era', whereas the more open experience of reading 'exhibits some of the social forms and orders, requirements and tasks and demands of the present and future era'. Kress clarifies the implications of this for teaching literacy to younger generations:

It is, I believe, simply impossible now to expect young people to read in the older manner, other than in a specialized form of learning, where clear reasons will need to be given about the constitution of that difference and the purposes of maintaining it. Where that is not done, the tasks of that learning are made difficult for many and impossible for some. The screen trains its readers in certain ways, just as the page trained its readers in its ways: the latter had its uses and functions and purposes, which were the uses and functions and purposes of the society in which it existed. The new form has its uses and functions and purposes in relation to new social, cultural, political and economic demands (Kress, 2003, pp. 162/3).

This leads Kress to the view that reading needs to be defined either very broadly, in terms of engagement with the world, as above, or very specifically, in relation to the processes demanded by the forms of text that people are actually being faced with reading in their day-to-day lives.

> 'Reading' needs either to be discussed overtly as the general human urge and capacity for deriving meanings from (culturally) shaped materials which are thought to be the bearers of meaning; or to be treated as a culturally and historically specific instance of that general capacity…. it is possible to talk about the general human capacities that are involved, both physiological and semiotic, and it is possible to attempt to describe how these capacities are shaped at a particular point in the history of a society in relation to the shape of what there is to be read. (Kress, 2000 p. 143)

This seems to me a very useful approach for teachers. On the one hand, we can take a broad view of reading as a human urge to engage with the world to make meaning. This separates literacy and reading from an exclusive focus on books and print media. It allows us to take in broad notions of 'reading' situations, places, artifacts and people, which are clearly important life skills relevant to an educated literate adult. The focus on meaning-making underpins the reader's capacity to act upon the world and change it.

On the other hand, we can understand that reading consistently changes. We can use this insight to analyze the specific social and historical moment we are currently living through, identify what there is to be read and think about the specific literacy practises that will support the reader most effectively in making meaning from the texts they might and do deal with.

Let's consider then what is required of a reader today.

Reading, more specifically

Alberto Manguel, in his *History of Reading* (1997), illustrates very effectively some of the significant ways in which reading has changed over time. Striking examples that can be cited include the fact that, until the tenth century, reading in Western Europe appears to have been understood exclusively as reading aloud. Silent reading, which is now the norm, was either unknown or considered an oddity (Manguel, 1997, p. 43). Or the fact that in ancient scrolls and manuscripts there is no punctuation or space between words (Manguel, 1997, p. 48). New technologies have regularly transformed literacy practises: the printing press comes immediately to mind, but humbler technologies – like the biro, or the telegram, or the invention of spectacles, or social institutions like the Universal Postal Union that linked European countries in a common postal system – also revolutionized reading and writing (Manguel, 1997, p. 43; Vincent, 2000, pp. 1–3; Hannon, 2004, p. 20).

In relation to more recent technological changes, David Reinking writes about the differences between printed and digital texts. Basing his thinking on Salomon's work in the late 1970s, which suggested that printed and digital texts may be distinctly different media which make different cognitive demands and require different ways of processing text, Reinking argues that there are five main areas of difference for the reader (Reinking, 2005). Digital texts, he argues, create literal rather than metaphorical interactions with readers – they are dynamic in that they can be manipulated by the reader and so respond to readers' needs and interests. Secondly, they enable information to be organized and accessed in non-linear formats, for example, through the use of hypertext. Thirdly, digital texts employ a broader range of symbolic elements than print texts to carry meaning (a wider range of fonts, animation, audio, film). They are more open than printed texts in that they offer opportunities for accessing supplementary information during reading, through hot links, and finally, digital texts create new pragmatics for written communication (for example, email has its own conventions).

Elsewhere, Reinking has claimed that reading in multimedia environments is inherently more engaging than reading print (Reinking, 2001). He argues that the digital experience of reading is more active because of the interactive features of the medium and easier to understand because more help is available to the reader. He thinks that digital texts can meet a wider range of social needs than print texts and generally finds that they 'tend to be less serious and philosophical and more playful, rhetorical and concrete' than printed texts, whose 'inert features … make reading essentially a solitary psycholinguistic process' and a 'static, silent, introspective and typically serious' matter (2001, p. 177).

These judgments tell us more about David Reinking's personal preferences than they do about whether texts are inherently more engaging in one medium or another. Clearly, there are many playful print texts and plenty of serious philosophical material online. Book reading is often shared and screen reading is often solitary; introspection, silence and seriousness are not, in themselves, unpleasurable or unrewarding. Nevertheless, Reinking's arguments, like his identification of the different text features, alert us to the importance of engagement, interest and interactivity in modern understandings of the reading process.

This emphasis on the importance of interest and engagement is more than just the obvious point that reading relies upon readers making the effort to actually read and comprehend what is in front of them. Both Kress and Reinking comment on the relative openness of screen reading: the variety of reading paths and points of entry and exit into and from the text that are made available. The text itself, in these cases, requires an active, interested reader ready to engage and to identify what Kress calls 'principles of relevance' to their own meaning-making. Responses and choices are built into the text structure in ways that are less common – though not altogether lacking – in more traditional print texts.

The reader's active engagement is also central to the development of reader-response theory, which has been highly influential in the teaching of literary texts in schools. Wolfgang Iser's seminal work *The Act of Reading: a Theory of Aesthetic Response* (1978) emphasizes the reader's role in creating meaning: according to Iser 'the meaning of a literary text is not a definable entity but, if anything, a dynamic happening' (1978, p. 22). Interpretation is understood as an interaction between the reader and the text. What the reader brings to the text affects the meanings that are made; multiple readings or interpretations are thereby legitimated. This, of course, profoundly affects the ways in which texts are taught in school. If the dominant theory of interpretation suggests the authority of the text and the author, literature teaching will focus on exegesis and appreciation. But since the pedagogic work of Rosenblatt, and Lunzer and Gardner in the 1970s, the emphasis in schools has been on accessing, questioning and reinterpreting literary (and other) texts to develop response and create new readings.

The position of the reader in relation to the text and the nature of how the text should be interpreted and understood are philosophical, but also deeply political, matters. Decisions about who is taught to read and how they are taught relate closely to what reading is under-stood to be. In nineteenth-century America, it was a punishable offense to teach slaves to read. In Victorian Britain, for working-class people, learning to read was about compliance and authority: the Bible and standard grammars were the core texts, and, until well in to the twentieth century, children from the lower classes were expected to leave school once they had achieved the necessary 'standard' of decoding and literal comprehension. Inherent in both of these examples, of course, is an acknowledgment of the liberatory and trans-formatory potential of fluency and breadth in reading. As Dickens, Hardy, or Frederick Douglass illustrate so graphically, regulatory systems of schooling or exclusion were tailored to maintain hierarchical distinctions between classes and groups, to attempt to preserve the reading privileges of a powerful elite (Douglass, 1845; Dickens, 1854; Hardy, 1896; Simon 1960). Writing – in the form of composing and having a voice, rather than merely being able to take dictation – was considered even more of a threat to the established social order. Hannah More, for example, who promoted education through the Sunday School movement, thought that writing was likely to unsettle the lower classes; she is quoted as saying 'I allow of no writing for the poor. My object is not to make them fanatics, but to train up the lower classes in habits of industry and piety' (Cowburn, 1986, p. 105).

In contrast to earlier notions of reading, then, modern theories conceptualize readers as active in bringing personal interest and experience to a relatively open text in order to create interpretations that are nuanced to their own circumstances. For teachers, this raises questions about the pedagogies that support and develop these characteristics. Are we drawing on the best theoretical resources when we teach reading? Do school practises promote the transformatory potential of reading and writing or inadvertently contribute to outmoded systems of control and restriction?

Reading, pedagogically

Reinking describes his ideal reader as 'light-hearted' (2001). This offers an appealing contrast to the gradgrindery of nineteenth-century images of young readers toiling over joyless tasks designed to elicit respectful, officially endorsed readings. A light-hearted reader will be confident, not too timid, open to finding value and enjoyment in the text.

Light-heartedness is not, of course, a characteristic closely associated with students in school systems that rely on test-driven pedagogies. Even students who do well academically consistently report low self-concept and high anxiety when they face high stakes testing, and students who struggle with or fail tests lose the sense of progress, success and enjoyment that motivates further engagement (Wilkins, 2004; Berliner, 2006). As Paris and McNaughton point out: 'The increasing emphasis on high-stakes testing may motivate children for the test, but the unintended consequences may be overwhelmingly negative for children's motivation to read, particularly for children already at risk' (2010, p. 19).

Fear of not making the grade tends to act as a spur to behavior in school and in work, but reliance on such extrinsic motivation is likely to produce learning and behaviors that are short term and instrumental (Sanson and Harackiewicz, 2000). Deficit discourses and a focus on identifying and recording minor distinctions and levels do not encourage the reader to feel confident, independent and engaged. Yet these are precisely the characteristics needed to establish the foundations of productive reading across the life course.

Paris and McNaughton comment that reading is about more than enjoyment and trying hard (2010, p. 13). At the heart of what is needed, as we have seen above, is engagement, which requires intrinsic motivation, cognitive and social knowledge and strategies (Guthrie and Wigfield, 2000). Focusing on engagement brings these cognitive, social and psychological aspects together with the behavioral and emotional dimensions. Also, the idea of engagement 'calls attention to the enactment of motivated reading in specific situations', which is, of course, the essence of what happens in lessons in school (Paris and McNaughton, 2010, p. 13).

What then are the characteristics of engaged reading? One important and easily observable characteristic is what Csikszentmihalyi (1990) calls 'flow', a term he uses to describe deep immersion and concentration in a task with all its concomitant pleasure and sense of mastery. Flow in this sense can be observed in many activities – playing sport or music, painting or building, for example; it bridges superficial divisions between work and leisure/pleasure. It refers to times when a task or activity is going well, and when the doer has a sense of control and achievement. In reading terms, it might be used to refer to occasions when it is hard to put a book down or move away from a screen, or what have been called 'binge' reading behaviors shared by both adults and young people (Hardy, 2008), or the lure of the next book in a series, or by the same author, or the next DVD in a box-set.

What are the pedagogies that support students' experience of flow in reading? Clearly, readers need time, and a situation that allows them to concentrate. Neither of these is self-evidently easily available to students in schools. Time in lessons is understood through metaphors of production and efficiency, and orthodox 'good' lessons often involve multiple short activities and changes of direction. Control in these lessons rests with the teacher rather than being ceded to the learner. Independent reading is squeezed in to fill short time slots, or squeezed out because specific learning objectives cannot be readily identified in advance of the activity. Group reading is often atomized, interrupted by the teachers' questions, focused on extracts that are left hanging, or selected to illustrate a particular teaching point. As teaching practises, these are not necessarily right or wrong, but if flow is a sign of deep engagement in reading, it seems worth encouraging in school.

Pace is an important aspect of flow and of engagement in reading more generally. As Margaret Mackey points out in her study of young adults' leisure reading: 'One of the most significant qualities of reading print is the power of the reader to control pace' (Mackey, 2007, p. 105).

Out of school, re-reading a passage or a chapter is usually an option; in school the reader is not always in control of the pace. Too slow a pace can leave the reader floundering for meaning, distracted or bored. Too fast a pace can have the same effects, or result in the 'surface skating' that Bearne and Cliff Hodges consider particularly harmful to young readers who have just gained a degree of fluency. As they put it, 'If you are struggling with a text, you have to be engaged with it in some sense. But if you glide over its surface you never have to get to grips with it at all' (Bearne and Cliff Hodges, 2000, p. 10).

The optimal pace will depend upon the reader's level of fluency, but also on the reason for reading the text. As Mackey points out (2007, p. 147), skilled readers use their discretion to arrive at 'good enough readings' which allow them to find a balance between retaining a degree of momentum in the reading process and accountability to the text itself. The 'good enough' reading will vary according to the reader's familiarity with, for example, the text type, subject matter and language, but also in relation to why the text has been chosen and what the reader wants from it. These choices, and the strategies associated with them, are eminently teachable in school. So, too, is an encouragement to re-read texts; Robert Protherough noted in 1983 that the pleasures and benefits of encouraging students to re-read texts are largely ignored after the early years of education, yet returning to favorite books and stories is a notable feature of adult reading behaviors.

All of this depends, of course, on the reader having a sense of curiosity about the text. Curiosity will sustain a reader through a challenging text, contribute to a sense of flow and help the reader determine what constitutes a good enough reading. Teachers have many well-established methods of encouraging students' curiosity through, for example, questioning, predicting, trailing ideas. But above all, teachers need to be free to respond to what their students are curious about. This is likely to be an eclectic mix that starts, in Alistair West's terms, 'with texts rather than literature' and, as Richard Andrews puts it, 'separates books from literacy' (West, 1994, p. 128; Andrews, 2001, p. 143).

Conclusion

The implication of these points, I think, is that the curriculum can be fashioned to show students how reading can help them explore their interests and develop new ideas and perspectives. In pursuit of the literate future adult, students need to be encouraged to follow interesting ideas, characters or themes, and helped to make connections between texts in different forms and genres and from different cultural milieux. School reading should be about encouraging students to become commentators on their reading, sharing their enthusiasms, following trends and research interests – exploring the kinds of readers they want to be, and 'taking cultural action in the world'. Alistair West underlines the point: 'Students must be free to make their own cultural and literary affiliations; our responsibility is to help them to a greater understanding of the implications of their own and others' choices' (West, 1994, p. 129).

Since this is about building, rather than imposing, a reading identity, the teacher's professional role involves listening, suggesting, extending and developing the reader's critical literacy skills. This requires flexible, analytical adults who are willing to read with and on behalf of their students to open up new possibilities for them.

For the students, these processes are about more than just building cultural affiliations and a social identity as a reader; they are also about exploiting the cognitive benefits of reading. Reading is in part about creating possible worlds and then reflecting on them. As Olson puts it, readers 'shift from thinking about things to thinking about representations of those things, that is, thinking about thought' (1994). The processes are also about respecting the emotional and therapeutic potential of reading. Is there any reason why teachers shouldn't take older children's fascinations with tales of misery, heroism, celebrity, the uncanny, bizarre or sentimental as seriously as they take younger children's interest in magic, toys and talking animals? Shouldn't teachers help young people grapple with the kinds of questions about right and wrong, fiction and fact, and how to live a good life that pervade both popular and highbrow culture?

Critics often have firm views about what children and young people should be reading in school. Luke and Carrington, for example, comment disparagingly on the 'parochial' nature of reading curricula that offer disadvantaged students a diet of 'relevance' to 'suture the home-school mismatch and transition problem' (2002, p. 242). They are similarly skeptical about what they call 'fantasy literacy' – reading that offers readers escape from the here and now, a practise that they argue is based on the idea that 'a rich, imaginative literary focus will build self-esteem, expand psychological horizons and world views, and create a "love of literature"' (2002, p. 242). They argue instead for a 'glocalised' literacy, a reading of the local that connects with 'other possible worlds, a curriculum approach that focuses students' work with texts on the analysis of the flows of effects between this time-space locality and others' (2002, p. 243).

In fact, of course, the different literacies are not necessarily discordant with one another. The local, the escapist and the 'glocal' could very well be dimensions of an individual reading profile that was responsive to a student's curiosity and stimulated the flow of ideas within different political, social, cultural and aesthetic frameworks of thought. It seems reasonable to think that, at different times in our development, we might all want to see ourselves reflected in what we read, to escape to a fantasy world, comfort ourselves or explore political ideas through reading. First and foremost, school needs to convince students that reading is a lifelong resource that can offer them all of these things – and many more.

References

Andrews, R (2001). *Teaching and Learning English*. London: Continuum.

Bearne, E. and Cliff Hodges, G. (2000). 'Reading Rights and Responsibilities'. In Davison, J. and Moss, J. (eds), *Issues in English Teaching*. London: Routledge.

Berliner, D. (2006). 'Our impoverished view of educational reform'. *Teachers College Record, 108*(6), 949–95.

Cowburn, W. (1986). *Class Ideology and Community Education*. London: Routledge.

Csikszentmihalyi, M. (1990). *Flow: The Psychology of Optimal Experience*. New York: HarperCollins.

Dickens, C. [1854] (2007). *Hard Times*. London: Penguin.

Douglass, F. [1845] (1973). *Narrative of the Life of Frederick Douglass, an American Slave*. Garden City, NY: Anchor Books.

Freire, Paulo (1987). *Literacy: Reading the Word and the World*. Westport, CT: Greenwood Publishing.

Guthrie, J. T. and Wigfield, A. (2000). 'Engagement and Motivation in Reading'. In Kamil, M. L., Mosenthal, P. B., Pearson, P. D. and Barr, R. (eds), *Handbook of Reading Research,* 3. Mahwah, NJ: Lawrence Erlbaum Associates, pp. 403–22.

Hannon, P. (2004). 'The History and Future of Literacy'. In Grainger, T. (ed.), *The RoutledgeFalmer Reader in Language and Literacy*. London: RoutledgeFalmer.

Hardy, C. (2008). *To Read or not to Read: Adult Reading Habits and Motivations*. Saarbrücken, Germany: VDM Verlag.

Hardy, T. (1896/1994). *Jude the Obscure*. Harmondsworth: Penguin.

Iser, W. (1978). *The Act of Reading: A Theory of Aesthetic Response*. London: Routledge & Kegan Paul.

Kress, G. (2000). *Before Writing – Rethinking the Paths to Literacy*. London: Routledge.

—(2003). *Literacy in the New Media Age*. London: Routledge.

Lankshear, C. and Knobel, M. (2003). *New Literacies: Changing Knowledge and Classroom Learning*. Buckingham: Open University Press.

Luke, A. and Carrington, V. (2002). 'Globalisation, Literacy, Curriculum Practice'. In Fisher, R., Brooks, G. and Lewis, M. (eds), *Raising Standards in Literacy.* London: RoutledgeFalmer, pp. 231–50.

Lunzer, E. and Gardner, K. (1979). *The Effective Use of Reading.* Oxford: Heinemann.

Mackey, M. (2007). *Mapping Recreational Literacies: Contemporary Adults at Play.* New York: Peter Lang.

Manguel, A. (1997). *A History of Reading,* London: HarperCollins.

Olson, D. (1994). *The World on Paper.* Cambridge: Cambridge University Press.

Paris, S. and McNaughton, S. (2010). 'Social and Cultural Influences on Children's Motivation for Reading'. In Wyse, D., Andrews, R. and Hoffman, J. (eds.), *The International Handbook of English, Language, and Literacy Teaching.* London: Routledge, pp. 11–21.

Protherough, R. (1983). *Developing Response to Fiction.* Milton Keynes: Open University Press.

Reinking, D. (2001). 'Multimedia and Engaged Reading in a Digital World'. In Verhoeven, L. T. and Snow, Catherine E., *Literacy and Motivation: Reading Engagement in Individuals and Groups.* New Jersey: Lawrence Erlbaum Associates, pp. 177–204.

—(2005). 'Multimedia Learning of Reading'. In Mayer, R. E. *The Cambridge Handbook of Multimedia Learning.* Cambridge: Cambridge University Press, pp. 355–74.

Rosenblatt, L. (1978). *The Reader, The Text, The Poem: The Transactional Theory of the Literary Work.* Carbondale, IL: Southern Illinois University Press.

Salomon, G. (1979). *Interaction of Media, Cognition and Learning.* San Francisco, CA: Jossey-Bass.

Sanson, C. and Harackiewicz, J. (2000). *Intrinsic and Extrinsic Motivation.* San Diego, CA: Academic Press.

Simon, B. (1960). *Studies in the History of Education, 1780-1870.* London: Lawrence and Wishart.

Vincent, D. (2000). *The Rise of Mass Literacy.* Cambridge: Polity Press.

West, A. (1994). 'The Centrality of Literature'. In Brindley, S. (ed), *Teaching English.* London: Routledge, pp. 109–16.

Wilkins, J. M. (2004). 'Mathematics and science self-concept: an international investigation'. *Journal of Experimental Education, 72*(4): 331–46.

6

Teaching Shakespeare with Film Adaptations

Jane Coles

Chapter Outline

The ready availability of popular film versions of Shakespeare plays on DVD and other digital formats, coupled with the rapid development in classroom technology over the past decade (Jewitt et al., 2009) have had the potential to radically change the traditional relationship between secondary school students and the printed playtext. Teacher surveys published over the past ten years (see for example, Batho, 1998; Stibbs, 1998; Martindale, 2008) indicate that very nearly every English teacher complements the study of a set Shakespeare text at Key Stage 3 (11–14) or 4 (14–16) with reference to a DVD or video adaptation. There is, however, much less empirical evidence about the use to which these moving image versions are commonly put: for instance, how teachers construct the cultural and historical relationship between playtext and adaptation within the classroom, or the way students are positioned as readers of the different textual modes. The purpose of this chapter is to explore some of the pedagogical possibilities raised by use of moving image Shakespeare and to consider some examples of teachers' practise taken from classroom-based research data.

Background

For nearly 20 years teachers in English state schools have been statutorily required to teach two Shakespeare plays to all students aged between 11 and 16 years. Precise forms of national assessment and testing of Shakespeare may have changed in the intervening years, but teacher concerns with issues of entitlement and access for the full range of student 'abilities', particularly in urban comprehensive schools, have remained central (Kress et al., 2005). From the outset, Shakespeare was constructed in the National Curriculum as the *de facto* embodiment of English cultural heritage (McEvoy, 1991; Coles, 2004; Moore, 2006), and very specifically as Literature (located within the programs of study for reading), rather than as drama for performance (Franks, 1999). Moreover, as Buckingham and Jones (2001) comment, successive UK governments have emphasized print-centerd culture at the expense of new forms of media within education policies, a position that is increasingly out of step with students' cultural lives outside of school. As noted by Burn (2010), film's relationship with English has been hindered historically by condescending attitudes towards the mass media inherited from Leavis (Leavis and Thompson, 1933), institutionalized during the past twenty years in curriculum struggles over cultural value and the primacy of print over visual production. According to a recent film industry report: 'film education is still on the margins of the formal curriculum' (BFI et al., 2008, p. 8), despite a general acceptance by media educators that:

> In the same way that we take it for granted that society has a responsibility to help children to read and write … we should take it for granted that we help children and young people to use, enjoy and understand moving images; not just to be technically capable but to be culturally literate too. (BFI et al., 2008, p. 1)

This statement reflects expanding concepts of literacy as a complex set of social practises situated in an increasingly technological world (see, for instance, Lankshear and Knobel, 2003). Yet this rich concept of literacy has only been partially translated into government policy documents. Thus, while the latest National Curriculum document (QCDA, 2007) places moving image and multimodal texts within the reading curriculum and urges teachers to include 'non-linear and multimodal texts' in the range of texts students should encounter, lengthy lists of recommended literary print texts ('heritage' and 'contemporary') dominate the program of study for reading. Film texts are absent from the National Curriculum's recommended canon of fiction, despite film having been established as a narrative art form for more than a century. Although teachers have 'shown the film of the book' to support the reading of English literary classics for decades, this practise is not officially recognized. So, in the National Curriculum's explanatory notes for reading at Key Stage 3 (QCDA, 2007, p. 71) teachers are invited to explore Shakespeare in performance alongside reading the playtext, where performance includes theater productions and classroom drama, but omits film productions. Significantly, only one of the GCSE examination boards in England and Wales has used the opportunity of curriculum and assessment changes at Key Stage 4 (as from September 2010) to offer scope for explicitly assessing students' responses to film versions of Shakespeare alongside the printed text (see below).

Considering how much Shakespeare is taught each year in English secondary schools, and therefore how many film versions of specific plays are presumably viewed, there has been surprisingly little research as to what is actually happening in classrooms. Evidence arising out of Rex Gibson's national Shakespeare project suggests little uniformity in the way teachers make use of film Shakespeare in the classroom (Gibson 1998), and, indeed, other commentators' conclusions are contradictory. Leach (1992), Goodwyn (2004) and Burn (2010) suggest that the most common practise is for teachers to show students a single film version, where the decontextualized film merely supports reading of the print text. This view is supported by Martindale's teacher survey which indicates that English teachers in the main regard film versions as little more than useful visual tools, affording easy access to the play in performance and an overview of plot and character, '… thereby allow[ing] more time to be spent on close study of the language in particular scenes' (2008, p. 20). In contrast, Stibbs' (1998) teacher survey conducted a decade earlier suggested the most common practise then to be critical comparison of clips taken from diverse screen productions.

This is a practise exemplified in Marshall's more recent classroom-based research where a class explore divergent interpretations of *Henry V* through a comparison of Olivier's and Branagh's film texts (Hodgen and Marshall, 2005). Kress et al.'s multimodal overview of English teaching in urban schools (2005) supplies additional qualitative evidence in its detailed description of a GCSE sequence of work based on *Macbeth*. In this the teacher combines film, drama and text: the teacher's strategy is to start the textual work with film, a cultural mode she assumes her students will find most accessible, then move to the reading of one brief witches' scene in depth (including a comparison of two moving image versions); this is followed by collaborative drama activities based on the scene, and then written coursework as the final stage of the process. Film is used to provide students with a sense of the play's plot, rather than being interrogated on its own cinematic terms.

Kress et al. comment on the extent to which the text of *Macbeth* becomes fragmented in this pedagogic model, where students' reading is heavily mediated by the teacher through worksheets and writing frames. The underlying assumption appears to be that students in urban classrooms are not capable of reading and responding to more than one scene from the printed Shakespeare playtext (particularly in the limited class-time available); film's status in this teaching sequence is positioned at the opposite end of the literacy spectrum, reduced to that of an undemanding, illustrated teaching aid.

A radically different relationship between film and playtext is constructed by Durran and Morrison (2004). In their work in a Cambridge comprehensive school, book and film (in this case, *Macbeth* and *Romeo and Juliet*) are afforded parity and taught side by side. 'Film does not just serve the study of literature … each film version asks students to consider its own textual structure, and the reasons for its construction' (Durran and Morrison, 2004, p. 19). Students analyze stills taken from different moving-image versions of the play and explore the 'grammar of shots in sequence' (Durran and Morrison, 2004, p. 20). Provided with laptops, students are positioned as active readers of digital film text, and invited to navigate it in a non-linear fashion. Not only that, this study suggests that systematic analysis of film, an exercise in 'close technical reading – both of film and of Shakespeare' (Durran and Morrison, 2004, p. 17), encourages students to study the printed playtext more closely, a conclusion leant support by Bousted and Ozturk (2004) in their work with undergraduates reading *Silas Marner* alongside watching a film version. Burn (2010, p. 356) concludes that this kind of comparative teaching, drawing on both media and literary critical traditions, 'implies a parity of cultural value, rather than a hierarchy privileging literature'.

Classroom-based research

I want to turn now to look at some examples from my own classroom-based research and focus on the way four English teachers use film when teaching specific Shakespeare plays. In my wider research, I am interested in considering the ways in which Shakespeare is constructed through competing discourses in the secondary classroom, and what sense students make of it. Samples of practise discussed here are selected from the wider body of data collected for this exploratory case study. In total I observed nearly thirty hours of English lessons in two contrasting London comprehensives, with a focus on two year 9 classes studying *Macbeth* and two year 10 classes, studying *Henry V* and *Romeo and Juliet* respectively. The lessons were video-taped, transcribed, coded and then analyzed thematically (Miles and Huberman, 1994). The four teachers, whose experience ranges from newly qualified status to long-established head of department, and whose training is in drama or Media Studies, were interviewed separately at the end of the sequence of lessons; these interviews were recorded, transcribed and similarly analyzed. I particularly want to focus here on the work of the two teachers of year 10 (15- to 16-year-olds) classes, although within the scope of this chapter I am only able to offer glimpses of key moments from my classroom data.

All four teachers in my sample make use of film versions of the Shakespeare play under study and in interviews all are in complete agreement that 'a decent film version' is a crucial aspect to successful Shakespeare teaching at KS3 and 4. What might be surprising is that, despite the availability of a number of alternative productions of each play, each teacher adheres to a single version for use with their class. Marie (names of teachers anonymized) shows Polanski's *Macbeth* (1971) with her mixed attainment year 9 class; Felicity uses the 1978 RSC version of *Macbeth* (director, Trevor Nunn) with her middle set year 9; Beth shows Kenneth Branagh's 1989 film of *Henry V* to her mixed attainment year 10 group; and Pip's middle set year 10 class watch Baz Luhrmann's 1996 film, *Romeo + Juliet*.

In contrast to practise described in research elsewhere, in the lessons I observed none of the teachers make comparisons across available alternatives, even to look at how key scenes have been interpreted by different directors. In effect, Marie, Felicity and Pip show the film/video version in a fairly concentrated unedited block, spanning two or three lessons with little or no accompanying discussion. Marie's class watch the whole of Polanski's *Macbeth* while she is absent during two cover lessons before beginning the unit of work on the play. Felicity's class watch the video of *Macbeth* once they have begun to read the opening scenes of the play, after some preliminary work on Shakespeare's life and times. Pip reads the opening scene of the play after some discussion about film conventions, then shows the opening sequence of Baz Luhrmann's film; the class get to watch the whole film between lessons four and six. In contrast, Beth stages the viewing of the film version of *Henry V* across a number of lessons so that it runs more in sequence with the small amounts of reading her class undertake. My interviews with the teachers indicate that there is little consensus between them as to how each film might be organized structurally within the series of lessons and that this aspect of their Shakespeare teaching is less consciously theorized than others. None of the teachers read more than a third of the published playtext with their classes – and the two year 10 classes read considerably less.

Both Baz Luhrmann's *Romeo + Juliet* and Roman Polanski's *Macbeth* prove to be popular with their student audiences, yet the status of moving image texts in these classrooms is an uncertain one. Because the focus of study ultimately remains the literary text (as is demanded by the specific national assessment systems in place at the time of the research) it results in each teacher performing a sleight of hand, whereby students encounter the majority of the play through film but write a conventional 'lit crit' essay about fragments of printed text as if they had read the whole. Hence, students who assume the film adaptation is 'the' version have to be corrected when preparing their assignments and reminded of the primacy of the printed text.

Pip and Beth appear to construct *Romeo and Juliet* and *Henry V* in film terms for their year 10 students right from the start. In Pip's opening lesson she invites her students to recall films they have seen which have dramatic opening scenes before she shows them Luhrmann's interpretation of *Romeo and Juliet* Act 1 scene i. Although the viewing is prefaced by asking the students to notice how the filmmaker dramatizes the opening scene, and to consider the way 'the hate between the two families is set up', Pip's subsequent whole-class questioning is entirely focused on impressions of character:

> **Teacher:** … so what kind of person is Tybalt then?
> **Kursheed:** Mean.
> **Meera:** He doesn't care.
> **Teacher:** He's mean, he doesn't care.
> **Robert:** He's quite rough.
> **Teacher:** He's quite rough (.) What do you mean by rough?
> **Robert:** [inaudible].
> **Anjna:** He thinks he's cool.
> **Teacher:** [Nods] Yes, he thinks he's cool, he's the king of cats, he thinks he's very, very cool indeed. And he's a very angry character isn't he? And so [T turns to face board] what kind of words can we use to describe Benvolio then? [T begins to write on board].

This extract is typical in the way the students are expected to draw generalized, quasi-literary conclusions about character and events from a very specific film adaptation. The Luhrmann film remains a continuing reference point in Pip's classroom throughout the series of lessons, but it is always to be mined for plot information or character recognition and rarely, if ever, analyzed as a film. Pip resolutely refers to 'the play' in class discussions even though students' comments (such as a student suggesting that Mercutio 'looked like he was on drugs'), indicate it is the film text that they are cross-referencing, even after they have read parallel extracts from the playtext.

Perhaps not surprisingly for an experienced Media Studies teacher, Beth introduces students to *Henry V* through the medium of film. In the first lesson I observed (the third lesson in the teaching sequence) Beth asks students to deconstruct the image of King Henry's first entrance in the play (at the opening of Act 1, scene 2) using a still photo captured from Branagh's film version. Students are positioned by Beth as 'viewers of Henry', a perspective that enables them to distance themselves from stock literary responses around 'character'. Consequently, their contributions focus on the trappings of kingship and on this entrance as a dramatic moment:

Teacher: … Other words people came up with? Richard?

Richard: Powerful.

Teacher: Brilliant! Why powerful?

Richard: Because he made an impression, he's coming out of darkness, the doors opening, it's lightening him up.

Dexter: He's wearing a robe.

Teacher: He's wearing a what?

Dexter: [gestures with his hands] He's wearing all robes, like a cape—

S: [interrupting, humorous tone] Cape! He's not Superman, you know!

Dexter: [deliberately finishing what he was saying] —they make him look scary.

Ss: [several start to shout out].

Teacher: [amused] Because robes are always scary? [she gestures next student] OK, guys! Ade, what else have you got, please?

Ade: I just put powerful and scary.

Teacher: Powerful and scary. OK. Bode, what did you put?

Bode: I put dark, manly figure.

Teacher: Brilliant, yep, OK. Cem?

Cem: The light's on him, it means God's on his side.

Teacher: Fantastic. I really like that: the light's on him so God's on his side. I like that one a lot. OK, Karen.

Karen: Secrecy because he's in shadow.

Teacher: Brilliant, secrecy, I like that. [A few Ss call out] No, don't call out! We need to hear comments. Yeah, Bode?

Bode: Shady.

Teacher: Why shady?

Bode: Because you can't really see his face, yeah. You can only see bits where the light comes in.

By working multimodally, students are co-constructing an initial reading of Henry that begins to capture the ambiguities inherent in Shakespeare's king figure, ambiguities that help explain the variant (and sometimes contradictory) readings of the play. Later in the same lesson, after watching the beginning of the film on DVD, Beth outlines reasons for the

English going to war; she is able to explicitly build on Cem's comment about God being on Henry's side, developing a sense that interpretation in this classroom is produced dialogically, out of interaction between all parties. Beth's approach is unique amongst my sample of four teachers in decentering Shakespeare's text: Branagh's film version quite consciously remains the key reference point throughout the observed lessons. This helps to shift the act of reading away from conventional parameters of literary meaning in terms of character, plot and feature spotting. Students' impressions of Henry are not character-based in the conventionally idealist sense (i.e. how he comes across *as a person*). Instead, students are encouraged to approach the play as a performed drama, and to consider Henry as a dramatic figure whose actions have significant political, social and personal consequences.

In Beth's classroom, role-plays and improvisation arise as an extension of watching the film. At times students are asked to predict events or decisions through drama, at others to develop an aspect from a section of the play they have watched on film. For example, during one lesson Beth asks one student to be Henry and another to be the French Ambassador presenting the King with a mystery gift:

Teacher: Right, OK, Henry (.) Henry now comes in, OK, and I want someone here to stand at the front and be Henry. Yeah. OK, Owsun. [Owsun gets up and moves to front] And I want somebody else to come [turns to Owsun] come and stand over here where there's a bit of space. OK, Henry has just come in (.) walked in through this door. He's now um (.) he's now standing there and the French Ambassador (.) I need a volunteer to be the French Ambassador [a few Ss make stereotypical French sounds] don't worry about the language, you're going to give Henry a present.
[Several Ss put up hand and call out].
Unur: I don't mind!
Teacher: OK, Unur [S gets up and come to the front] OK, the French Ambassador … [T hands over large box] How do you think the French Ambassador is feeling as he walks up to Henry to give this present?
Unur: Scared and nervous.
Teacher: Scared and nervous. Right. Why are you feeling scared and nervous?
Unur: Because he's afraid he might get killed.
Teacher: And he's representing his country. Kadife what were you saying?
Kadife: Might get killed.
Teacher: Might get killed. Good.
Richard: He shouldn't, he's an ambassador.
Teacher: Yup, he shouldn't do, because he's an ambassador, he should be protected, but he's a bit worried. OK. What do you think (.) Graham, what do you think is the message you, er, he is going to say? He's already had a message that Henry wants to invade France. What do you think the French Ambassador is going to say to that?
Ss: [various, making stereotypical French sounds].
Teacher: Listen! Dexter?
Dexter: We don't want war, we want to make peace.
Teacher: We don't want war, we want peace, OK. But what else might, probably, the King of France think if the King of England writes and says, I want your country?
S: [in French accent] Idiot!

Teacher: Idiot. Perhaps.
Ade: War!

Students are next invited to predict what might be in the parcel (suggestions include 'a bomb', 'a head'), then Unur, in role as the Ambassador, passes over the box, and Owsun is directed to open the present (which he does in suitably dramatic fashion). The teacher leads a whole-class discussion as to what tennis balls might symbolize; all students are then asked to jot down what they think Henry's response is likely to be. These ideas are read out to the class, following which students watch this scene on film and then have a look at photocopied extracts from Henry's actual speech:

> **Teacher:** … We'll hear a few ideas, what's Henry going to say and then (.) … I'm then going to very, very quickly show you a little bit of what Henry does actually say …
> **Ade:** [in role] 'He's suggesting I should go play tennis. This is a great insult. If he wants to play with me, we'll play on the battlefield'.
> **Teacher:** Brilliant. Yeah. [indicates another S with hand up] Right, OK, Dexter? OK, listen!
> **Dexter:** [in role] 'How dare you! The cheek! I should kill you for the thought against a King!'
> **Teacher:** Good. Right, Karen?
> **Karen:** I don't want to.
> **Teacher:** Go on! Or shall I read it then? [moves across to Karen. Reads her work] 'Is this a joke? OK, if he wants to stick tennis balls, um, then [she consults Karen] off with his pig-head. He's got another think coming! I want his head and when I do, I'll play tennis with it and let that be a warning to him!' OK, excellent!

Improvisation, role-plays and film are inextricably linked here in the reading process, often with students drawing on their own experiences and cultural knowledge within the collaborative framework of drama. For instance, when students are in small groups considering what a leader might say to rally their troops, Kadife asks Beth: 'Were people living in England in them days, were they all Christians?' Cem pursues this line of thought and asks Beth what would have happened in Henry's day to someone who was not a Christian. Later, adopting the role of leader, Unur incorporates the words, 'Do it in the name of Allah' into his motivational speech to the class. These students are simultaneously behaving as social actors and dramatic actors (Franks, 1996; Neelands, 2009), a fusion that has the potential to help bridge the gap between the Shakespeare text and students' own cultural understandings – a fusion I would argue that is made easier by the decentering of the 'sacred text'.

Conclusions

Echoing findings from Kress et al.'s research (2005), access as a concept is a key concern for each of these London teachers, and it underpins every aspect of their approach to Shakespeare, including pedagogy and film selection. For example, Beth chooses Branagh's version of *Henry V* because it is 'pretty accessible'; Pip talks about Luhrmann's *Romeo + Juliet* in terms of modernization and relevance, and, along with Marie, states that a film aids pupils' understanding of the plot and characters. Felicity is critical of the RSC video production of *Macbeth* for being less accessible (she calls it 'the big turn-off') and in interview regrets using it with her class, suggesting that this televised stage production is appropriate for top sets only. Across these classrooms film's role is subordinated as a cultural form, pressed into service as a simplified substitute for the 'real thing'. Holderness (1985) suggests that the act of adaptation, reconstructing Shakespeare for screen, is potentially a radical process that disrupts conventional ways of reading and thinking about the text. But the way in which film is employed in these classrooms may well achieve the opposite, by suggesting that this specific production represents 'the' authoritative interpretation of the text:

> Conventional ways of using film with Shakespeare present some problems … watching a single version of a Shakespeare play can flesh out the story for pupils in a way that constrains the imagination … such films are still generally read as extended, linear works, positioning the viewer through the force of narrative. (Durran and Morrison, 2004, p. 17)

There is a school of thought that Shakespeare's printed plays are merely 'pre-texts' (Wheale, 1991, p. 214), incomplete in themselves until transformed by performance (Reynolds 1991). My interviews concur with Martindale's questionnaire data (2008) indicating that English teachers appreciate the importance of performance, and welcome the benefit of film in providing easy classroom access to a professional performance of the play.

That teachers generally do not draw students' attention to the differences between film and theater as performance modes is problematic, particularly with, say, Baz Luhrmann's *Romeo + Juliet*, which with its high-tech digital editing techniques shifts the playtext into a multimodal space more closely related to pop videos and electronic games geared for the teenage market. Shakespeare DVDs that can be viewed non-linearly on large or small screen, including laptops, have the capacity to completely change the concept of performance, and of the play's relationship to its audience (Worthen, 2007). This in itself could be a fruitful area for exploration in classrooms, along with comparisons of the playtext and the screenplay.

Teachers' appreciation of film versions of Shakespeare does not in itself raise films' status as texts. Despite frequent references to film and television texts by teachers in the classroom, moving image versions of specific plays are rarely if ever interrogated on their own terms. Ultimately literary culture is tacitly afforded superior status in each of the classrooms I researched. Although Pip begins the unit of work on *Romeo and Juliet* by making links with her students' existing cultural knowledge of popular film, this is abandoned once the printed text itself is introduced. Even in Beth's classroom, Branagh's film text is supplanted by fragments of printed text once students begin to write their (heavily scaffolded) GCSE coursework essay. Moreover, the notion of textual authority is strongly marked in these classrooms. Despite at least three of the four teachers clearly feeling committed to enabling students to interpret the play for themselves, the majority of the lessons I recorded in both schools frequently position the students passively in the reading process and strongly suggest that there is ultimately a 'correct' way of thinking about the play, one that students need to reproduce in their exam or coursework essays. My observations of teachers working within curricular and assessment constraints provide a glimpse into just how difficult it is to avoid reproducing authoritative readings of Shakespeare's plays in the classroom, and the relegation of film as a low-status medium to support the reading of high-status printed text. When interviewed, two of the teachers are even slightly defensive about showing the film, suggesting that this is somehow not a valid part of English lessons. For example, Pip says, 'You always feel a bit of a cop-out teacher if you're showing the video, but I do think they do get so much out of it'. A common theme running through each of the teacher interviews is that film's main purpose is to provide a sense of the plot and the main characters, so that only small sections of the printed text need to be read. The phrase 'filling in' is used in this context by more than one teacher, putting film very much in its place.

Any assessment system that purely focuses on the printed text will tend to treat a Shakespeare play as a piece of literature, rather than as a playtext for performance. My research indicates that it also results in a degree of dishonesty whereby teachers substitute the film for the printed text in lessons, yet construct essay assignments for their students which for the most part rely on them ignoring the film version. Therefore it is an interesting development that one GCSE exam board (the Oxford and Cambridge and RSA Examination Board, or OCR) introduced in Autumn 2010 assessment of a set Shakespeare play that explicitly raised the status of film adaptations by requiring students to compare playtext and performance text (moving image, audio or live performance). Support materials produced for the OCR by Film Education provide teaching resources underpinned by a clear rationale:

> Film … is a popular medium and by teaching young people the critical skills with which to deconstruct both directors' interpretations of Shakespeare's texts and the texts themselves, teachers have an opportunity to approach the subject afresh. The combination of classic texts reconstructed by modern filmmakers goes to the heart of the debate about the position of Shakespeare in schools and provides teachers with a rich source of stimulus material for their students. (2010, p. 5)

Film Education's approach to the study of Shakespeare and film assumes that the reading process is both active and critical. The teaching support materials exemplify this approach, including, *inter alia*, comparison of book and film as commercial objects, a focus on differences between film and theater language and techniques (for example, how 'character' is constructed in each medium), and exploration of historical perspectives on notions of cultural value.

New technologies offer the potential to make diverse 'Shakespeares' available in the classroom, multimodal forms that have the capacity to subvert the kind of 'heritage' Shakespeare beloved of politicians. There is a rich seam of literary and cultural understanding to be mined within the classroom in comparing the ways in which playscripts have been adapted and reshaped according to the specific medium. This helps to place emphasis on audience and purpose, and on the ways different productions are received rather than seeking 'essential' meanings residing in the text (Clarke, 1995). Such an approach would serve to shift moving-image adaptations to the center of pedagogic attention, so that the specific social and historical context of production is given prominence (Goodwyn, 2004). Students can begin to explore how Shakespeare has been re-read and re-interpreted at different historical moments, and adapted to fit new modes of production whether theatrical, literary or digital. Not only is this pedagogy based on a 'model of literacy that can travel across semiotic modes and cultural forms' (Durran and Morrison, 2004, p. 17), but I would argue it comes much closer to meeting the National Curriculum's declared aim of helping students appreciate why Shakespeare's plays have remained popular and influential over time.

References

Batho, R. (1998). 'Shakespeare in secondary schools'. *Educational Review, 50*(2), 163–72.

BFI, Film Education, UK Film Council and EMC (2008). *Film: Twenty-first Century Literacy*, BFI, Film Education, UK Film Council, EMC.

Bousted, M. and Ozturk, A. (2004). '"It came alive outside my head." Developing literacies through comparison: the reading of classic text and moving image'. *Literacy, 38*(1), 52–7.

Buckingham, D. and Jones, K. (2001). 'New Labour's cultural turn: some tensions in contemporary educational and cultural policy'. *Journal of Education Policy, 16*(1), 1–14.

Burn, A. (2010). 'A Very Long Engagement: English and the Moving Image'. In D. Wyse, R. Andrews and J. Hoffman (eds), *The Routledge International Handbook of English, Language and Literacy Teaching.* pp. 354–66. Abingdon: Routledge,

Clarke, S. (1995). 'Is "NC" English never changing? Shakespeare and the new information technologies'. *English in Education, 29*(2), 12–19.

Coles, J. (2004). 'Much ado about nationhood and culture: Shakespeare and the search for an "English" identity'. *Changing English, 11*(1), 47–58.

Durran, J. and Morrison, C. (2004). 'From page to screen and back again: teaching literature through moving image; teaching moving image through literature'. *English Drama Media*, 16–22.

Film Education (2010). OCR GCSE English Literature, Unit 661: Shakespeare and film. Available online at: http://www.ocr.org.uk/download/sm/ocr_48119_sm_gcse_unit_a661_film_res.pdf [accessed 10 December 2010].

Franks, A. (1996). 'Drama education, the body and representation (or, the mystery of the missing bodies)'. *Research in Drama Education, 1*(1), 105–19.

—(1999). 'Where the action is: how drama contributes to the art of the teaching and learning of English'. *English in Education, 33*(2), 39–49.

Gibson, R. (1998). *Teaching Shakespeare.* Cambridge: Cambridge University Press.

Goodwyn, A. (2004). *English Teaching and the Moving Image.* London: RoutledgeFalmer.

Hodgen, J. and Marshall, B. (2005). 'Assessment for learning in English and mathematics: a comparison'. *The Curriculum Journal, 16*(2), 153–76.

Holderness, G. (1985). 'Radical Potentiality and Institutional Closure: Shakespeare in Film and Television'. In J. Dollimore and A. Sinfield (eds), *Political Shakespeare*, pp. 182–201. Manchester: Manchester University Press,

Jewitt, C., Bezeimer, J., Jones, K. and Kress, G. (2009). 'Changing English? The impact of technology and policy on a school subject in the 21st century'. *English Teaching: Practice and Critique, 8*(3), 8–20.

Kress, G., Jewitt, C., Bourne, J., Franks, A., Hardcastle, J., Jones, K. and Reid, E. (2005). *English in Urban Classrooms: A Multimodal Perspective on Teaching and Learning.* London: RoutledgeFalmer.

Lankshear, C. and Knobel, M. (2003). *New Literacies: Changing Knowledge and Classroom Learning.* Buckingham: Open University Press.

Leach, S. (1992). *Shakespeare in the Classroom.* Buckingham: Open University Press.

Leavis, F. R. and Thompson, D. (1933). *Culture and Environment.* London: Chatto and Windus.

Martindale, S. (2008). 'Shakespeare on film: viewing Shakespeare inside the classroom and out'. *English Drama Media*, 10, 19–22.

McEvoy, S. (1991). 'The politics of teaching Shakespeare'. *English in Education*, *25*(3), 71–8.

Miles, M. and Huberman, M. A. (1994). *Qualitative Data Analysis.* Beverly Hills: Sage.

Moore, A. (2006). 'Curriculum as Culture: Entitlement, Bias and the Bourdieusean Arbitrary'. In A. Moore (ed.), *Schooling, Culture and Curriculum,* pp. 87–99. London: Routledge.

Neelands, J. (2009). 'Acting together: ensemble as a democratic process in art and life'. *Research in Drama Education*, *14*(2), 173–89.

QCDA (2007). *The National Curriculum: English.* London: Qualifications and Curriculum Development Agency.

Reynolds, P. (1991). 'Unlocking the Box: Shakespeare on Film and Video'. In L. Aers and N. Wheale (eds), *Shakespeare in the Changing Curriculum,* pp. 189–203. London: Routledge,

Stibbs, A. (1998). 'Between desk, stage and screen: 50 years of Shakespeare teaching', *Educational Review*, *50*(3), 241–8.

Wheale, N. (1991). 'Scratching Shakespeare: Video-teaching the Bard'. In L. Aers and N. Wheale (eds), *Shakespeare in the Changing Curriculum,* pp. 204–21. London: Routledge,

Worthen, W. B. (2007). 'Performing Shakespeare in Digital Culture'. In R. Shaughnessy (ed.) *The Cambridge Companion to Shakespeare and Popular Culture,* pp. 227–47. Cambridge: Cambridge University Press,

Films

Branagh, K. (dir., 1989). *Henry V*. Universal Pictures.

Luhrmann, B. (dir., 1996). *William Shakespeare's Romeo + Juliet*. Twentieth Century Fox.

Nunn, T. (dir., 1979). *Macbeth*. RSC/Thames Television.

Polanski, R. (dir., 1971). *The Tragedy of Macbeth*. Playboy Productions.

7

Film, Literacy and Cultural Participation

Mark Reid

Chapter Outline

English needs to start from an idea of education, before an idea of the subject.

(Medway, 2010)

For some years I have been working on behalf of the British Film Institute (BFI) promoting a version of literacy that includes film (Reid, 2009). My starting point is always a definition of literacy as 'being able fully to participate in a culture'; the implication is that one cannot participate fully in twenty-first-century culture without a grounding in the moving image. As the late Anthony Minghella put it, 'It is vital and obvious that understanding, manipulating, and appreciating the film sentence should be an accepted part of the education system' (Minghella, 2005).

What I would like to do here is explore, and then formalize, a participatory definition of literacy that includes the 'film sentence', and then illustrate it with examples from work at the BFI.

Let us start with a straightforward question: what does it mean to be literate? And answer with an example from Gee (1990). A man goes into a bar. It is a Hell's Angels' bar, and the man wants to pass as a Hell's Angel. So he wears leathers and denims, biker boots. He wants to look the part, so he grows his hair long, and grows a beard. This process takes several months. In everyday life he is a stockbroker, so he knows his accent and idiom would immediately give him away – so he watches biker films, and reads biker magazines and practises biker talk, a process that also takes several months. But when he finally goes into the bar, and speaks to the bartender, in spite of all of his preparation, he is still identified as a charlatan. It seems that there are a set of beliefs, values, assumptions that Hell's Angels subscribe to, that our character is not aware of. No matter how perfectly he replicates the appearance of the Hell's Angel, underneath he is still a stockbroker. His daily acculturation is as a stockbroker; in order to 'pass' as a Hell's Angel, he would have to immerse himself in their habitus, and absorb their beliefs and values, those attributes that are embodied in dress, language, body language. (Although to some extent it is also true that taking on the outward appearance of a discourse enables you to 'let it speak through you', as it were. Discourses are embodied, as well as separable, ideologies. Maybe more 'taking on' the appearance of different discourses would help students perform better.)

James Gee (1990), from whom the example above is taken, wrote about literacy as an immersive, total discourse system, what he called 'saying (writing)-doing-being-valuing-believing combinations … which integrate words, acts, values, beliefs, attitudes, and social identities as well as gestures, glances, body positions, and clothes' (Gee, 1990, p. 142). To be literate, (my paraphrase) is 'to participate *fully* in a culture' (my paraphrase), where a culture is more than a loose collection of people assembled contiguously together, but rather a community of people who share values and beliefs, behaviors and practises.

Take artists for example. 'Being an artist' entails more than developing and establishing a repertoire of craft skills – like painting, or sculpting. Artists group themselves into discourse communities governed by very implicit rules – of language, dress, behavior, even belief. As if to take this makeover of identity seriously, some of them even change their names, to signal their change of state, their membership of a non-civilian order. (Andrew Graham Dixon talks about the art community as a clerisy – a priesthood; just like a religious order, its members sometimes change their names, and follow a dress code.) In short, literacy is not just about writing; it is about whole value systems, and about the cultures that people participate in. The language that you use is just one marker of the culture you are a part of.

This is a long way from film, which is where I work, and where I want to take this chapter. But it establishes a central tenet for English: literacy is not about text types, or meaning-making systems (modes), or about the vehicles that carry these messages to us (media). It is about accessing, inhabiting and critiquing culture as 'a whole way of life', as Raymond Williams put it (Williams, 1958, p. 54). And the role of educators is to support people in accessing a range of forms of life beyond those they already inhabit, as other educators did for us.

The special role that English has is that it is concerned first of all with the imagination: how people have imagined new and different worlds, and re-presented the worlds they already know. The structuring of experience in materials that have been adapted for this purpose – in film, theater, poetry and prose – is our subject. But these forms reach beyond themselves, and their closed interpretive systems and communities; novels, films, TV programs change both the way we see the world, and sometimes, the world itself. So, to go back to the quote that opened this chapter, our role is to enable people to change, or develop, or extend, the way they read, watch, listen, and think, in ways that help them participate in society. This, to answer Medway, is 'the idea of Education that English should start from' (Medway, 2010).

Theroizing literacy as participation

Here is a model of how an individual participates in society, through the act of making something.

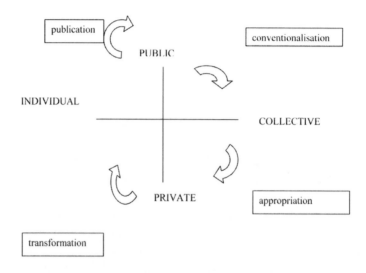

Ross et al. (1993) after Harre (1983)

A social model of the arts as a 'making process'

What this diagram presents is a heuristic for conceiving how a child relates to the wider social world, as mediated through the act of making something. For Ross et al. the made objects were from the arts of sculpture, painting, dance, but it serves equally well as a model of making in literacy: the relationship between reading and writing, between self and other, and between a child's present context and the traditions they have access to.

Following the cycle clockwise from the top, we first of all witness the absorption (or *conventionalization*) of a newly made object, or text, into a collective meaning or set of practises. This is typically how a new film, poem, novel or painting (Martin Scorsese's *Goodfellas*, say (Scorsese, USA, 1990) joins a pre-existing set of other films, novels etc. in the public domain (Scorsese's body of work; gangster films; films about New York or about Italian American life) and then changes that set of examples, either subtly, or in a major way. The set, or sets, of examples, we call genre, and a film artist like Scorsese will change our sense of what the genre is, and can do.

The new work, welcomed to the collective realm, doesn't have to be made by an internationally recognized artist: works by children sometimes enter larger collective bodies of work, anywhere where a work of art enters a community and a communal memory: in the sixth-form Media Studies department I used to work in, video work from previous years' students served as a reference point for us, and for our students, and the same was true on a larger scale for the exam boards who collated and disseminated the best of student work.

In the 'private' quadrant of the cycle, individuals absorb, internalize, or in Ross et al.'s terms *appropriate*, the sets of meanings, techniques and strategies that come with either a specific film or poem or painting (there's the famous 'restaurant tracking shot' in *Goodfellas*, for example, or its bravura opening), or are absorbed more generally from a set of works within a genre (children's internalized sense of the dialog and characterization in soap opera, for example). In either case, we make texts personal to ourselves; their strategies, moments, features enter a personal canon or repertoire. With some people – those embarking on making something – not just film, but any work of art – the special, personally associated meanings and tropes and features of *Goodfellas* will become part of their personal lexicon. What T. S. Eliot (1920) said about poets ('immature poets imitate; mature poets steal; bad poets deface what they take, and good poets make it into something better, or at least something different') applies just as well to other art forms: filmmakers will be (and have been) influenced by powerful examples of a genre, whether consciously or unconsciously, and some of them will quote from it, or remake it into something new.

In the third quadrant, the *transformative* stage, the internalized meanings and feelings and associations bump into the materiality of the maker's chosen form: if it is written language, then some things can be said, and others not. If it is visual art, then some things can be shown, and others not. If it is film, then the resources of film – sound (speech, music, sound effects), pictures (and how they're framed and designed, and what's in them), and time (how long shots last; how shots are juxtaposed with each other, and with sound) – enable some things to be shown, reproduced, revealed, and not others. The material and form – and generic rules – allow and enable some things to be said and shown, and proscribe others. As Elliot Eisner puts it:

> Transforming the private into the public is a primary process of work in both art and science. Helping the young learn how to make that transformation is another of education's most important aims. (2002, p. 3)

And later, considering how the imagination acts transformatively on its objects, how it is more than a passive looking glass on which other images are reflected:

> Yet there is a difference between recalled images and their imaginative transformation. Were we limited to the recall of the images we had once experienced, cultural development would be in trouble. Imagination gives us images of the possible that provide a platform for seeing the actual, and by seeing the actual freshly, we can do something about creating what lies beyond it. (2002, p. 4)

The *publication* phase of making is the presentation of the made work to the outside world. This does not have to mean publishing in a global sense, in which everyone in the world potentially accesses the work; instead it is the presentation of work to an audience outside the self – maybe only classmates, family and friends, a teacher. On the identity matrix above, it's the work moving from individual to public. And then, in Ross et al.'s terms, the work, once made public, joins the swim of humanity: 'The child's products are offered as additions to the conventional wisdom of society, and she herself becomes a bearer of the culture.' (Ross et al., 1993, p. 54).

In arts education, the notion of the publication of children's work – its presentation to an outside audience – is now recognized as fundamental. But the conditions in which this happens are crucial to whether the child's work actually *lives* beyond its own means. If a child's film, for example, is not shown in its entirety at awards ceremonies or celebratory screenings, then such presentations cannot fairly constitute publication in its fullest sense. Further than this, without maker and audience being able to talk about the work (or sometimes just the audience; artists can be notoriously reluctant to talk about their work, preferring it to 'speak for itself'), there is no real 'conventionalization' of the work in wider discourse. In order to become assimilated to a wider body of work, of form, and genre, works of art are given life beyond themselves, by social means. This is the purpose of book groups, film societies, adult education art courses, internet fan groups, arts reviewing: they are how works of art are given life and sustained within a culture, and they are given life often through language.

I want to argue that a child progressing through this whole cycle constitutes a moment of literacy, and literacy as social and cultural participation. The child who produces a piece of film melds examples and features of films she has seen, sometimes consciously, but more often without directly being aware of them, into her own personal film lexicon, into a piece of her own film, and possibly, shown to a 'public'. The whole process is one whereby a child joins the 'film conversation' – the set of discourses, and discourse communities that have built up around film over the past 115 years. There are subsets of film conversations that are more closely related to children, young people and film: around animation in schools for example (but also around home-made animations on YouTube), or around pieces of film made for assessment at post-16 study (Media Studies; Moving Image Arts), or among teachers (see Yahoo groups on film in Modern Foreign Languages). But these are all in the end part of a larger discourse group – the 'film community'.

On the face of it, the Ross model is not so different from other accounts of the creative process in education (see Burn and Banaji, 2010). But other accounts tend to follow a particular pattern: from planning/input, through making, to publication/sharing/output. What is crucially different about the Ross model is that it theorizes a relationship between four points and two axes that between them express a relationship between the individual and the social, and between the public and the private (lest this be confusing, the social or collective sphere is different from the public sphere: it is possible to be private and collective, as with Masonic groups, for example).

The movement between public/collective, and private/individual is one of the fundamental dynamics in society: it is how individuals create and maintain a sense of their own individuation, but from within a group, or set of groups. Social groups are made up of individuals that share some features in common, while individuals choose from the many common features at their disposal in order to incorporate their own uniqueness. Any act of creative 'making' – from babies learning to talk, to great artists changing the direction of painting, sculpture, or film – has a constitutive role in this transaction between individual, collective, private and social, and can be explained by it. Without the social or collective dimension of the matrix, we have a series of single voices in empty rooms, of work made in a vacuum. We have no conversation, in fact no public realm, in which to participate.

We know that creative learning is about the self, the 'expressive entitlement', but less about the self's central but subordinate role in participating in a culture. Contemporary public and policy discourse about education tends to follow the 'business ontology' (Fisher, 2011, blogging as *k-punk*) where the only purposes of education are instrumental and economic, where the training of children is as agents, serving the economy as its instruments. However, there is an alternative sphere, or ontology: the public space, or public realm. This place is created out of collective participation, and is collaboratively built. Being literate as a form of social and cultural participation is therefore more than an individual entitlement: it is a necessity if the public realm is to exist at all.

This is why a social, participatory model of literacy (or of creative practise more generally) is so important: it projects the maker, and her work, beyond herself, into the wider world, into history, into discourse, into language, into what philosopher Michael Oakeshott (cited in Ross et al., 1993) called 'the conversation of mankind.'

Film, identity, literacy – a case study

From here, I would like to examine some work we have been doing at the BFI that is illuminated by the Ross model – and which shows how film education can help children join 'the conversation of mankind'.

For two years now, the BFI has been participating in a program run by the Cinémathèque Française – the Paris-based, French sister organization to the BFI. In 1995, the Cinémathèque instituted an idea called 'Le Cinéma, cent ans de jeunesse'. ('Cinema 100 years' young', or '100 years of youth'). The year 1995 was the centenary of film, and the idea was to invite a group of filmmaking workshops to make films in the style of, and under some of the same conditions as, the Lumière Brothers – for many people the originators of film as we know it. Each year subsequently, the program has taken an aspect of film language – light, camera movement, depth of field, framing, color – and set out an education program around it. The program comprises watching – a double DVD is put together of clips from all over the world, and across film history – and a 'curriculum' of specified exercises and tasks (playful experiments that enable children to try out some of the techniques they will have seen in the DVD of clips), culminating in a final 'film essai'. I use the word 'curriculum' deliberately (as opposed to 'project' for example), in the sense of a set of prescribed steps and activities and offered resources supporting them, underpinned by a set of pedagogical principles. The program takes around two terms, or 50 hours, to complete.

In our first year of involvement, the theme was 'camera movement'. Better still, it was framed as a question: 'Pourquoi bouge le camera?' (Why move the camera?) Thus, all the work produced by children became a set of possible answers to that question. The program began with a two-day training seminar in Paris. Alain Bergala, the critic whose ideas have informed much of the Cinémathèque's work over the last twenty years (summarized in his book *L'hypothèse cinéma*, 2006), led the seminar, with a discussion of the many dimensions of camera movement in the history of cinema, starting with the Lumière Bros', early experiments with travelling shots, a long look at Stanley Kubrick's *Barry Lyndon* (USA, 1975), and a film called *July*, by Kazak director Darezhan Omirbaev (Kazakhstan, 1988). All of the clips used in Bergala's presentation (which itself ran to some seven hours over two days) were compiled and distributed on a double DVD soon after the training session.

The exercises for the Camera Movement year encouraged very short experimental pieces: contrasting film of moving objects, and moving cameras, with static shots and objects, for example. As many of the projects operate within school buildings (if not always school time), many of the exercises featured moving shots through school corridors, replicating, or referencing, travelling shots from Gus Van Sant's *Elephant* (USA, 2003), or Woody Allen's *Everyone Says I Love You* (USA, 1996), or Kubrick's *The Shining* (USA, 1980). You can watch some of the examples of the exercises made by children (http://100ans.cinematheque.fr/100ans20092010/?page_id=17), put 'Cinema cent ans de jeunesse 2009/10' into your search engine and click on 'quelques exercices realises' in the right hand toolbar.

In 2009/10, we worked with three groups of young people: one group of around ten Year 8 boys from a boys' school in south London, another of six Year 9 boys from a mixed secondary school, also in south London, and a group of Year 10 girls on a BTEC (vocational qualification from the Business and Technology Education Council) Media Production course at a girls' school on the outskirts of south-east London. The first group of boys came to BFI Southbank every Wednesday after school, for two to three hours, between October and May; the second group of boys worked on and off through the Spring term of 2010; the girls' group followed the program as part of their curriculum, on a Friday, between November and May. The Cinémathèque program allows for this flexibility: our after-school BFI group worked through a compressed version in eight weeks, while the BTEC group spent a day a week for over a term.

I should like to focus just for a moment on the exercises carried out by our groups. The early exercises of one of the groups, who came to BFI Southbank once a week after school for the duration of the project, were characterized by filmed 'group rucking': the filming activity was an excuse for portrayals of play fighting. Later, when we asked for story ideas, their responses were typically about filming more violent stories. A second group, based at their school in south London, took a different tack in their exercises, choosing to film long single-take travelling shots along corridors, past and through groups of students, following a single character – a compilation of footage that became incorporated into their final *film essai*.

The second group had watched more of the DVD clips as part of their preparation: when we asked them at the end of the project which films had an impact on their final outcome, they all said the clips from *The Shining* (Kubrick, USA, 1980), in which there are many shots of the young boy travelling along corridors on his tricycle. The boys remembered in particular the heightened sound effect as the tricycle moved from carpeted to polished wooden floor – and it may be significant that a number of the group had been identified as being on the autistic spectrum, which sometimes presents as a heightened sensitivity to sound. In terms of the arts cycle, it may have been that the exposure to, and internalization of, some of the Kubrick work, came out explicitly in the exercises and completed films.

It is significant here that when young people are given access to examples of how expert creators make use of the language they have access to (the 'rhetorical tropes' that make up the expressive repertoires of a mode like film, or writing), they have the potential to move away from what might otherwise be their default story-telling techniques. In many film education settings (especially outside the formal sector) there can be a tendency on behalf of group leaders and educators not to want to scaffold, shape, or otherwise influence children's choice of story-telling resources, possibly based on a limited version of a 'liberation pedagogy', in which children were felt to be most creative when no artificial limits were set to their creativity (see a discussion of this tendency in film education in Reid et al., 2002). However, what we are finding in the Cinémathèque program is that children and young people welcome examples of work by filmmakers who have had to answer similar questions as themselves ('why and how will I move my camera?'); children can then choose (or not choose) to respond to or accommodate those ideas.

The choice of the word 'essay' to describe the final outcome in the Cinémathèque program is interesting: the origin of the word, in French, means 'a trying out', an experiment. The program does not encourage children to feel that they will be making a complete film, but rather a summation of some of the ideas and techniques they have been learning, practising and experimenting with. In a world where very many children (in the UK it may be as many as 100,000) make a single film in their school lives, this distinction is important: if a film is cast as your first attempt, the implied expectation is that you will go on to make many more films. Also, to go back to Anthony Minghella's conception of the film sentence, it is possible that these film exercises are more like playing with phrases and sentences, and then combining them into a couple of paragraphs, than embarking on complete stories.

In 2009/10, between them, the two boys' groups produced five completed *film essais*: one school producing four, shorter films, quite early on in the year, and the other group producing a longer, overall group piece. The four shorter films focus very closely on the film essai rubric (see https://markreid1895.wordpress.com in the July 2010 posting), particularly the moment of revelation that closes each film. In contrast, the single longer film (http://100ans.cinematheque.fr/100ans20092010/?page_id=16) incorporates a much wider range of camera movement as its defining feature. The girls' group produced four films that interpreted the rubric more loosely, combining aspects of the exercises with the final *film essai* (their examples are also included at: https://markreid1895.wordpress.com).

At the end of the program, in June, all the participating children and young people between 8 and 18 years old (by 2011 around 400 young people from Spain, Italy, Portugal, the UK, as well as France), had showed their work in Paris. But this was not a celebratory awards event; there we held three all-day presentations of work, in which children interrogated each other, as peer filmmakers, about technique, choices, accidents, sources in their work. Serge Toubiana, Head of the Cinémathèque, and Costa-Gavras, its Chair, joined in the conversation for a couple of hours, showing work they had made as well.

For the boys' group in the first year of our participation, there were many opportunities to present their work in public. Early in the year, four of them presented their exercises, and what they were learning about camera movement, to a group of teachers on a film language INSET day (originally an IN-SErvice Training day when schools sessions are not required to be run and staff undergo training). Another six of them came to Paris, and presented to their peers in the daunting 400-seat Lotte Eisner cinema. And finally a couple came and presented their work at the BFI. The opportunity for publication (or exhibition) in more than one context has meant the boys have become adept and confident at speaking to their work in public, and becoming quite unusually reflective.

Back to the model

The Cinémathèque program, viewed as a cycle, maps onto the Ross et al. (1993) model like this. The initial impetus – the viewing and discussion – is an instance of appropriation, where participants – students and facilitators – familiarize themselves with new ideas, forms, and sample answers to the central question 'why move the camera?', but it also is a kind of conventionalization, where a community of practitioners take on a new formal category in their chosen art form (why move the camera?) and explore examples of cinema through the prism of this new category. The films chosen for the training, and the DVD of clips, thus become repositories of 'camera movement' techniques, as well as whatever other generic category they already belong to. Kubrick's *The Shining*, in other words, becomes a 'camera movement' film.

The conventionalized, appropriated examples and central question are internalized by the participants and made their own, not just through watching the clips, but through playing with technique: filming a travelling sequence; comparing static and moving shots and objects; filming a fleeting encounter between three unrelated characters. These exercises have something of the traditional rhetorical exercise about them (Lanham, 1993). In the medieval school and university curriculum, rhetoric was the vehicle through which students were trained in the language arts, and in thinking and behaving morally, by means of imitating rhetorical tropes in great works. Classic texts were not studied for ennoblement alone, but were copied, adapted, re-presented as an apprenticeship in cultural participation. Richard Andrews (2010, p. 258), refers to the progymnasmata of Renaissance rhetoric – exercises in which genres were modelled and then imitated by apprentice writers and speakers – and in the Cinémathèque program, apprentice filmmakers are doing the same thing: copying, internalizing, transforming stock techniques as demonstrated by the masters of cinema.

This is the process of internalization, following the third quadrant of the Ross model: the student or child takes the example of the thing from out of the world, and transforms it into his own thing, in his own voice. In Ross et al.'s (1993) terms, this is where the child uses publicly available aesthetic conventions and forms to order his own feelings. What is unusual about the Cinémathèque program is how the processes of filmmaking – which start with film viewing – are drawn out, decompressed and elaborated over time. The exercises that are prescribed as preparatory, playful preludes to the final 'film essai' enable explicit internalization of some of the conventions of film, before the student is invited to mobilize them in a final 'high-stakes' production. The process is private, internal and essentially inaccessible from the outside (from a teacher's perspective, for example). The process of transformation is only knowable after the fact, when a new object is presented for publication.

The application of the arts cycle model to this particular approach to film education illuminates both film education and the model itself. Ross et al.'s model presents an essentially isolated and internalized sense of making and yet filmmaking is a social, collaborative experience. In education settings – and in the film industry more widely – single, controlled, hermetically sealed film creation is extremely rare. Children making animations in primary schools do so in groups: they collaborate on story-making, scripting, shooting, voicing their work. Students at higher levels are required to create film (in A level Film and Media Studies, or BTEC Media Production for example) in groups, allocating roles as they would in the film industry. So how can this transformative phase of the making process still be internalized, and private, among a group of individuals? One possibility is that a filmmaking group creates for itself a single, collective, subjectivity (Mitchell, 2001): for the purpose of making a particular film, an agency is constituted solely for the completion of the task. And the process of transformation, of gathering the resources to hand and applying to them the constraints of the task (Sharples, 1999), is more often than not conducted in language. For just as buildings can be said to be created in conversations between architects, clients and site managers so films are often created through talk between their participant makers.

The process of filmmaking is therefore elaborated in talk; but it is further elaborated in that it is a process that has a number of clearly defined stages: first, in conceiving a story or scenario; second, in planning out a series of shots and sequences, and maybe drawing or designing them; third in shooting those images, or ones like them; then in combining the chosen images, and 'post-producing' sequences, with the addition of extra sound, transitions, effects; and then, probably shooting more footage, and recombining it with the existing material. This extended creative process distinguishes film from other modes: it is not possible with film to 'shape [it] at the point of utterance' (Britton, 1982, p. 139[1]) in an improvisatory sense, as it is with writing or speech; nor is film all preparation and rehearsal until it becomes performance. (Dance, as Wim Wenders notes when interviewed about his film *Pina*, has no way of archiving itself; all it can be is the performance – *Sight&Sound* magazine, May 2011).

Conclusions

Consider the implications of the relationship between forms of representation for the selection of content in the school curriculum. Learning to use particular forms of representation is also learning to think and represent meaning in particular ways. How broad is the current distribution? What forms of representation are emphasized? In what forms are students expected to become "literate"? What modes of cognition are stimulated, practiced, and refined by the forms that are made available? (Eisner, 2002)

Eisner very eloquently and clearly makes the case for the school curriculum concerning itself with a wider range of modes of representation than just speech and writing. He means the whole curriculum, I imagine (see BFI publications *Look Again* (2003) and *Moving Images in the Classroom* (2000)), but even in its own backyard, English should have accommodated and given equal prominence to film, drama, comics and graphic literature, and radio, by now. He is right that new(er) modes enable us to think in different ways (Tufte, 2004), but the larger argument is that the public realm is now constituted out of the still and moving image as much as it is by the printed and spoken word. If we are serious about children participating in this realm, and these cultures, on their own terms, and adding to and enriching them, then a practise that follows the models above begins to develop a body of work in which children and young people take a more active role in 'the film conversation'. They will be essentially 'talking with' filmmakers of the past, and from around the world, on issues of common interest: how to move the camera, and why; how to use depth of field to tell stories; how to use color, light and sound expressively. They will become more adept at presenting, and reflecting on, their own work, and at interrogating the work of others – not just their peers, but more celebrated filmmakers as well.

The Cinémathèque program itself emphasizes other aspects of 'film literacy' that we can learn from in wider literacy: the importance of practise and play in making sentences of any kind; the centrality of shorter units of meaning in the creation of new texts; the importance of setting constraints in a task, but constraints that enable and scaffold new understandings.

---

1   Well, not entirely. Jonas Mekas, in the compilation of 'diaries, notes and sketches' he called Walden, effectively 'shapes at the point of utterance' with a 16mm camera.

The importance of repeated opportunities for working with film, as opposed to the 'one shot' which is more typical for young people. Practice, experiment and play; constraints, sustainability and long-term engagement; the sense of oneself as an artist or maker whose work and role is taken seriously; learning from, adapting, reproducing, critiquing the work of those more experienced; all of these elements contribute to the ability of a child to 'participate fully in a culture', to join 'the conversation of mankind'.

References

Allen, W. (1996). *Everyone Says I Love You*. (USA).

Andrews, R. (2010). 'Moffett and rhetoric'. *Changing English: Studies in Culture and Education, 17*(3), 251–60.

Bergala, A. (2006). *L'hypothèse cinéma*. Paris: Cahiers du cinema.

BFI (2000). *Moving Images in the Classoom*. London: BFI.

—(2003). *Look Again*. London: BFI.

—(2012). BFI/Cinémathèque (blog) https://markreid1895.wordpress.com [accessed 30 November 2012], 92.

Britton, J. (1982). 'Shaping at the Point of Utterance'. In *Prospect and Retrospect: Selected Essays of James Britton*. Portsmouth, NH: Boynton Cook.

Burn, A. and Banaji, S. (2010). *The Rhetorics of Creativity*. London: Creativity, Culture and Education.

Cinémathèque Française (2012). *A Nous le Cinema!* http://100ans.cinematheque.fr/100ans20092010/?page_id=17 [accessed 30 November 2012], 92.

Eliot, T. S. (1920). ' "Philip Massinger", a biographical essay'. In *The Sacred Wood*, London: Methuen. http://en.wikisource. org/wiki/The_Sacred_Wood/Philip_Massinger [accessed 30 Novemeber 2012].

Eisner, E. (2002). *The Arts and the Creation of Mind*. New Haven: Yale University Press.

Fisher, M. (2011). 'blogging as "k-punk" '. http://k-punk.abstractdynamics.org/archives/007489.html [accessed 4 May 2011].

Gee, J. P. (1990). *Social Linguistics and Literacies: Ideology in Discourses. Critical Perspectives on Literacy and Education*. London: Routledge FalmerPress.

Harre, R. (1983). *Personal Being*. Oxford: Blackwell.

Kubrick, S. (dir., 1975). *Barry Lyndon*. USA.

—(dir.,1980). *The Shining*. USA.

Lanham, R. (1993). *The Electronic Word: Democracy, Technology, and the Arts*. Chicago: Chicago University Press.

Medway, P. (2010). 'English and Enlightenment', *Changing English: Studies in Culture and Education, 17*(1), 3–12. Oxford: Blackwell,

Minghella, A. (2005). Speech at the launch of the Charter for Media Literacy, http://www.google.co.uk/url?sa=t&rct=j& q=&esrc=s&source=web&cd=1&ved=0CDEQFjAA&url=http%3A%2F%2Findustry.bfi.org.uk%2Fmedia%2Fword% 2Fc%2Fr%2FMedia_Literacy_Charter_Launch.doc&ei=vYC4UN_iNtHasgbwz4HoAw&usg=AFQjCNFlnDTa5NW4 Bvo1JBjMr4RSvR_riw&cad=rja [accessed 30 November 2012].

Mitchell, S. (2001). 'Questions and Schooling'. In R. Andrews and S. Mitchell (2001), *Essays in Argument*. London: Middlesex University Press.

Oakeshott, M. (1977). *Rationalism in Politics and Other Essays*. London: Methuen.

Omirbaev, D. (dir., 1988). *July/ Shilde*. Kazakhstan.

Reid, M. (2009). 'Reframing literacy: a film pitch for the 21st century'. *English, Drama, Media*, Issue 14 June 2009, NATE.

Reid, M. et al. (2002). Evaluation report of the Becta Digital Video Pilot Project. Coventry: Becta. http://homepages.shu.ac.uk/~edsjlc/ict/becta/research_papers/what_the_research_says/dvreport_241002.pdf [accessed 21 July 2014].

Ross, M., Radnor, H., Mitchell, S. and Bierton, C. (1993). *Assessing Achievement in the Arts.* Buckingham: Open University Press.

van Sant, G. (2003). *Elephant.* (USA).

Scorsese, M. (dir., 1990). *Goodfellas.* USA.

Sight&Sound (2011). Wim Wenders interviewed by Nick James. May 2011 Issue.

Sharples, M. (1999). *How We Write: Writing as Creative Design.* London: Routledge.

Tufte, E. (2004). An interview with Edward R. Tufte, at www.edwardtufte.com/tufte/s15427625tcq1304_5.pdf [accessed 4 May 2011].

Williams, R. [1958]. 'Culture is ordinary'. In I. Szeman and T. Kaposy (eds) (2011), *Cultural Theory: An Anthology.* Oxford: John Wiley & Sons, pp. 53–9.

Part 3
Writing

What is Writing? What's it For? 8

Michael Rosen

Before thinking about how to help children and young people (or indeed ourselves) to write, perhaps it is worth thinking for a moment about what writing is for. The simple answer that people usually give to that question is 'communication'. Clearly, that is true, but it is not the whole story, nor does it really explain why we do it, when we have other very good communication devices, speech, radio, TV and phones, for example.

There are several strong reasons for writing. Here are some:

1. It conserves thought – or a form of thought, anyway. Speech, radio, TV and phone conversations are mostly in a fast current. They can be preserved in recorded form but mostly our actual use of these forms is to take part or to listen and then move on.
2. For the person doing the writing, it involves a special kind of organization of thought. This is slower than speech – which is itself important – but it also involves a use of language that is different from speech in many ways. (I will come back to that.)
3. Writing can be long-distance. That is to say, writing is usually conserved on fairly permanent materials: originally clay tablets and stone, bark, animal skins, wood, papyrus, paper, digital forms and so on. So it has the potential of lasting and travelling to places far from the original writer both in space and time. We read Greek inscriptions. Someone on the other side of the globe writes and we can read it.

4. Writing can be read out loud. This may seem obvious and absurd, but it is why and how drama and the media have developed. Most drama and media entertainment involves people reading and/ or learning something that has been written down. In other words, we have developed forms of communication and entertainment that look as if they are speech but are in fact a particular kind of mongrel: spoken-writing (or in the case of song, sung-writing). This is a crucial part of written culture but is not usually described as such. Millions of people worldwide are engaged in jobs and leisure that involve writing things down (and/or editing them) in order that they will be spoken or sung. In passing, I will say that education has traditionally overlooked this crucially important function of writing, or if not overlooked, it has downgraded it. How many exam papers include a section on writing e.g. a playscript, a filmscript, a sketch, a song, a radio announcement, a short intro to a chatshow ... and so on?

5. Some writing is not really for 'communication' in the traditional sense. People do it for themselves: diaries, shopping lists, notes and certain kinds of poem. It is as if we understand that by writing something down for ourselves we make it easier for us to organize our thoughts, keep hold of things, find out what is important, easier to remember and so on.

So what actually is writing?

It is of course a way of capturing language but by and large it is a way of capturing only one kind of language: i.e. 'written language'. That is to say, you can make strenuous efforts to make writing represent daily speech, but a transcript of conversations is usually rather unsatisfactory as a form of communication.

Societies have developed various ways of capturing language in writing. The system I am using now ('the alphabetic principle') is an evolved attempt to capture or represent the sounds we use when we speak. English has around 44 phonemes (small segments of sounds) and 26 letters in the alphabet. So the letters are combined in various ways to represent some more of the phonemes.

It is not a failsafe system. There is hardly a phoneme in English that is represented in the same way every time. Think of 'meet' and 'meat' for example. And even a sound like the 'm' of 'meat' is represented by 'mm' in 'humming'. Conversely, some letters, when found in different contexts represent different sounds: 'ou' in 'wound' and 'sound' – or even the two ways to say 'wound'.

Then again, because English has never been regularized, it carries with it a long historical baggage of 'fossilized' remnants of previous pronunciations, interferences, typographers' reforms and much else. This explains why we write 'fight' and 'debt' and 'don't', etc.

All language has grammar – that is to say a system by which parts are strung together to release ideas, commands, questions, thoughts, feelings. In a school context, it is easy to think that grammar is one thing – 'sentence grammar' – but in fact, if we remember that grammar is about stringing parts together, we can see that there are other grammars: the grammar of conversation, the grammar of paragraphs, the grammar of songs and so on. So, for example, a conversation might go like this:

'You going out?'

'Mm?'

'You going out?'

'Yep.'

We might ask, what is the grammar of 'Mm?' It is perhaps one of the most used units of communicative sound in everyday usage. We might give it a name: 'interrogative particle' or 'interrogative expletive'. It performs a crucial grammatical function, which gets a vital communicative response: the repetition of the misheard or misunderstood question. Apart from when I am writing dialog, this 'Mm?' is hardly ever used in what we usually call writing. (As it happens I can think of one way in which it could. If I was writing, say, a stream of consciousness piece of prose, trying to represent my flow of thoughts, I could find myself interrupting myself with a 'Mm?')

My point here is that writing does not only represent phonemes. Clearly it represents words. It can represent meaningful and not-so meaningful sounds. Mostly, it has the job of putting a particular kind of language on the page: the sequence of language we call sentences. Again, I will say, though – not always. Songs, TV scripts and film scripts are full of non-sentence grammar.

The written sentence is mostly an example of standardized language. The story of who did the standardizing is itself very interesting because it was done mostly by people who thought that standardization was about making things correct according to rules belonging to another language: Latin. Standardization is a fantastically useful tool because it offers common ground between people who use a given language in different ways when they speak. However, it is not quite as neutral as that, because the standard written English resembles some people's speech more than others. As a general rule, the more education someone (or their children) has, the more time a person (or their children) spends in a job that involves writing: these people's speech will more closely resemble standard written language than that of those people (or their children) who have less education, and who work in jobs not requiring writing.

In other words, we might observe that it is generally more difficult for the offspring of people with less education and/or people who work in jobs with little or no writing to make the jump from their own speech to the standard written language. It is a bigger leap for them to make. There are many diverse conclusions we might draw from that observation.

How do we learn to write?

One of the interesting things about learning to write is that it is a process that for some of us goes on for all our lives. I am still learning to write. In the past couple of years, I have learned how to tweet. Before that I learned how to text. I am not very good at writing 'chapter books'. I'm still teaching myself.

In schools, we mostly ask young people to write things that they do not actually say. Good thing too, some might add – what children say is mostly inconsequential, or incorrect; the job of schools is to take them to a new level, show them great thoughts and correct English. In general terms (not expressed quite like that!) I would agree. Yes, schools should be places that take all children and students to that place where they can produce standard English and where they have encountered ideas and knowledge produced by great thinkers and writers.

The crunch comes, though, in thinking about how we do that and if we ask ourselves the question, are there systems in place in education that appear to penalize some students even as we try to take them to these new places?

I will make an analogy: let us say that there are two islands. On one stand the children and students using language in their own ways, spoken and written, mostly informally, chatting, texting, watching TV, listening to music programs on the radio and so on. On the other island, are educated people writing reports, reading broadsheet newspapers, engaging with politics, writing long letters to authorities or to each other, planning holidays, asking for explanations and so on. And let us say, it is the job of schools to help as many young people as possible to get from their island to the other.

Then we need certain kinds of what we might call 'transitional processes' or bridges or boats to assist the young people. These vehicles, I would suggest, will not be the same as living on the other island. They will need to include aspects of the students' island, otherwise, some will never get across.

Getting across

Here are some of the strategies that I think help children get across:

1. I am not sure that very young children fully know and understand that there is a link between what they themselves say and what can be written down. My observation is that many of them are inducted so quickly into the written form of language that they do not know that it can represent many of the things they say and hear their friends and family saying. Sticking to my analogy, we dump on the 'other island' without the means of knowing how or why they got there.

   I don't think this is only a problem for very young children. In our anxiety to get the children writing standardized English, we quite often neglect those other functions of writing that are valid and (if we need that justification) economically useful, e.g. script-writing, song-writing and so on.

   If part of our job of teaching writing is to connect young people to its usefulness and pleasure, then I think we need to find occasions in which a) they can represent their own speech and b) they can have a go at performing the kinds of writing that underpin much of what they like seeing and hearing.

2. We can treat the standard written form as a static body of knowledge that has to be learned. The traditional way of doing this was to break the language down to its units and functions and ask students to learn, let us say, subject–verb agreement, punctuation rules, correct formation of the past tense and so on.

No one knows if this is appropriate or useful. There is no evidence to suggest that this system of teaching results in more children and students writing better.

From an educational perspective, there is another approach. This is to treat the written language (or any aspect of language) as a phenomenon analogous, say, to a material or an aspect of nature such as landscape or space. What we usually try to do in education in respect of materials and aspects of nature is to offer students a mixture of methods: information, investigation, discovery, discussion, exercise, feedback.

So, if we are looking at the properties of matter – solid, liquid and gas – teachers might begin with stating the outlines of the whole process, then invite students to come up with their observations of solids turning to liquids to gases. We might set up experiments in which this happens, or, better still, invite the students to come up with their own experiments that might show this. And then we might ask them to draw conclusions about what causes the transitions between the three states of matter (upwards and downwards) and then ask them to think about ways in which these processes are used in everyday life (refrigeration etc.).

Now consider if we used or adapted that method of teaching in relation to writing. At the heart of it would be the idea that language can be observed, the students' own observation and discussion would be useful in the learning process, they could come up with experiments to see what works and what does not work in language, you might devise some experiments, and you could discuss conclusions.

To be honest, it mystifies me why we think that the scientific process and the learning of scientific processes should be restricted to the sciences. Language is a phenomenon created by humans. It is in us, around us, observable, capable of being snipped out of context and looked at under a metaphorical microscope and put back into context. It is quite possible to 'do things' to language to see what happens and for us to discuss that.

Mostly, we think that is a good way for children and young people to learn science. I would suggest that it is a good way for them to learn about language too. So, perhaps one of the things we need to do is develop teaching strategies for investigating language in a scientific way. One simple way to do this is the fridge magnet method. Have piles of words on single bits of paper and get students to combine them. What works and what does not work. If it does not work, why not?

If it works, what are the rules governing why it works? Are they rules? Are there alternatives? Why is it possible to swap one kind word for another in some parts of a sentence and not in others?

A full engagement with this will actually produce the main rules of sentence grammar and the main names and functions for words in the context in which they are used.

Alternatively, another method of observation is to take language in use. Take, say, the opening lines of different language-use: e.g. the opening lines of a play, a novel, a song, a chat-show, a film, an opinion column in a newspaper, an instruction manual, a sporting commentary, an instruction from the local council, a political speech, a history textbook – and so on.

What is similar, what is different about these different ways of writing? Why are they different?

Writing

I suggest that at the heart of every bit of writing is a question: 'why write?' The more that children live in a world in which they are not reading very much and don't write very much outside of school, this is a burning question. It is comparatively easy to repeat over and over again that learning to write will get them a good job (though some of them may see their parents doing little writing but are in work). What is much harder is to explain why the very next piece of writing, the piece of writing that they are about to do, is worth doing.

In other words we have to find purpose and meaning in the writing tasks we set them. This means that we have to think of what will happen to the writing. If there are people on the receiving end of my writing who will be interested in what I am writing, then this helps me want to write, to write well and to write in ways that they will understand and enjoy.

I believe that if we want children and young people to write and to write well, then we have to think all the time of varied output and varied reception. That is to say, we should get them thinking of who they are going to interest, why are they going to interest them, and how this can change in order to keep their audiences interested.

So, perhaps the starting point for writing is to think: who are we writing for today? If the answer to that question is usually I am writing in an exercise book for the teacher to mark, then I would suggest that this is not enough. Nowhere near enough. We desperately need other alternatives, e.g.:

- making booklets, books and magazines for distribution around the school and/or locally
- a short play that will be performed
- a factual report on any event that they or their peers have taken part in to be put into a class or school blog, bulletin, magazine, wall-magazine, school website, etc.
- a speech for a class debate
- poems or songs for a concert or for wall display, blog, school website
- a film script for a script that will be shot, edited and shown
- letters to the local or national paper about matters that concern them.

In other words, writing is connected to the real world of the students themselves, the school, parents, grandparents and the wide world.

In this context, many of the concerns you have about accuracy and standard English can be addressed as 'editing', and you can make explicit that the purpose of standard English is to make it comprehensible for all readers – and that is why it has to be 'standard'. You can even rotate the job of sub-editing so that everyone can see that there is 'writing' and there is 'editing' – that job you do to polish and get writing standardized.

But what to write?

Take any of the genres I have mentioned and the first stop with any of them is not a toolkit but real examples of real writers' writing. These are your models or 'scaffolds'. Again, take the children and students through investigation and discovery. Are these good bits of writing? Why? Collect the answers, discuss them. Consider how these can be imported into the 'our writing'. Make this a permanent feature of your teaching about writing just as it is for all people who write for a living. I can assure we spend an enormous amount of time looking at other people's writing and wondering what it would be like to do that sort of thing ourselves.

If it is helpful, when investigating real writers' writing you may want to use any of these questions about the texts:

- How does the piece open? Does it arouse our interest? If so, how or why?
- Are the sentences the same length? Do they vary?
- Are there things in the text that are not clear? Do you think that's the fault of the writing or is it something that you can't figure?
- How would you improve the text?
- If we had to draw a line across a page to imitate how we feel as we read, what would that line look like if we said 'more interested' is high up, 'less interested' is low down.
- Put the text away and repeat any part of the text to your partner. What bit did you remember? Why do you think you did? What was it about the writing that made it easy to remember. Now find a part that you did not remember. Why was that hard to remember?
- Can you re-tell the main drift of the text? Try it on your partner.

Then,

- What can you imitate about the way the text is written?
  What if you wrote about something slightly different and did it by replacing some of the words in the text in front of you with words of your own? Does that work? So, if it's a piece about visiting a castle from a Sunday newspaper, say, can you replace 'castle' with a place you have visited, and then swap the words to do with 'castle' in the text with words about your visit?

(That by the way is what most writing is like! We stick to the same structures but swap certain elements in the structures. Really! That's why it's an important experiment for children and young people to play with.)

Some people have said that all fiction starts out from more or less the same idea: someone or some people lack something or need something or are suffering something: i.e. some kind of problem or dilemma that needs to be solved. They then spend the rest of the story trying to find it or get it or reach it or solve it. On the way, they face problems and obstacles. Sometimes they are helped. The writer has the choice of trying to make it harder or easier for the main character(s) to find a solution(s). The writer can make the obstacles seem real to the hero, while the reader knows they're not. The writer can make the helps real or bogus. The writer can distract the reader with what looks like a good solution or a real danger but then this turns out to be a red herring.

This core set of ideas (that I have expressed in the previous paragraph) are worth bearing in mind as you teach the writing of fiction, but telling children and young people about them may or may not help them write good fiction. It may well be too dry and too abstract for them. It is usually best (in my experience) to get them thinking about one core element of the above: setting up problems, dilemmas and 'lacks' and inventing ways of getting out of them. Brainstorming is the most productive way of writing fiction that most of us know of. It is important not to do too much of it, or you do not want to write the story, though!

Collecting

An important job in learning to write is learning how to collect language, stories, sayings, words. Writers do this all the time, in a variety of ways. Here are some that will be helpful to you.

- Create a language wall. Call it something funny or interesting like 'Our word museum' or better than that! Make it a place where you and the children collect lines from songs, poems, stories; funny signs that you have spotted; interesting things you have heard people say; quotations from websites of great or interesting things to think about; headlines from newspapers; words in other languages, especially if they include languages from the children in class or the school. Keep this wall going all year. Feed in new stuff from websites, poems, songs, funny words that you have come across or do not know the meaning of. Every now and then start a lesson on writing by getting the class to pick words or phrases on the wall as starting points for a brainstorm and then some writing.
- Do a family literacy project in which the children collect sayings, proverbs, stories, narratives, songs, poems from parents and family members. These can be factual or traditional, made-up or remembered. Get the children to make 'language maps' where they create a family tree, putting in people in their family and words or expressions that go with each member of the family, typical sayings, jokes, or examples of how they speak or sing or use language. Many grandparents have stories of migration, loss, funny accounts of how their children (i.e. the children's parents) were naughty. Any of these can be collected and written up and circulated in booklets, books, blogs, school websites. This could be turned into a local history project mixing factual narratives with traditional, along with e.g. recipes. There is an increasing number of these appearing online. I know of one that took place in Hackney which was called 'A Taste of Hackney'. To do such a project shows real writing in action.
- Do a whole-school project around a text that has many meanings and many possible outcomes, e.g. *The Tempest*, the Greek myths. Across key stages many kinds of writing can take place: historical, geographical, fiction, poetry, song, critical, drama and film scripts, letters and so on. The advantage

of this approach is that it develops momentum as more than just one class is involved. Teachers cooperate and help each other to develop new and better pieces of writing, and the children themselves talk about what they are doing with children from other classes. Parents and the wider community can become involved in something that seems to be interesting a whole school.

- Bring real writers into school. This does not only mean writers like me! Yes, bring in writers of fiction, poetry and non-fiction along with story-tellers and drama groups. Consider who writes in your local community: local journalists, people writing reports of different kinds, graphic designers who have to move typefaces and chunks of writing across screens; local printers thinking about how best to set out an invitation, or a family tree or whatever. Get such people to come into school and work with a small group of children on a specific project with a particular outcome, e.g. a blog page or a page on the school website. Again, this is literacy in action in the real world. Such people talk about writing in ways that are practical and real.
- Consider adopting an author for a term. This will involve discovering as much as possible about why and how a writer writes (or wrote). Make it an open-ended investigation that all the class can engage in.

Reading

You will have seen that I have slipped quietly from writing to reading. There is a good reason for this: the two are inseparable. In truth, when we write, we write by taking bits out of our treasure store of what we have read. This is sometimes expressed as 'we write with what we read'. This is called 'intertextuality'. Our heads are full of texts taken from TV, books, instructions, films and of course the things people say around us. However, the things that have been written down (even if they are being spoken as on TV or in a film) have a special place in our writing process, because they are in that special mode of language that is writing. This is the kind of language that does not usually break off mid-flow, repeat itself, interrupt itself – and all the strange broken quality of spoken language. Written language also has to make things extra clear in ways that spoken language can do. When we speak we fill our speech with words like 'there', 'it', 'he', 'them' and so on. That is because we know what the speaker is talking about because he or she is pointing or nodding or using intonation to indicate what he or she means. In writing, we have to struggle to be more precise.

Part of learning to write is to learn how to be this precise, be more complete in making sentences, discovering ways of making the sentences flow and link to each other.

Some people think that the best way to learn that is to be given a toolbox of instructions, learn them, do exercises in them and then apply them. I personally do not think that this is a great way to go about it because I see more often than not writing that is strangely stilted and includes arbitrary uses of words that do not seem to have much to do with the subject in question.

Another approach starts from reading. This approach says that the best way to encourage good writing is to read loads of it – in other words, part of the job of teaching writing is to ensure that the children and students in front of you are reading widely and often. The only way this will happen is if they learn to read for pleasure, i.e. to read when you are not there. To bring this about, you have to set up the experience of 'browsing'. Only then do you discover what you do not want to read, as well as what you do want to read. This requires time in a library, choosing something to read, giving it a go – rejecting it if it does not work, or persevering if it does. Some say that there is strong evidence to suggest that children reading silently to themselves for 20 minutes a day are in effect embedding the language, structures and strategies of the written mode into their minds so that when they come to write they can draw on these strategies. It is, if you like, analogous to what foreign-language teachers call 'immersion'. We ask the children to 'immerse' themselves in the written mode, accessing it, processing it, deriving satisfaction and pleasure from it, making meanings from it, retaining it.

So, part of school that is interested in getting children to write well is a well-stocked school library, a trained librarian spending some time each week updating and keeping the place going, a school staff thinking and talking about books for children and young people. a staffroom and departmental rooms full of books of many different kinds, up to date magazines and book pages about books, e.g. from *Books for Keeps, Carousel,* the *Guardian,* the *Sunday Telegraph* and so on. Pin book reviews up in staffrooms and on classroom walls. Look at book websites on the web. Use Booktrust, the National Literacy Trust and the Reading Agency. Create a 'conversation about books' in the classroom and in the school. Have a 'book of the week', have assemblies where teachers and children talk about books they've read, create book swaps where people swap books they've read for books that others have read.

However, there are some children and parents that this will not reach. In order to involve everyone you will need to create a children and/or parents' committee – 'reading champions' if you like, to come up with ideas to keep the reading momentum going. Encourage these champions to initiate projects. Remember, new books are coming out all the time. Once a group of parents and children connect with the newness and buzz around the newness and freshness of this, the publishing industry will provide some momentum of its own.

What is vital is to connect the children and young people's writing with this reading. They can write 'in the style of' favorite kinds of books or texts. They can write recommendations of what to read. They can do interviews with readers and writers. (There are models for this in *Books for Keeps* and *Carousel,* for example.)

Even more importantly, the children's own writing should be seen in continuum with the published writers' writing. The children's booklets and books, blogs and web content for the school bulletins, etc. must be constantly put alongside and integrated with the published writers. This gives it status and enables the children and students to make comparisons and to up their game.

And after all, this is what we all want.

Thinking, Talking and Writing: What Lies Beneath?

9

John Keen

Chapter Outline

Talking and writing

Take an ordinary object and describe it in a way that both enables and prevents a reader from working out what you are referring to. Make it too easy and it will just be a description, too hard and it will turn into a gnomic enigma; but if you can get the balance right you will have composed a riddle. An example written by a year 7 student after reading, discussing and sometimes solving Anglo Saxon riddles (e.g. *water made bone*), might help us to imagine the process of creation from the moment of choosing an object to the riddling form of words.

> I have felt the sharp stones and the hot sands. I am a shield for weary men on the march. I am broken in like a frisky colt, comfortable as a hand on a bow.

Where did this 12-year-old writer go to find those phrases? Did she somehow feel *the sharp stones and the hot sands*, or was she thinking of a scene from a film? The *shield for weary men on the march* might have had its origins in a film or a book, something Roman perhaps, and the *frisky colt* surely came from her reading, but for *broken in* there might also have been a kinesthetic memory of the pinch and rub of new shoes that didn't quite fit. *Comfortable as a hand on a bow* is a nice piece of misdirection – *a hand*, not a foot, and *a bow*, a weapon, not, say, a glove – justified, tenuously but ingeniously, by the idea of a part of the body wearing something into shape through constant use. Whatever the specific immediate or cultural experiences this student was drawing on, something had to happen in her mind either before she started writing or as she was in the process of putting pen to paper, or more likely both, for her to be able to compose this riddle. If we asked her she might be able to tell us where she got her references from, but it is more likely that as far as she was concerned they just appeared.

Faced with trying to understand an experience that is beyond conscious access, what can we do? The obvious thing is to accept it and live with it, as most people do – the unconscious processes that lead to the act of writing things down just happen when the occasion arises and the how of it is best left to the psychologists.

And psychology does have ways of bringing some of the hidden processes to the surface, leading to theories about how writing happens. One method is to elicit *think-aloud protocols*. You get someone to talk aloud about what they are thinking at the same time as they are writing, or sometimes after they have finished writing, generating data that can give valuable clues about the processes of composition that happen beneath conscious awareness. Here is an example from one of the early pioneers of research into writing processes using this method, Stephen Witte (Witte, 1987, p. 402). It is a protocol elicited from a student, Pat, writing about education in the USA and it shows the student's thinking aloud leading up to writing the sentence: *During the past thirty years, the American education system has been influenced and changed tremendously*. The numbers in brackets are Witte's division of the whole, quite long, utterance into short sections for reference purposes. The three dots (…) represent pauses in the flow of speech.

(30) Well okay … let's do a … (31) what's gonna be the thesis on this … (32) how about the educational system? (33) … the educational system in America has … uh … transformed itself from … a … (34) golly … a … a … (35) god that doesn't make any kind of sense … (36) the educational system in America … (37) no … (38) during the past thirty years … the American public education system has been influenced and … a … a … changed in … a … myriad of ways … a … number of ways … a lotta ways … (39) during the past thirty years the American education system has been influenced and changed in … a … a number of ways … (40) … um … okay … (41) <u>During the past thirty years, the American education system has been influenced and changed</u> … a … ways … <u>tremendously</u>. (42) … um … okay … now that's what we are gonna be working off of …

The explorations leading to the for-now-final version of the essay's opening sentence include a lot of verbal composing out loud, with pauses, questioning and tentative, unfinished statements as well as alternative phrases being tried out, judgments on, rejections of and amendments to proposed sentences and rewordings of phrases for different levels of formality. It is very similar to the kind of collaborative talk that goes on when students try to work out a problem among themselves. Here, for example, is a transcript of a small group of UK 16+ students discussing, among other things, why we gossip.

- why do we gossip?
- I don't know
- um (.) to talk about things
- I think it's to um relay useful information across to other people
- oh yes I think that's true
- mm
- um sometimes but that's not what gossip tends to be (.) rumors
- malicious rumors
- gossips aren't always malicious though
- no true
- they can be useful information like you said
- mm mm
- and if you want to um tell somebody something like (.) that that I've told him not to say anything about (.) so I say (.) listen don't talk to people about that
- yeah it could be quite useful though to know that
- right my auntie she's a widow and um she plays golf with my mother (.) you know (.) anyway so my mother tells everybody she's a widow because (.) like she's thinking about what people might say (.) what's your husband do or anything (.) that's quite useful to know

The structure of Pat's think-aloud protocol is similar to that of these students' discussion of the folk linguistic term *gossip* – a task in one case and an issue in the other followed by some tentative suggestions, some of which are explicitly rejected, leading to a definite outcome: a piece of realized written text in the think-aloud protocol and an anecdote which pins down some of the general ideas being discussed in the exchange among the four students.

In some ways Pat's protocol is reminiscent of the egocentric speech that proved such a fruitful source of debate for Jean Piaget and Lev Vygotsky in the mid-twentieth century. Egocentric speech is language used by children, and sometimes by adults, to talk to themselves, particularly when they are trying to solve a problem. For example, a child might say *That one goes there and this one goes here* when they are trying to solve a jigsaw puzzle and an adult might use exactly the same words while they are trying to assemble an item of flat-pack furniture. In his early research Piaget (1926) took the view that generally we grow out of egocentric speech in the same way as we might discard any other childish habit. However, Vygotsky saw it as a surface manifestation of something that gradually goes underground and is transformed into a thinking process:

> Our findings indicate that egocentric speech does not long remain a mere accompaniment to the child's activity. Besides being a means of expression and of release of tension, it soon becomes an instrument of thought in the proper sense – in seeking and planning the solution of a problem. (1987, p. 31)

The experience of ideas and topics surfacing, submerging and resurfacing will be familiar to anyone who has listened to students exploring an issue that genuinely engages them. For example, look at how the group of 16+ students discussing how gossiping was once identified with witchcraft move between the issues and their own experiences and concerns.

- gossiping is telling stories
- yeah
- I've got another essential question
- 'cos sometimes it's a laugh (.) well so-and-so fell over down the hill yesterday in the snow
- I've got another essential question
- it wasn't snowing yesterday
- why (.) why (.) why (.) you said that women got burned and everything (.) why didn't men if they
- because men were never thought of as witches
- no (.) women were thought of as witches
- wizards
- no but wizards
- E—'s dad's a wizard
- no he's a magician you twit (.) he did my birthday party
- it was generally older women (.) with black cats
- spinsters

As teachers we want to see these characteristics of openness, playfulness and willingness to listen and interact when students prepare for writing. To use one of Vygotsky's key ideas about how learning happens, we want this quality of dialog and social interaction to become internalized so that students will be able to switch naturally into exploratory mode when they are preparing to write something:

> Every function of the child's cultural development appears twice: first on the social level and later on the individual level … all the higher functions originate as actual relations between human individuals. (Vygotsky, 1978, p. 57).

Presumably there was a similar process to Pat's protocol and the students' exploration of gossip taking place with the student who composed the riddle about a pair of worn sandals. Perhaps once she had pictured the footwear – her own? – that was to be her topic she recalled a seaside holiday with a beach with rocks and sand, leading to *I have felt the sharp stones and the hot sands*, then her next step was to decouple the item from her own experience and relate it to something more exotic, *weary men on the march*, so reinterpreting the sharp stones and hot sands as more distant landscapes and more sinister intents. Then the associations of war and conflict suggested by *men on the march* may have activated the images of horse riding and archery. That might have been what happened, or it might not; but it has to have been something like that, and it certainly involved reaching into experiences and memories, rejecting some, shaping half-formed ideas into words, playing with different possibilities, and learning to write in the process of doing these things.

Writing and prewriting

For writing, the learning is in the struggle to engage non-conscious knowledge, to bring language, experience and knowledge together, to activate understandings that have been internalized through exchanges with other people. One important purpose for the teacher therefore must be to facilitate exploratory processes that enable students to access experiences, values and linguistic capabilities, to create a space and conditions where young writers can think and imagine things through for themselves. One example of how this could be achieved can be seen in the different perspectives of a class of year 7 students in a UK school writing stories about incidents in their lives. In this scheme of work on personal writing students discussed significant moments in their lives by sharing pictures and photographs, acted them out through mimes, wrote first drafts of significant memories then peer assessed and redrafted these before celebrating their accounts through reading them aloud.

This teacher's chosen prewriting activity was the use of mime by the students to enact incidents in their lives as part of the process of preparing to write about their memories. For example, three students worked together to mime an account of one student's first day at primary school, with the initial tears and trauma of separation from mother followed by making friends and playing with another student. Another group mimed the rituals of baggage check-in, document checks and boarding an aircraft, followed by take-off and the moment when the plane hit severe turbulence.

The teacher's main rationale for using mime for prewriting was that detail is important in conveying events, actions, feelings and characters both through mime and through writing. In particular some of the finer detail about emotions and reactions, such as in the first-day-at-school mime the boy's desperate lunge towards his mother as she walks away and leaves him with the school teacher, can be dramatized in ways that might be difficult to achieve in a cold first draft written account. In some of the mimes, nuances of character emerged that might be hard to convey in writing; for example, the pilot in the aircraft mime conveyed cheerful friendliness at first, then professional calm under pressure as his stage army of two passengers panicked. Another example of the emergence of character was of two girls miming being driven to school by the mother of one of the students with lots of jerking backwards and forwards and sideways. It emerged that the girl's mother was a very bad driver. The students' teacher stressed that the student probably wouldn't have written that, but that she felt safe conveying it through mime, with the element of humor adding a layer to their engagement with their audience during the mime itself. The teacher also believed that mime was able to activate memories and events, especially the feelings and perceptions associated with these. In addition, to make their mimes successful the students had to think about how their audience would see and interpret their actions and expressions, in the same way that writers need to be aware of how their writing will be read and understood by readers.

The teacher's concern to enable students to use mime to explore some of these issues emerged, among other things, in the students' attention to detail in their written accounts. One student had written an account of a sudden snowfall prompting the family to dig out little-used sledges:

> Eventually we found two sledges which were covered in dust and cobwebs. In fact there were some dead spiders inside the sledges, it had been so long since they had been used.

Peer assessing this account, one of the student's classmates identified the use of detail as a strength to build on:

> Instead of just saying it was really old he says it was covered in cobwebs with lots of spiders.

Another student wrote a long account of a primary school sports day where he was taking part in a number of events. A fellow student given the role of peer assessor and critical friend focused on his use of details:

> Student A: You give every single detail about your day.
> Student B: Is that good or bad?
> Student A: Good and bad – some details give you information but some of them are boring.

Discussions such as these remind us that writing is part of a wider matrix of linguistic and social processes which include talk and action and thinking and reading as well as the act of putting pen to paper. An example of how these modes interrelate can be seen in the following example. This is an extract from a teacher's summary of a scheme of work that used a process approach, including exploratory and prewriting activities, with a year 8 class as preparation for writing about personal experiences.

> Students had read *The Diary of Anne Frank* and we had a whole-class discussion about why her story was worth telling. We discussed diaries, first-person narratives and dramatic monologues.
>
> In a paired activity, the students had to decide on three criteria that a personal story would need to make it worth sharing or that it would need to have to make it interesting. These were pooled during another whole-class discussion and a 'criteria for success' list was created that all the students were happy with.
>
> In groups of three, the students had to tell their 'story' orally. They loved this bit. Other members of their group could ask questions and draw out additional information. They discovered that they all wanted to know about how the narrator had felt about certain incidents and that seemingly insignificant details were helpful in creating a picture in their mind, for example what the weather was like on that day.

What happens in language-users' minds?

As we might expect, different researchers characterize prewriting, and what counts as the prewriting phase of the writing process, differently, including what kind of activity counts as prewriting and how long the process is considered to last. Janet Emig's (1971, p. 39) definition of prewriting is reasonably clear and comprehensive. Prewriting is:

> that part of the composing process that extends from the time a writer begins to perceive selectively certain features of his inner and/or outer environment with a view to writing about them – usually at the instigation of a stimulus – to the time when he first puts words or phrases on paper elucidating that perception.

The problem is that while it is easy to know through simple observation when someone puts pen to paper or fingers to keyboard, it is much more difficult to know when someone begins to perceive something, at least without access to their thought processes.

There is evidence from recent work in neurological engineering on BCI (brain–computer interfaces) that some very limited direct access to people's inner linguistic processes may be possible. This research was mainly motivated by efforts to gain access to the thoughts, or rather the neural correlates of subvocally realized words, of people with locked-in syndrome, that is, severely paralysed but fully aware. Some recent work (Kellis et al., 2010), has succeeded in directly obtaining the unique electrical patterns picked up by closely spaced electrodes on the surface of people's brains, of potentially useful words like *yes, no, hot, cold, hungry, thirsty, hello, goodbye, more* and *less*. This method has the potential to provide 'the underpinnings of an intuitive and rapid BCI for communication' (Kellis et al., 2010, p. 7). A team led by Brian Pasley at the University of California, Berkeley Campus (Pasley et al., 2012), was able to use electrodes on people's skulls to pick up the neural activity as they thought of certain words; this information was turned into a spectrogram, a visual representation of sound frequency and amplitude, then from that into a form of audible speech.

Just as thinking of a word is quite different from thinking about something, these experiments in rudimentary mind-reading are a long way from detecting how a sentence is generated just before, or possibly while, a speaker vocalizes it. However, they do provide tantalizing evidence that something is going on under the surface when we use language. So if we want to write or to teach writing effectively we have to make some imaginative effort to get in touch with the non-conscious activities that lie underneath the act of composition and can't simply treat writing as a stimulus–response/input–output activity.

If we were looking for an artistic rather than a scientific expression of this view, we could turn to D. H. Lawrence's account of his students writing in 'The Best of School', particularly the moments when the students, for most of the time engrossed in composing their stories, look up from their writing:

And one after another rouses
His face to look at me
To ponder very quietly
As seeing, he does not see.

And then he turns again, with a little, glad
Glad thrill of his work he turns again from me
Having found what he wanted, having got what was to be had.

This account gives us a dimension that the scientific versions generally omit, the *little glad/ Glad thrill* of communicating an experience, of finding a shape to something you want to say. Writers and teachers know that without this the whole process is a sterile exercise, an opportunity for students to show that they can include features and devices or pack otherwise banal narrative with adjectives and adverbs as required by the mark scheme. Neither of the two neurobiological papers cited above says anything explicitly about the affective side of the work of the scientists involved, but it is impossible not to imagine, for example, the exultation of a locked-in person finally being able to communicate in their ten-word pidgin, or to share the sense of wonder at directly 'hearing', albeit at several removes, an unvocalized word that someone else is merely thinking of.

Thinking, writing and social interaction

If Vygotsky was right in claiming that what goes on inside people's minds at the non-conscious level must have its origins at some stage or another in the sociocultural matrix of talk and symbolic action that defines and regulates our thinking and our use of language, then writing too must be in some sense collaborative and a product of interrelated social factors, even if the act of transcribing is most often carried out by one person alone. We can see why it is so important for teachers to be aware of these social elements by examining what happens when they are brought to bear on the process of composition.

The following extract is from a personal account written by a year 7 student about his trip from the northwest of England to Middlesbrough in the northeast with his uncle to see his first premier division soccer match, between Middlesbrough Football Club and Manchester United Football Club. The account consisted of the following sections:

Section 1   Preparation and packing
Section 2   The train journey to Middlesbrough
Section 3   Walking to the stadium
Section 4   Going into the stadium
Section 5   Watching the match
Section 6   Evaluation of the experience

Here is the student's first draft of Sections 3, 4 and 5:

> *Draft 1*
> On the way to the stadium there were loads of shops selling caps to hotdogs or magazines to flags. We were a little bit late so as soon as we got there the whistle blew. We scored within seconds and the crowd went wild. I remember one second we was sitting there and the next second it was as if there was a big explosion and the crowd flew off their seats. That happened several times.

The scheme of work of which this story was part included several opportunities for students to discuss and peer assess each other's accounts. It is impossible to know what his classmates said to this student about his story, but reading between the lines of his third draft we can get a sense of the steer they might have conveyed:

> *Draft 3*
> When we were walking to the Theatre of Dreams there were loads and loads of tiny little shops selling memorabilia and souvenirs. When we got inside we were a little bit late and we barely had time to sit down before the whistle blew. We scored the first goal in seconds all thanks to Ryan Giggs. The crowd went wild and so did I. That happened a number of times and we ended up winning 4–1.

There are some stylistic enhancements in the later draft, including a more specific reference with *the Theatre of Dreams* for *the stadium*, addition of modifiers – *shops* becomes *tiny little shops* – and enhancement of the precision of description where *as soon as we got there* becomes *we barely had time to sit down before … .* But these changes occur alongside the deletion of a carefully crafted description in which the dramatic image of *a big explosion* had been framed by the parallel structure *one second … and the next* and followed up by the vivid metaphor *flew off their seats.*

The cumulative effect of these alterations is to produce, in Draft 3, a text with a different set of narrative goals from the earlier draft. While Draft 1 aims to convey personal experiences from the narrator's point of view, with the specific and evocative *caps to hotdogs or magazines to flags* and the metaphor-enhanced description of the crowd's sudden excitement, Draft 3 plays up those effects that would be most meaningful to a reader who was a member of the soccer-supporting community. The name of Middlesbrough's stadium, *the Theatre of Dreams*, would resonate with such readers. They would also take it for granted that memorabilia and souvenirs includes caps and flags as well as many other items; they would be interested in how many goals were scored and who scored them, and would already know what it felt like to be in a crowd that *went wild* and so wouldn't need to be told. The transition from *the crowd went wild* to *the crowd went wild and so did I* may represent a performative claim by the writer to membership of a social group, soccer supporters, with its own norms, expectations and linguistic register. The writer may have used the whole redrafting process as an opportunity to write himself into membership of this community, at least in his own mind, much as people generally may, according to Judith Butler (1990), enact their gender identities performatively. Fiona Webster's (2000, p. 4) explanation of a key idea in Butler's account of gender identity may relate very directly to the personal account of this student's abrupt shift of focus from personal experience of a specific football match to membership of a community of social and linguistic practice.

> … gender is performative, according to Butler, in the sense that it is not a stable or fixed point of agency, but rather is an identity category created and constituted through "a stylized repetition of acts" (1990, p. 140). Its meaning is constituted dramatically and contingently through sustained social performances which take place in the context of the regulatory conventions and norms dominant in society (1990, p. 33).

The shift in implied audience between Draft 1 and Draft 3 is accompanied by corresponding changes in dialogic expectations. By losing content relating to the more personal aspects of the experience, the specifics of *caps … hotdogs … magazines … flags* and the *big explosion* passage, Draft 3 reduces opportunities for an engaged and empathetic reading by readers who are not soccer fans. Instead the power of the soccer register is deployed to construct a more esoteric stance for the narrator, altering the status of the account from evocation to code.

The fact that this writer was prepared to concede so much to one socially powerful sector of his audience suggests that enabling students to achieve dialog between writer and reader in the classroom might be more complicated than simply exhorting students to help and support each other in their writing.

Planning and writing or planning as you write?

Galbraith and Torrance (2004, p. 64) have identified two main compositional strategies used by writers – a *revising strategy* in which writers 'work out what they want to say in the course of writing and content evolves over a series of drafts' and a *planning strategy* in which writers 'concentrate on working out what they want to say before setting pen to paper, and only start to produce full text once they have worked out what they want to say'. If this suggests that there is a clear and unambiguous dualism between planning and writing, then it is a misleading distinction. It might be more productive to think of the talking, reading and thinking that make up planning and the process of writing as inextricably entangled, with a dialectical relationship between the act of writing and the process of finding what you want to say. It is difficult, if not impossible, to observe this process of *dynamic composition* directly, and think-aloud protocols can only hint at it. But it may be possible to see it in action if we compare consecutive drafts of pieces of writing as they are being composed.

The following example consists of two drafts of an account by a year 7 student of an incident that happened to him while he was on holiday with his family in Malta.

Draft 1
A time in my life I will always remember
My story starts when I went to Malta with nana grandad and cousin. One of the days we went to a cafe in the Silent City when a cat jumped on my knee and attacked me.

After responding to questions about his story from classmates, the student developed his story as follows:

Draft 2
The Ferocious Felion
My story starts when I was 11 and I went to Malta with nana grandad and cousin. It was nice there but it was cold. One of the days we went to the Silent City which is an ancient site where you're meant to be silent. We were getting hungry so we went to a cafe to get something to eat. When a ferocious cat jumped on me. It was big and white with giant teeth and claws. Next it started to scratch me and bite me.

On a dynamic interpretation of the composition process, the writer discovers what he or she wants to say, at least in part, through the act of composition itself, that is, by interacting with the text as it is being created. This act has at least the following components:

1. Writing something.
2. Checking that what has been written
   a. makes sense in itself;
   b. coheres with the text or episode that it is part of.
3. Checking whether other parts of the text need to be adjusted as a result of 2a and/or 2b and making any necessary adjustments to the text.
   In the composition of some texts, further checking and adjustment may be necessary or desirable, for example:
4. Checking whether incidental topics or themes introduced in what has been written need to be, or could be, developed, and making necessary adjustments.

The major transformations between Draft 1 and Draft 2 of the student's account of his experience are as follows:

Draft 1 – Draft 2
1. Change of title from *A time in my life I will always remember* to *The Ferocious Felion*
2. Addition of *when I was 11*
3. Addition of *It was nice there but it was cold*
4. Deferral of *we went to a cafe* to a later point in the story
5. Addition of *which is an ancient site where you're meant to be silent*
6. Addition of *We were getting hungry*
7. Addition of *to get something to eat*
8. Change from non-capitalized *when* to capitalized *When*
9. Addition of *ferocious*
10. Substitution of *me* for *my knee*

11. Deferral of *attacked me*
12. Change from *and* to full stop
13. Addition of *It was big and white with giant teeth and claws*
14. Addition of *it*
15. Elaboration of *attacked me* to become *it started to scratch me and bite me*
16. Addition of *Next.*

Transformation 2, addition of *when I was 11*, is an example of a change that has only minor effects on the composition of the text beyond itself, namely ensuring that the new information is integrated grammatically using *and* and *when*. However, several other transformations have implications for the text beyond themselves and their immediate textual environments.

Transformations 2–7 give background information, whereas Transformations 1 and 8–16 relate to the main incident of the story. We might imagine the student pausing after he has made Transformations 2–7 but not yet 1 or 8–16. This is something like what he would see:

> A time in my life I will always remember
> [Section 1] My story starts when I was 11 and I went to Malta with nana grandad and cousin. It was nice there but it was cold. One of the days we went to the Silent City which is an ancient site where you're meant to be silent.
> [Section 2] We went to a cafe when a cat jumped on my knee and attacked me.

We can see that Section 2 is pretty tame compared to Section 1. Section 1 now has subjectivity with *nice* and *cold*, explanation with the account of *the Silent City* and a touch of drama with the phrase *an ancient site*. By contrast the wording of what should be the main incident of the story, *a cat jumped on my knee*, suggests affectionate domesticity rather than a sudden violent event. The general phrase *attacked me* lacks drama and impact. The event of going to the café is missing motivation or explanation.

This dynamic perspective on a text that is in the process of being realized might help us as readers to appreciate how and why the student remedies the gap in rhetorical effect between the two sections by enhancing his description of the cat, and of the cat's attack on him. As well as emotive effect, the addition of *ferocious* in Transformation 9 gives a kind of justification, if not an explanation, for the cat's attack. Transformation 13, the boldest addition to the account, draws on strands prefigured in earlier transformations, including reference to sensory experience introduced in earlier transformations as *cold*, *silent* and *hungry*, now extended to *white*, and use of the adjectives *big* and *giant* help to justify the use of the word *ferocious*.

Grammatically, Transformation 15 is the most complex in the account. Again, strands are prefigured, and may have been activated, by earlier transformations. In particular the conjoined noun phrases *giant teeth* and *(giant) claws* correspond closely to the verbs *scratch* and *bite*. The lack of specificity in the use of *me* rather than, say, *my face* or *my knee* endows the cat with added agency in the same way as *jumped on me* does, again helping to justify the force of the word *ferocious*. The narrator's feelings of shock and pain are not made explicit, but the inference is easily drawn, especially by extrapolating from the line that includes *cold ... hungry ...*

This analysis may be speculative, and the writer himself may give a different account of how he composed his story, just as he may not recognize explicitly how his Freudian misspelling of *feline* as *felion* sensationalizes the animal in line with his general strategy of talking the incident up for effect. However, if it is even partially valid it shows that students can make sophisticated judgments about tone, effects and nuance in their own writing. It also shows that they can deploy their judgments procedurally to enrich and enliven their writing, in this case by redrafting, even if they may not be able to articulate the rationales for their revisions explicitly and declaratively.

Conclusion

What has become the standard method of facilitating students' writing in the UK – analysing a model text into features of the text-type it instantiates, then getting students to apply those features in composing their own texts – is attractive to teachers with targets to hit for students' attainments because its outcome can often be a piece of student's writing that complies with a required set of approved genre features.

A fairly characteristic example of this analysis-and-application approach to teaching from a trainee English teacher is as follows:

> I showed a clip from the film *Robin Hood* in which the lead character delivers the persuasive speech called 'Liberty by Law'. Students had a transcript of the speech and were asked to identify the persuasive techniques used as well as answer questions about the effects of its language and structure. I then asked the students to write a speech to the Headteacher persuading her that there should be more school trips.

This approach assumes that it is possible to identify the load-bearing features of a piece of discourse explicitly and declaratively, and comprehensively, and that it is not only possible but productive to use the individual features abstracted from the model or exemplar text in composing a text that applies those features in a new context.

But by reducing a text to a set of items of declarative knowledge and the act of composition to the relatively simple problem of filling out and exemplifying those items, the standard approach to teaching writing bypasses large parts of the writer's struggle to pull disparate elements of content and language together and therefore places limits on what students can learn procedurally about how to write. Why did the trainee teacher cited above think he needed to give students a model for their writing? Did he feel perhaps that the task of writing and delivering a speech to their head teacher was so contrived that it needed justification from an official source? Perhaps he didn't think his students would be able to compose a sufficiently persuasive speech without being led by the hand in this way. It may be that he needed to feel a measure of control over his students' compositional process and that simply asking them to write a speech to deliver to the head teacher gave too much control to them. Or perhaps the habit of reading first and writing second has become so ingrained in the way we teach writing in the UK that it simply didn't occur to him to consider alternative approaches.

Currently the main alternative approach to genre-based strategies for teaching writing is the process approach, though this is not used extensively or in any systematic way in UK schools. Process approaches to teaching writing are based on the principle that while writing composition is often messy, unsystematic and opportunistic, processes such as *exploring*, *prewriting*, *drafting* and *revising* can help students to develop the complex procedural skills necessary for them to become independent writers.

The main focus of the process approach is as much on the learning that takes place as students use the process of composition to test out relationships between elements of written text and to explore different forms of expression in their writing as it is on the written outcome, the finished text. Process approaches, effectively carried out, can place students as writers at the center of their own learning, giving them authorship of the texts they write in a way that mere adherence to genre conventions never can. A year 7 student from the same class as the girl who wrote the conundrum about the sandals expressed the essence of this idea in riddling form:

> Lift it up and scrawl, scribble, there I am. I denote such pride. The queen and the baker know me.

While the writing process is made possible by complex interactions between speaking, reading and writing, there are some aspects of our identity as language users that can only be expressed in writing. The signature, like the style, is the person.

References

Butler, J. (1990). *Gender Trouble: Feminism and the Subversion of Identity*. New York: Routledge.

Emig, J. (1971). 'The composing processes of twelfth graders'. *NCTE Research Report No. 13*. Urbana, IL: National Council of Teachers of English.

Galbraith, D. and Torrance, M. (2004). 'Revision in the Context of Different Drafting Strategies'. In G. Rijlaarsdam, L. Allal, L. Chanquoy and P. Largy (eds), *Revision: Cognitive and Instructional Processes. Studies in Writing*, 13, 63–85. Dordrecht: Kluwer.

Kellis, S., Miller, K., Thomson, K., Brown, R., House, P. and Greger, B. (2010). 'Decoding spoken words using local field potentials recorded from the cortical surface'. *Journal of Neural Engineering*, 7(5).

Lawrence, D. H. (1977). 'The Best of School'. In V. Pinto and W. Roberts (eds), *The Complete Poems of D. H. Lawrence*, rev edn. Harmondsworth: Penguin Books.

Pasley B. N., David S. V., Mesgarani N., Flinker A., Shamma S.A., Crone, N.E., Knight, R.T., Chang, E.F. (2012). 'Reconstructing speech from human auditory cortex', *PLoS Biol* 10(1): e1001251. doi:10.1371/journal.pbio.1001251

Piaget, J. (1926). *The Language and Thought of the Child*. London: Routledge & Kegan Paul.

Vygotsky, L. (1978). *Mind in Society*. Cambridge, MA: Harvard University Press.

—(1987). *The Collected Works of L. S. Vygotsky, Vol. 1, Problems of General Psychology: Including the Volume Thinking and Speech*. New York; London: Plenum.

Webster, F. (2000). 'The politics of sex and gender: Benhabib and Butler debate subjectivity'. *Hypatia, 15*(1), 1–22.

Witte, S. (1987). 'Pre-text and composing'. *College Composition and Communication, 38*(4), 397–425.

10   Writing, Reading and Rhetoric

Terry Locke

This chapter begins with some considerations of the term *dialogue* and argues that a dialogic framing of subject English is conducive to a view that reading and writing are both involved in acts of textual engagement. It then goes on to tackle the thorny question of the place of metalinguistic knowledge in the English classroom. This section begins with a brief review of the various arguments that have raged about the relationship between the teaching of grammar and writing performance, and shifts the ground somewhat to argue that metalinguistic knowledge finds its place in the English classroom in relation to the text producer as critical reader. It then revisits and develops a theme foreshadowed in Chapter 2, showing how a rhetorical view of English constructs the *reader/viewer* and *writer/rhetor/designer*, arguing that explicit knowledge of language (grammar in a broad sense) is inextricably bound up in the "arts of discourse". It then proceeds to show how a rhetorical model of English might be reflected in classroom practise.

English as dialog

Act II of Arthur Miller's play, *The Crucible* begins with the following dialog:

> ELIZABETH: What keeps you so late? It's almost dark.
> PROCTOR: I were planting far out to the forest edge.
> ELIZABETH: Oh, you're done then.
> PROCTOR: Aye, the farm is seeded. The boys asleep?
> ELIZABETH: They will be soon. *And she goes to the fireplace, proceeds to ladle up stew in a dish.*
> PROCTOR: Pray now for a fair summer.
> ELIZABETH: Aye.

My guess is that this extract illustrates the most common understanding of the word 'dialogue' in the English classroom – something that students are more likely to read and occasionally perform than write. In this example, there are two speakers, a husband and wife, who are producing a chain of linked utterances. A number of things are going on. We can see this as the enactment of a 'reconnection' ritual, or an exchange of information. But (in line with speech act theory), these sentences are not just saying things; they are also doing things (Locke, 2004, p. 76). For instance, while Elizabeth's first question *looks like* a simple question, there is an accusatory edge to it. They both know that Proctor has a history of infidelity. Elizabeth's subtext might read: 'I fear you've been with Abigail'.

Elizabeth and Proctor are both producing utterances and responding to the utterances of the other. The meaning of each utterance and the lexical items that constitute it is determined by the immediate context. Each utterance is shaped by the utterances that precede it and by the response that is anticipated or hoped for – what Bakhtin calls 'addressivity' (1986, p. 95). Bakhtin describes this dialogic aspect of an utterance in the following way:

> The utterance is filled with *dialogic overtones*, and they must be taken into account in order to understand fully the style of the utterance. After all, our thought itself – philosophical, scientific, and artistic – is born and shaped in the process of interaction and struggle with others' thought, and this cannot but be reflected in the forms that verbally express our thought as well (1986, p. 92).

It is clear in this exchange that there is something of a struggle going on: Elizabeth's hurt and resentment, and Proctor's defensiveness and desire to please are reflected in the style of their utterances.

But there is a larger sense of dialog at work here in this scene, which is made clear in lines that occur later:

> PROCTOR: Are you well today?
> ELIZABETH: I am. *She brings the plate to the table, and, indicating the food:* It is a rabbit.
> PROCTOR, *going to the table:* Oh, is it! In Jonathan's trap?
> ELIZABETH: No, she walked into the house this afternoon; I found her sittin' in the corner like she come to visit.

PROCTOR: Oh, that's a good sign walkin' in.
ELIZABETH: Pray God. It hurt my heart to strip her, poor rabbit (1958, pp. 261–2).

The *overtone* imbuing Proctor's use of the word 'sign' relates to his evocation of a Puritan way of thinking which obsessed about signs and their meanings, in particular, signs read as portents of damnation or salvation. Let me bring in Bakhtin again here:

> Any speaker is himself a respondent to a greater or lesser degree. He is not, after all, the first speaker, the one who disturbs the eternal silence of the universe. And he presupposes not only the existence of the language system he is using, but also the existence of preceding utterances – his own and others' – with which his given utterance enters into one kind of relation or another (builds on them, polemicizes with them, or simply presumes that they are already known to the listener). Any utterance is a link in a very complexly organized chain of other utterances (1986, p. 69).

In Bakhtinian terms, Proctor's utterance, where he uses the word 'sign', is not just a response to utterances Elizabeth has made previously. It also has an *intertextual* relationship with countless texts – sermons, perhaps, or the texts of Puritan divines – which have constructed a discourse around signs and their meanings, and which Proctor's utterance is 'presupposing'. Drawing on this intertextual knowledge, Proctor is indicating that the Almighty is smiling on them both.

The word utterance I'm using here (following Bakhtin) is not restricted to oral language. It refers to a stretch of discourse bounded by a change of speakers and characterized by *finalization* (a sense of completion, a particular purpose and typically formal shape). There is another kind of intertextual dialog going on here, of course. This chapter I am writing is an utterance and also needs to be thought of as part of a *chain of utterances* and therefore intertextually situated. I've referred in a 'manifest' way (Fairclough, 1992) to certain *preceding* utterances from Bakhtin and Miller. This chapter is further characterized by addressivity, in that I'm 'taking into account possible responsive reactions' (Bakhtin, 1986, p. 95). Like any utterance, this chapter also has an interdiscursive relationship with other texts (Fairclough, 1992; Locke, 2004, p. 43). By the way I am framing my argument, I am subscribing to a view of the relationship of texts and speakers that reflects a discourse (or way of thinking about things) of *dialogism*. I am aware, as I write in this way, of other writers who subscribe to a similar discourse (Bakhtin, 1986, of course, but also, for example, Andrews, 1992, 2010; Parr, 2010).

What has all this to do with subject English? Well, first and foremost English concerns itself with the study of textual practises as socially constructed (as literacies), cognitive, and technologically mediated in various ways. In the preceding paragraphs, I have been showing how the producer of an utterance is also a 'reader', first of those utterances that may be thought of as preceding him/her and to which he/she is responding, and more broadly of the wider social context into which his/her utterance is being issued in order to serve a particular function – to inform, to persuade, to narrate, to describe, and so on. The tasks of text production and dissemination cannot be separated from the task of reading, and one's qualities as a reader of texts and situations have a direct impact on one's capability as a writer/composer. In the next section of this chapter, I argue that an understanding of the role of 'grammar' in the English classroom needs to be framed by an acknowledgment of this relationship.

Metalinguistic knowledge in the English classroom

As mentioned in prefatory remarks to *Beyond the Grammar Wars* (Locke, 2010, p. viii), a battle has raged for over 100 years now about grammar and its place in the English/literacy classroom, with many participants, including politicians, policymakers, teacher professional associations, linguists, teacher educators and educational researchers. The battle can be reduced to the question: does explicit knowledge about language contribute positively and productively to a learner's repertoire of textual practises as readers (viewers) or composers (makers) of texts? If the answer to this question is yes, then two further questions follow:

1. *What* explicit linguistic or grammatical knowledge are we talking about? and
2. *What* pedagogical form might this positive contribution take?

In what follows, I attempt to summarize emerging findings in respect of these questions, before returning to a consideration of how a view of the reader/writer nexus discussed previously can illuminate this topic.

In 2004, a systematic review was undertaken by an English Review Group based at the University of York and in association with the Evidence for Policy and Practice Information and Co-ordinating Center (EPPI-Center) of the University of London (Andrews et al., 2006). The research question for this review was: 'What is the effect of grammar teaching in English on 5–16 year olds' accuracy and quality in written composition?' The Review focused on two aspects of 'grammar teaching': the teaching of formal sentence grammar/syntax and the teaching of 'sentence-combining'. In relation to the first of these aspects, the teaching of formal grammar/syntax, the review asserted that it 'appears to have no influence on either the accuracy or quality of written language development for 5–16-year-olds' (2006, p. 51; see also, Hillocks, 2006 p. 45). Such a result was hardly surprising. The Review really was traversing old ground. Elley et al. (1979), one of the three studies viewed as of reasonable quality, had drawn a similar conclusion almost 30 years before. The EPPI Review finding was controversial in England and Wales, because in that setting a policy decision had been made to mandate the teaching of formal grammar (of a sort) and huge amounts of money had been invested to support that policy.

The Review's second finding was that teaching 'sentence combining appears to have a more positive effect on writing quality and accuracy' (Andrews et al., 2006 p. 51). Comparing its first finding with its second, Andrews and colleagues wrote:

> The teaching of syntax appears to put emphasis on 'knowledge about' the construction of sentences. Sentence-combining suggests a pedagogy of applied knowledge – at its best, applied in situations of contextualized learning; at its worst, drilling (2006 p. 52).

So far, let us note that the research focus has been on writing rather than reading, where writing is being treated as a discrete activity. Secondly, a certain knowledge *about* language (what Hillocks, 2006, calls 'declarative' knowledge) is found to be ineffective in helping improve knowledge, whereas applied or procedural knowledge in relation to a particular pedagogical practise is found to have a moderately positive effect on writing. Thirdly, the focus of the knowledge *about* language is on the sentence: parts of speech, parts and kinds of sentences, rules of usage and so on.

For a number of reasons, the EPPI Review ignored Australia, where an entirely new approach to the 'grammar question' was being implemented by genre theorists (see Chapter 2 in this book), who built an approach to writing pedagogy in part on a foundation of Hallidayan systemic functional grammar (e.g. Halliday and Hasan, 1985). According to a member of the Genre School, Frances Christie, the 1970s in Australia saw the emergence of two schools of thought on language and language learning in schools. These groups, which she terms *linguists* and *non-linguists,* had a number of features in common, including disenchantment with traditional English teaching, 'with its joyless pursuit of parts of speech and correction of "faulty sentences"' (Christie, 2004 p. 149). However, the groups 'differed sharply about what should constitute knowledge about language for teachers, and about how such knowledge should be used' (Christie, 2004 pp. 149–50). Influenced by Dartmouth and the personal growth model of English espoused by John Dixon (1975) and others, the non-linguists saw teachers as language growth facilitators and 'eschewed linguistic knowledge, on the grounds of its alleged preoccupation with 'structure' and indifference to meaning' (Christie, 2004 p. 150). Operating out of a less individualistic discourse than the non-linguists, the linguists constructed the child as a social being:

> growing in participation in complex sets of social processes, where language was an essential resource for articulating experience and knowledge, and where language itself was an interesting phenomenon to speculate about and to learn (2004 p. 150).

The linguists were committed to teachers mastering an extensive metalanguage and applying this in their classroom programs.

Australian references are missing from the EPPI Review because: 1) the Australian Genre School was more concerned with program implementation than research (especially randomly controlled trials); and 2) because Hallidayan grammar was a 'top-down' approach that focused on language in use, the relationship of text to context and only secondarily on grammar at the level of the sentence. Halliday's contribution to the debate about grammar was to suggest that the most appropriate grammar for school use was one based on meaning and function rather than rule (a suggestion taken up by Ron Carter in the ill-fated LINC

Project in the UK, see Carter, 1996.) The meaning of any feature of language was viewed as dependent on the function it was required to serve in a particular context.

It needs to be stated that a top-down approach to grammar does not require one to use systemic functional grammar. In the US context, Martha Kolln's 'rhetorical grammar' is top-down but non-Hallidayan (Kolln, 1996). However, the uptake of systemic functional linguistics as an answer to the first of my questions above – *what* knowledge about language – has widespread advocacy. For example, Fairclough adopts it in his approach to critical discourse analysis (see Fairclough, 1992). Kress and van Leeuwen use it as a basis for their development of a grammar of visual design (see Kress and van Leeuwen, 2006). A number of contributors to *Beyond the Grammar Wars* are firm advocates of systemic functional grammar: Christie (2010); Janks (2010), French (2010) and Unsworth (2010), among others. Moreover, there is some research emerging on its pedagogical efficacy, even with primary-aged children. French (2010), for example, provides evidence that children can learn a range of grammatical concepts and even enjoy learning and applying them. In respect of the *utility* of children learning grammar, she makes the claim that 'grammatics was found to be useful to students across a number of dimensions of their school literacy programs', enabling them to develop: 1. conscious control of their writing; 2. critical understandings in their reading; 3. improved expression in reading aloud: and 4. improved punctuation of direct speech (2010 pp. 215–16).

It is interesting, I think, that the focus of the Grammar Wars has been on arguments about the impact of grammar teaching on writing. Where the use of explicit linguistic knowledge is advocated as integral to approaches to English focused on reading – critical literacy, for example – one finds virtually no dissent on the matter. Ruth French's research (just cited) is a good example of a case being made for grammar's utility across a range of dimensions of literacy, including reading. It may be that as textual beings we are more aware of the nuanced use of language features in utterances we are receiving than in those we are in the act of producing. In the final section of this chapter, I will be suggesting that as producers of texts in rhetorical situations, it is when we are in 'receptive mode' that we are best able to consider the choices available to us as artists of discourse.

The text producer as reader and rhetor

Both research and theory, then, support a place for grammar in the English classroom that is top-down, practically oriented and contextualized. What a contextualized yet effective pedagogy drawing on explicit grammatical knowledge might look like in practise, particularly in relation to writing, is still a matter of research (see Myhill, 2010). Another open question is the extent to which this explicit grammatical knowledge needs to be systematized to be effective? Does the 'grammar at the point of need' argument leave too much to chance? Despite these questions, however, there is a further, overarching consensus one finds in the current literature on the grammar question. This relates to the importance of rhetorical framing and the focus on choice. Figure 10.1 offers a rhetorical view of textual reception/ production. I am using it here to do two things: 1) to emphasize how complex the task of text production *is* (compared with reading) and the extent to which text-producers are not only called upon to be readers, but to be different *sorts* of readers at different stages of the text production process; and 2) to highlight the issue of choice.

Unit planning in English classrooms is typically dominated by two kinds of focus. The first of these is theme-based, where a topic is chosen for exploration across a range of texts. (Critical literacy lends itself to theme-based planning.) The second is medium- or genre-based planning, where a teacher may decide to involve her students in a novel study or a newspaper unit. To relate the previous discussion to the actualities of the English classroom, I will discuss the steps a teacher might follow in planning a *rhetorical unit*, underpinned, as I stated in Chapter 2, by the following statements:

- People construct texts with a view to achieving a desired result with a particular audience.
- Text is a product of function (form follows function).

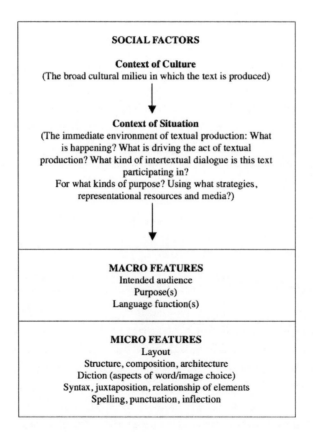

Figure 10.1 A rhetorical view of textual reception/production

- Texts are generated by contexts. Social/cultural contexts call forth texts.
- All texts assume a kind of social complicity between maker and reader.
- The expectations of people participating in such acts of complicity become formalized in the conventions of genre.
- These conventions can apply to such language features as layout, structure, punctuation, syntax and diction in the case of print texts, with other configurations of features operating for other modes and modal combinations.
- In a rhetorical approach, literature is not devalued but revalued.

Establishing a social context

The first step is to choose (perhaps in negotiation with the class) a social situation where a number of participants are responding to a crisis or are involved in a project or a campaign of some sort (for example, a wilderness area is under threat from development, or the school is experiencing an outbreak of bullying). The example I will be using for illustrative purposes is the situation where there is a cultural or environmental heritage area that is not well known. In this instance, a number of people decide that it would be a good idea to publicize this heritage area.

In terms of Figure 10.1, this step calls for a recognition of the context of culture. A 'reading' of this context means an engagement with some of the discourses that underpin various texts that in some ways engage with issues of cultural and environmental heritage, some of which may be in contradiction with one another: discourses related to environmentalism, development (including job creation) and tourism (see Morgan, 1996, for an example of the last). It would not be inappropriate for a teacher to invite students to engage in a critical reading of one or two such texts, showing how various linguistic features position readers to take up a particular position in regard to the *value* of a cultural or environmental heritage in relation to other values.

Mapping the immediate context

In this step, students become far more specific in identifying various participants in a social situation? What types of people might be involved? What interest or lobby groups are present? What are their agendas? What oral, written or multimodal texts might these individuals and groups be involved in reading or producing? Are these identifiable genres? What models (exemplary texts) of these genres can teacher and students access?

This step relates to the 'Context of Situation' in Figure 10.1. In recent work that addresses challenges posed by the increasingly multimodal character of the textual environment, Gunther Kress goes beyond traditional notions of grammar, to establish some 'principles for meaning-making' (2010, p. 239) in the immediate context of communication. If contemporary meaning-making is increasingly being made via 'multimodal ensembles', the question arises as to the language that might best be used to name the 'categories, entities, process and relations' that exist in these ensembles. Kress addresses this issue by drawing attention to the 'resources for meaning-making' potentially available in a given social situation, each with its own particular 'affordances'. He then proceeds to show how these resources can be strategically (or rhetorically) deployed for effect by individuals doing 'semiotic work … in their social lives' (2010, p. 243). In this model, three factors dominate, 'the rhetor/designer, resources and principles of design' (Kress, 2010, p. 249).

> Now, the question, first and foremost, is one of resources and choices: of a reliable account of the social environment; a clear sense of who the audience is; what its criterial characteristics are; of my social relations with that audience? From that follow questions about resources available and resources to use: modal and other semiotic resources such as genre, discourse, media. Simultaneously too, there is the question: what resources shall I use for the representation of *this* content, these meanings? Resources and principles are now the focus and choice is the ruling criterion … . [And then] The meaning-maker – in full awareness of the social environment; of the requirements of the audience in relation to that which is to be communicated; of the affordances of the semiotic resources – *designs* the semiotic entity, whether as text or other semiotic object (Kress, 2010, pp. 249–50).

In terms of the example I am using here, the 'rhetor' in the situation need not be an individual. It could be a group charged by a local council to produce a nature trail pamphlet, or a heritage trail pamphlet. Or it could be a group writing a submission against the building of a multi-story hotel that is viewed as infringing on the heritage site itself. Or it could be an individual producing a potted history of the area or a personage associated with it, or a poem, or folk song. In rhetorical unit planning, the choice of 'rhetor' and text is determined by the context of situation itself.

Modelling

In this step, teacher and students select for focus a range of genres that the context of situation gives rise to. In the case of a natural heritage site, after brainstorming the potential range of genres, a decision might be made to focus on poems, a television documentary and a nature trail pamphlet for the duration of the unit. In a manner not dissimilar to the modelling stage of the genre wheel (see Chapter 2), a teacher would be required to model to/with students a way of cracking the semiotic code of each genre. What kinds of linguistic and other semiotic features have played a role in making it an effective example of its type? What metalanguage is required to maximize the effectiveness of this code-cracking exercise? Figure 10.2 is an example of the 'inside' face of a nature-trail pamphlet that I have used in my own teaching with 12- to 13-year-olds.

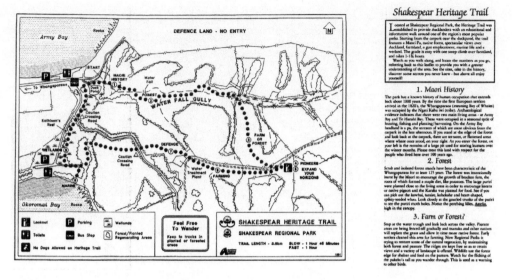

Figure 10.2 Shakespeare Regional Park: Nature trail pamphlet (inside face). Printed with permission by the Auckland Council. This brochure/map style is no longer used by council.

Deciding on steps of production

As a teacher moves students towards a focus on text making, decisions need to be made on the steps required for the successful production of the genre in question. Sometimes this will involve a teacher submitting themselves to the task of producing their own version of the chosen genre, though sometimes the steps can be worked out intuitively. Clearly, what is being planned for here is a text production process, different from but not incompatible with that advocated generally in process approaches to writing (Pritchard and Honeycutt, 2007), but one that is far more determined by the nature of the target text and the rhetorical situation. Below I offer an example of steps that might be undertaken in engaging students (in groups) in the production of a nature-trail pamphlet, a good example of what Kress (2010) calls a 'multimodal ensemble'. Before the process beings, students are given a 'production brief" (see Figure 10.3) which constitutes a set of constraints and which relates to the immediate context (above). The brief reflects a more dynamic and flexible view of genre than that practised by the Australian 'Genre School' (see Chapter 2) and adopts Hasan's view of genres as having *generic structure potential* – 'obligatory' elements (those that *must* occur); 'optional' elements (those that *can* occur); the possible placement for elements; and their potential for recurrence ('iteration') (Halliday and Hasan, 1985, pp. 55–6, 64, 108).

Size (opened out): A4

Text Function

Primarily to inform the reader about
what can be discovered through
visiting a bush reserve but also to sell
the idea of the benefits of knowing
about and enjoying our New Zealand
natural heritage.

Target Audience

Primary and intermediate students.

Mandatory Elements

- Folded, but not stapled
- Cover page
- Map with stations
- Key
- Pictures
- Printed text in segments

- Information box
- A range of scientific focuses.

Optional Elements

- Logo
- Photographs
- Choices for scientific focuses:
    o Trees, young and old
    o Plant varieties
    o Forest trees
    o Forest birds
    o Stratification
    o Epiphytes, parasites
       and fungi
    o Aliens
    o Arthropods
- Historical background to the
  area
- Maori uses of the bush, e.g.
  nikau, bracken root, totara
- The bush as a place of
  contemplation.

Figure 10.3 Nature trail pamphlet production brief

Step 1: Decide on the optional elements your group's pamphlet is going to contain.

Step 2: Visit to bush reserve. Each group member will need to have their own copy of a map of the reserve with the tracks (and any other features) clearly marked. Your task as a group will be twofold:

- Decide on a number of **points of interest** as you walk along the track. A point of interest might be a tree species, a land feature, an area of vegetation showing biodiversity, an item of historical interest and so on. These points of interest will become the stations on the map of your pamphlet.
- Take detailed notes of what you observe at each of your planned stations. Aim for accurate detail, not only of what you might be seeing, but also of sounds, smells and surface textures. Remember that you can leave questions related to species identification and other questions of a scientific or historical nature until after your trip.

Step 3: Using a sheet of A3 paper, decide on where your folds are going to be. (You can reduce your copy to A4 when your pamphlet is finished.)

Step 4: Once you have folded your A3, decide on *where* you are going to locate each of the elements in your pamphlet and *how much space* you are going to allocate for each element. This is a crucial step. It is a good idea to lightly pencil boxes on your mock-up to show location and size. (Remember you can modify the size and shape of these later.) Start with a decision on your cover page and map location.

Step 5: **Task allocation.** Each group member is to be allocated the production of a number of written and visual text production tasks. You should also appoint an Editor. The Editor's task will be to:

- Refine the shape and size of the elements that will comprise the finished pamphlet. (Use a new, clean, appropriately folded sheet of A4 cartridge paper for this.)
- Ensure that each group member knows the required shape and size of the segment of the A3 final copy sheet they are required to fill.

Step 6: **Drafting.** Group members draft, design and edit their allocated segments of the pamphlet. The style hand-out in your task sheet indicates ways in which your written text might be constructed. Ensure that your language is sharp and accurate. Research your facts. Remember who you are writing for and why.

Step 7: **Producing.** As a group decide on such things as font, style and size. Decide on the style of line you will be using for borders and boxes. Make decisions on colors. (Color photocopying allows for a final reduction of your finished copy from A3 to A4.)

Step 8: **Assembling.** Complete a paste-up of your group's finished text segments on your final copy sheet. Are there any gaps?!

Step 9: **Review.**

- How well did you work together as a group?
- What aspects of your finished product are you pleased with?

Deciding on specific learning outcomes and activities

The above steps provide a map for a production sequence. They are not a lesson plan. Lesson plans require teachers to formulate specific learning outcomes related to the stage in the text production process that students are at. For example, in respect of Step 6 above, a teacher might formulate learning outcomes in relation to such activities as peer conferencing, or the development of metalinguistic knowledge specifically tailored to what is required in the writing of a nature-trail 'station'. Figure 10.4 is an example of a 'station' from the nature-trail pamphlet shown in Figure 2.

Though a small text, there are linguistic features here that can be explored to enhance the choice-making of the young reader/rhetor/composer: imperatives, lists, technical language, phrase in apposition, use of the second person pronoun, and so on. In this instance, explicitly developed metalinguistic awareness has the potential to guide the young rhetor in the process of critically self-reflective re-drafting and editing.

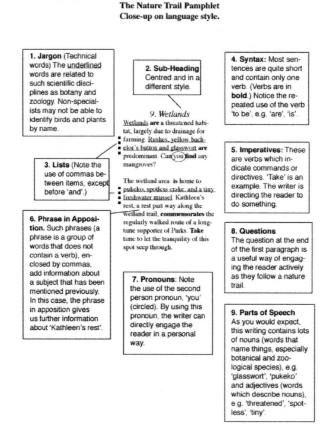

Figure 10.4 Grammar contextualized to the nature-trail pamphlet

Deciding on forms of assessment

Matters of assessment are dealt with at length elsewhere in this book. Sadly, summative assessment and qualifications regimes continue to operate as prime drivers of what happens in classrooms. Teachers may well find, for example, that in order to implement an approach to planning being illustrated here, they need to exercise a little bit of resistant cunning. Having said that, English teachers *do* have control of the way that they construct formative assessment practises in their classrooms, even when there is a disjunction between these and the summative assessment practises that impose themselves in various ways on their overall programs.

Of particular value, in a rhetorical approach to planning, is to have students (in reading 'mode') develop a set of assessment criteria themselves at the 'Modelling' stage above. In terms of the example used here, they would ask the broad question: 'What qualities make a nature-trail pamphlet successful?' To answer this question in some detail, reference can be made to aspects of Figure 10.1 and also to the kinds of structural, linguistic and other semiotic features found in successful models of the target genre. A set of criteria needs to be seen as a working document – something to be fine-tuned during the production phase of the unit. It can also be used as a checklist for students engaging critically as 'readers' of their own draft texts.

Conclusion

A nature-trail pamphlet is a 'real-world text' – one that requires the application of a number of semiotic modes in its production. In the real world of natural heritage trails, it is grasped by its users as they plot a course around a set of stations which help orient them to what a particular site has to offer. A pamphlet is a tactile thing; it has folds and edges and usually a glossy surface. Collectively, its producers are rhetors engaging in dialog in all sorts of ways with an array of precedent texts and utterances, and with an imagined audience of end-users. As rhetors, these text-makers are aware that a successful utterance in a multimodal environment is not just a question of getting the words right. It is a question of design – of style – of the exercise of choice in respect of composition, architecture, placement, illustration, and so on. In classical Greece, the rhetor was an adept at the arts of discourse. In these new digitally oriented times, the rhetor has become an aesthetician, adept in the arts of design.

References

Andrews, R. (ed.) (1992). *Rebirth of Rhetoric: Essays in Language, Culture and Education.* London: Routledge.

—(2010). *Re-framing Literacy: Teaching and Learning in English and the Language Arts.* New York: Routledge.

Andrews, R., Torgerson, C., Beverton, S., Freeman, A., Locke, T., Low, G., Robinson, A. and Zhu, D. (2006). 'The effect of grammar teaching on writing development', *British Educational Research Journal, 32*(1), 39–55.

Bakhtin, M. (1986). 'The Problem with Speech Genres' (V. McGee, trans.). In C. Emerson and M. Holquist (eds), *Speech Genres and Other Late Essays: M. M. Bakhtin.* Austin: University of Texas Press, pp. 60–102.

Carter, R. (1996). 'Politics and Knowledge about Language: The LINC project'. In R. Hasan and G. Williams (eds), *Literacy in Society.* London: Longman, pp. 1–3.

Christie, F. (2004). 'Revisiting Some Old Themes: The Role of Grammar in the Teaching of English'. In J. Foley (ed.), *Language, Education and Discourse: Functional Approaches.* London: Continuum, pp. 145–73.

—(2010). 'The "Grammar Wars" in Australia'. In T. Locke (ed.), *Beyond the Grammar Wars: A Resource for Teachers and Students on Developing Language Knowledge in the English/Literacy Classroom.* New York: Routledge, pp. 55–72.

Dixon, J. (1975). *Growth Through English (Set in the Perspective of the Seventies).* Edgerton: NATE/Oxford University Press.

Elley, W., Barham, I., Lamb, H. and Wyllie, M. (1979). *The Role of Grammar in the Secondary School Curriculum.* Wellington: New Zealand Council for Educational Research.

Fairclough, N. (1992). *Discourse and Social Change.* Cambridge: Polity Press.

French, R. (2010). 'Primary School Children Learning Grammar: Rethinking the Possibilities'. In T. Locke (ed.), *Beyond the Grammar Wars: A Resource for Teachers and Students on Developing Language Knowledge in the English/Literacy Classroom*. New York: Routledge, pp. 206–29.

Halliday, M., and Hasan, R. (1985). *Language, Context, and Text: Aspects of Language in a Social-semiotic Perspective*. Geelong, VIC: Deaking University.

Hillocks, G. Jr. (2006). 'Research in writing, secondary school, 1984–2003'. *L1 – Educational Studies in Language and Literature, 6*(2), 27–51.

Janks, H. (2010). '"Language as a System of Meaning Potential": The Reading and Design of Verbal Texts'. In T. Locke (ed.), *Beyond the Grammar Wars: A Resource for Teachers and Students on Developing Language Knowledge in the English/Literacy Classroom*. New York: Routledge, pp. 151–69.

Kolln, M. (1996). 'Rhetorical grammar: a modification lesson'. *English Journal, 85*(7), 25–31.

Kress, G. (2010). 'A Grammar for Meaning-making'. In T. Locke (ed.), *Beyond the Grammar Wars: A Resource for Teachers and Students on Developing Language Knowledge in the English/Literacy Classroom*. New York: Routledge, pp. 233–53.

Kress, G., and van Leeuwen, T. (2006). *Reading Images: The Grammar of Visual Design*, 2nd edn. London: RoutledgeFalmer.

Locke, T. (2004). *Critical Discourse Analysis*. London: Continuum.

—(ed.) (2010). *Beyond the Grammar Wars: A resource for Teacher and Students on Developing Language Knowledge in the English/literacy Classroom*. New York: Routledge.

Miller, A. (1958). *Collected Plays*. London: Cresset Press.

Morgan, W. (1996). 'Critical Literacy: More than Sceptical Distrust of Political Correctness?' In W. Morgan, P. Gilbert, C. Lankshear, S. Werner, and L. Williams (eds), *Critical Literacy: Readings and Resources*. Norwood, SA: AATE, pp. 35–46.

Myhill, D. (2010). 'Ways of Knowing: Grammar as a Tool for Developing Writing'. In T. Locke (ed.), *Beyond the Grammar Wars: A Resource for Teachers and Students on Developing Language Knowledge in the English/Literacy Classroom*. New York: Routledge, pp. 129–48.

Parr, G. (2010). *Inquiry-based Professional Learning: Speaking Back to Standards-based Reforms*. Teneriffe, Queensland, Australia: Post Pressed.

Pritchard, R. and Honeycutt, R. (2007). 'Best Practices in Implementing a Process Approach to Teaching Writing'. In S. Graham, C. MacArthur and J. Fitzgerald (eds), *Best Practices in Writing Instruction*. New York: Guilford Press, pp. 28–49.

Unsworth, L. (2010). 'Resourcing Multimodal Literacy Pedagogy: Toward a Description of the Meaning-making Resources of Language–Image Interaction'. In T. Locke (ed.), *Beyond the Grammar Wars: A Resource for Teachers and Students on Developing Language Knowledge in the English/Literacy Classroom*. New York: Routledge, pp. 276–93.

Part 4
SPEAKING AND LISTENING

Talk and Drama: Seeing Voices · 11

Anton Franks

Chapter Outline

I see a voice. Now will I to the chink
To spy an I can hear my Thisbe's face

(*A Midsummer Night's Dream*, Vi, 189–90)

Inquiry by looking through chinks

Playing Pyramus in the play-within-a-play, Bottom's comic utterance is, according to Hyppolyta, 'silly stuff', nonsense. Yet, clearly there is some serious intent in its contribution to the theme of the muddled, topsy-turvy world of relationships played out in *A Midsummer Night's Dream*. The theatrical convention of framing a play within a play draws attention to the adoption and playing out of different roles, which, in turn, facilitates a distanced view of playmaking and its depiction of the (sometimes comical) strangeness of human relations. Thus, in depicting and framing human interaction, drama can be likened to viewing social life through 'a chink'. Voices, of course, are intimately connected with a sense of the person, the 'speaking subject'. Voices are projected from the face through the mouth, accompanied by facial expression, gesture and posture, and directed towards others. Even if one cannot see the speaker, a voice conjures a strong sense of the material presence of the person doing the speaking. From this perspective, then, it is both strange and not so strange, comical and serious, that Bottom can 'see a voice'.

Investigating voices and talk in drama, either in discrete drama lessons, or as part of English, is the focus of interest here. The idea so fundamental to the making and viewing of drama, of making the strange seem familiar and the familiar appear strange, of viewing voices through a spy-hole or 'chink', is what drives this investigation of talk in drama lessons, albeit briefly. In making the opportunity for students to do drama, teachers provide conditions for learners to adopt a variety of dramatic roles, moving them from more familiar, everyday social roles through to more distant and imagined social roles. Doing drama allows students to be both participants and spectators of drama, to hold both the imaginary world created in drama and the real world simultaneously in view, a process that Bolton, drawing on Boal, refers to as *metaxis* (Bolton, 1984, pp. 141–2; Boal, 1995, pp. 42–4) To enable teachers and students to bring such complexity into view, describing and understanding diverse aspects of role-taking and its implications for learning, requires some distance and the adoption of an inquiry stance. Such a position of distance and inquiring is not easy to attain when teachers and students are engaged and involved in the flow of a drama lesson. Reflecting on his desire for an active, thinking audience, and allied to Boal and Bolton's use of the concept of *metaxis*, Brecht asserted that '[s]ome exercise in complex seeing is needed, though it is perhaps more important to think above the stream than to think in the stream' (1978, p. 44). Simultaneously 'to think in' and 'think above the stream', to adopt an engaged but critically distant perspective, is difficult to conceive. In Brechtian theater, his famous 'distancing effect', or 'estrangement' (from the German *Verfremdungseffect*) is achieved in part by bringing the artifice of theater into view through techniques such as songs, placards or direct speech to the audience that interrupt, and perhaps, disrupt, the flow of action on the stage. Brecht's purpose in developing these forms of theater was for imagined, dramatic action to feed back into the development of social life. Similarly, the purpose of putting forward an idea of the teacher as inquirer here is to promote the development of teaching and students' learning. In this instance, it is not theatrical techniques that provide the 'chink' through which to view students' drama from a critical distance, but 'lenses' provided in the ideas, practises and theories of others.

Talk in drama – real and not real

Talk, or speaking and listening, can be seen to be an intrinsic part of any lesson in school, of course. Unless one has in mind a lesson conducted completely through and about mime, imagining a lesson involving students in dramatic activity without talk would be impossible. In any learning context, the place, nature and role of talk is likely to be variegated, rich and complex; in drama, as part of learning, talk has particular and special functions. Not only is talk a necessary part of introducing, instructing, devising, presenting, reflecting and so forth on drama, for most types of drama activity, talk is a key as a mode of making meaning in drama itself. Talk, in its inextricable relation to gesture, posture, movement, facial expression and positioning, is woven into the very texture of drama. Drama presents an audience with imagined worlds, and so talk within drama is simultaneously real talk and imaginary talk, it is talk framed within quotation marks. The nature and qualities of talk within the drama is likely to be categorically different from the talk used to instruct, discuss and devise drama.

While it is relatively easy to make sweeping and generalized statements about the place of talk in school drama, its variety and complexity makes it rather more difficult to describe and analyze more precisely. The ambition here, then, cannot be to provide a full description and analysis of how talk in drama contributes to learning, but to gesture towards ways in which teachers might investigate talk in drama, to sketch its dimensions, indicating particular approaches to description and analysis. Again, like Bottom-as-Pyramus, the likelihood is that the voices of students and teachers will be seen but through a chink. The ultimate purpose of such investigations into the place and value of talk in drama is not simply for understanding as food for the intellect, albeit that there is intrinsic satisfaction in inquiry and analysis, but so that such understandings might feed back into practise so that both teaching and learning might be enhanced.

In the following sections, two short examples taken from observations of drama lessons will be presented. These instances of classroom activity are selected not because they are extraordinary or exemplary, but rather because they are ordinary, everyday examples of classroom practise. Recording these examples was not done electronically but by scribbling down written notes as the action unfolded in front of me, so they are rather sketchy, with some ellipses. Rough as they are, they will be used to illustrate two aspects of talk in the context of drama. The transcripts will give some sense of the activity in the drama and perhaps allow the reader to 'see' the voices that are represented. The first example is intended to show how drama can provide a context for students to extend their use of language. Through the adoption of dramatic roles in a shared imagined situation, students might be moved beyond everyday uses of spoken language. This will demonstrate how learners have access to varieties of speech and reach towards appropriate usage. Two broad frameworks of analysis will be applied, albeit sketchily, to illustrate how improvised dramatic speech can be described and understood. The second example is taken from a different lesson. Because drama lessons are by definition dialogic, and teachers play a pivotal role in leading the structure and dialog of lessons, the transcript will include the voices of the teacher as well as students talking *about* drama. Analysis will show how drama might provide contexts for learning, contributing to students' abilities to develop drama, ways of talking and thinking about drama, as well as assisting them in developing a wider repertoire of speech genres.

Courtroom drama – talking like a lawyer

The following transcript is taken from a lesson that took place in a large, culturally diverse school in south London with a year 8 class of students (aged around 13) who were designated as a 'low-ability' set. In previous lessons, they have been working around a playscript depicting the consequences when a group of youths throw stones from a footbridge over a motorway, causing a fatal accident. This is the last lesson in the sequence (as well as the last lesson of the school day) and the teacher prepares the students to conduct a court scene in which suspects are put on trial. The teacher plays the role of the teenager accused of throwing the stones. First she leads a discussion about courtrooms, their layout and procedures. Students then are divided into groups and are asked to prepare the cases for the prosecution and the defense, gathering up the evidence, preparing speeches and appointing two 'lawyers' for each team. Three students are appointed to sit on the 'judges' bench' and they set about moving a table to the front of the classroom (a large studio space). They arrange chairs in appropriate formations, theater-style, facing the bench, and setting a special chair for the 'witness box' in the corner, its back facing outward and angled so that it faces the 'courtroom' as well as the judges 'bench'. After 40 minutes of the lesson, the 'trial' is set to proceed. The groups advising the 'lawyers' take up positions in the main rows of seats, in front of which are two tables, facing the 'judges', for the 'lawyer teams'.

Prosecuting Lawyer 1: Where were you on Saturday night? Did you tell your mum that you killed someone? Remember, you swore to tell the truth.

Prosecuting Lawyer 2: A police officer saw the clothes you were wearing.

Defendant (the teacher): (petulantly) Everyone wears the same clothes.

The class in the body of the courtroom is silent, watching in rapt attention.

The teacher 'freezes' the action and comes out of role and asks the 'judges' (or prosecutors) to 'call on the defence to ask their questions'.

Defence Lawyer 1: OK you … were you at the scene of the crime?

Judge: A witness saw you.

Defendant [the teacher]: No one else was on the bridge.

Defence Lawyer 2: What time of day was it?

Defendant: 5.30.

Defence Lawyer 2: If it was dark the witness may be mistaken.

Judge 1: You may take your seats now.

Coming out of role, the teacher explains that people can ask their final questions …

Prosecuting Lawyer 1: Why are your fingerprints on the rock?

Judge 1: Order! Order! Prosecution sit down please. Defendant, come up please. What was he going to do if you didn't throw the rock?

Defendant: He was going to beat me up.

Judge: You may be seated. We will hear closing statements.

The groups reform to discuss the final statements. After twenty minutes, the 'court' reconvenes. There is much bustling and moving of chairs, reconstructing the 'courtroom'.

Judge: I call the prosecution. Hello! Order in the court!

It is nearing the end of the school day and concentration is wavering. The four 'lawyers' make very brief speeches that are difficult to capture because they are strutting around, clutching their lapels in a 'lawyer-like' manner whilst others in the class become restless and talkative. Hard against the end of the lesson, the teacher moves quickly to a 'jury vote', in which the whole class is involved, by show of hands. I am afraid to state that, as I failed to record the verdict, the reader will have to remain in suspense.

Analysis – multimodality and layers of language

There are two frameworks that I want briefly to bring to bear in analysis of spoken language in this short extract, the first a 'multimodal' framework that looks at in-role talk in relation to action and setting, the second, to look specifically at levels of language in use. Multimodal analysis draws from the work of Gunther Kress (1993; 2001), Kress and Theo van Leeuwen (2001) and colleagues, developed over the past 20 years or more. Work in this area draws forward social and functional approaches to semiotics developed in the last century (Bakhtin, 1986; Halliday, 1978, 1985; Vološinov, 1986) and uses them to examine the ways different modes of communication are combined and 'orchestrated' to make meaning in culture. Much current work in this area has been conducted in educational settings, in which multimodal social semiotics is used in analysis of teaching and learning (Jewitt and Kress, 2003).

Three key terms are associated with multimodal analysis: sign, mode and text. The concept of 'sign' is seen as a combination of form and meaning – in Kress's terms sign is 'form-as-meaning and meaning-as-form' (2003, pp. 37–44). The signs for 'lawyer', 'judge' and 'defendant' in the above excerpt are simultaneously given both form and meaning in the bodies, their position and action (including speech) of the actors. Signs, the material and media of communication shaped cultures over time into modes – in the above example, speech, gesture, posture, positioning in space and set can be seen as distinct modes that work together to make the meaning and give a sense of 'courtroom drama'. Modes always work in combination and are given instance and substance as 'text'. So the text in the above example, the 'courtroom scene', is formed out of a combination of the improvised drama performed against the improvised setting.

A key point is that talk-in-role in this 'courtroom drama' derives from the establishment of the whole dramatic scene. The layout of the classroom, however sketchily it replicates a courtroom setting, gives a sense of a courtroom, assisting the actors in the production of legalistic forms of speech. Some of the speeches betray traces of the struggle they experience at times to produce an approximation of the genre of speech – 'Did you tell your *mum* that you killed someone. Remember that you are under oath.' The relative positioning of the actors in the space of the classroom, embodies and substantiates the respective roles of judge, lawyer, defendant and court 'audience'. Speech in this context is both the prominent and dominant mode of making meaning, but its production rests on the intersection of the modes of space, movement and relative positioning.

Focusing down specifically on spoken language, I draw on a broad framework of analysis taken from the work of linguist Katharine Perera (1984). Perera draws a hierarchically layered model for the analysis of written or spoken text. The topmost layer is 'culture' that includes cultural settings, institutions, social relations, beliefs, expectations, conventions, power and so forth. In the drama, students' knowledge of the setting of the courtroom and expectations of behavior, conventions and power relations in the court between lawyers, judges and defendants is drawn on. Under culture is 'discourse', which includes varieties of speech and genres, as well as intended audiences and purposes. Discourse supersedes the 'textual' layer, for which strategies for organizing whole texts (including speeches) and sequencing are included. In descending order, there are layers that identify word order and syntax under the heading of 'wording', 'words' and 'substance', the material aspects of speech and writing. Utterances such as 'scene of the crime', 'the witness may be mistaken', 'you may take your seats now', 'I call the prosecution' and so forth, give evidence of the knowledge that students in this so-called 'low ability' group have of genres of speech, wording appropriate to the context of the courtroom (whether from direct experience or from film and television can only be open to speculation). The last recorded speech made by the 'Judge' – 'I call the prosecution … Hello! Order in the court!' – presents a neat example of how he interrupts the genre, inserting his informal 'Hello!' between the ritual forms of courtroom speech. Again, it is open to speculation whether it is evidence that he intends comical effect or that he is struggling to maintain the correct genre. What is notable, however, is that against a growing hubbub from the rest of the class, he does his best to remain in role, achieving this mostly through speech.

Making drama out of myths

The second, lengthier transcript is extracted from a lesson with another year 8 class, all girls from a variety of cultural backgrounds, in a school in east London. In this extract, the roles of the teacher, the varieties of her talk, including questioning, in-role narration, instruction and questioning, and responses of the students give an example of the dialogic aspects of talk, pointing towards the roles of talk in teaching and learning. Brief examples of student talk as they devise, present and reflect on drama are also evident below. Teaching and learning, and their relationship to talk and action are the focus of interest here.

A 'learning question' is up on the board as the class enter: 'Can I create a piece of drama that retells a section of a myth?' The teacher welcomes students and asks them to tell her what they did last week.

S: We sat in the circle and we had to figure out what blue was … we woke up one morning and everything is blue and we wondered what it was.

S: We came from a world where everything is grey and we're used to it.

T: And did you find out what blue was?

S: We did a piece of spontaneous improvisation and basically what A [the first student to speak] said.

T: How did you find out what blue was?

S: We made up a story.

T: Why'd you do that?

S: We made up a cautionary tale … a weird kind of story because we didn't have the technology.

T: So you were creating your own myth.

S: You used telling a story to find out what happened.

T: To find out what happened, to find out about the world. You made up stories to explain things. You made up stories to explain things.

The teacher continues, telling the students that they're going to explore a myth.

T: I'm going to come in as a character from it. What's that word?

S: Spontaneous improvisation.

T: No, no, another word.

S: Is it 'in role'?

The teacher nods and goes on to explain that they're going to be building a world of make believe together. If they remain in role, then the world of make believe will be like a balloon that will begin to rise, but if they come out of role, it will burst the balloon.

T [in role]: Oh thank you, thank you so much for coming. I'm really happy so many came. I don't know if you know my name? I'm Demeter, the harvest goddess. Some of you know my daughter, Persephone. Well, she was in the meadow, playing in the meadow. Were any of you there?

Ss: Yes.

T: Playing? And picking flowers? Did any of you see?

S: Yes.

T: What happened?

S: She was picking daisies.

T: Then something happened. The ground started shaking. Did you see it?

S: Yes, I was so frightened.

T: What happened?

S: The ground started to crack. It opened and swallowed her … A demon, something disgusting … the demon's face.

T: Someone told me it was Hades, King of the Underworld. Could that be right?

S: Yes.

T: Really ugly … What can we do?

S: We could send Hercules.

S: Ask Zeus …

The discussion continues for a while …

S: Send the strongest people in the kingdom.

The teacher tries to draw others, apart from the vocal few, into the discussion. A girl sitting next to the teacher goes into a long, complicated explanation that is mostly inaudible, but there are giggles from students around her.

T: [repeating the student's words] … a chariot, came out and he took her to the Underworld?

S: When he went, everything went black.

T: I have to go and look for her …

The teacher comes out of role.

T: Okay, some of you know the story of Persephone …

S: I learnt it in year 6.

The teacher tells a synoptic version of the story. As she does, hands go up.

T: Hands down. We're going to retell the story. What we're going to do now is …

There's excitement bubbling up from some in the class and the teacher pauses, waiting for silence and looking around the room.

T: You're going to get a piece of paper and you have to decide what's the most important [aspect to show] … you're going to tell the story in three frozen pictures.

The class is divided into six groups and allocated different areas of the drama studio to work. The teacher gives out slips of paper on which a section of the story of Persephone in the Underworld is written out.

T: Okay, five! [a departmental signal to stop to listen for instructions] C, what do you have to do?

S: You give us a piece of paper and we have to do three frozen pictures to tell the story.

T: What's on the paper, A?

S: On the paper is part of the story.

In their groups, students immediately get down to action. There is much gesturing, posturing and positioning. Below are some snatches from groups' conversations as they devise their presentations.

GROUP A

S: So, X is a monster … You can't move, okay? Then we move to the next one … Transitions … We're going to do three for Persephone … D stop it … push … sit down … no, don't sit down, bend down, smelling, pretend smelling the flowers and after that one of her friends is holding her hand …

GROUP B

S: … and after, you lot can be, like, looking in different directions … [she lifts her hand to her forehead, shading her eyes and looks, leaning forward slightly, her body leaning forward diagonally].

GROUP C

Four students are standing in parallel formation, facing each other, holding arms aloft and looking down on one girl sitting between them, her arms clasped around her drawn up knees.

S: You're going to say 'Crack!'

GROUP D

S: You lie down … not like that [she demonstrates how she wants it, then points to another student] She's the king, you know, the god of the Underworld. You're supposed to be powerful. Do that! [She demonstrates a gesture, her arms outstretched and describing an arc from parallel with her hips and swinging above her head].

The teacher interrupts the group-work.

T: Five! Five! Five! [She waits a second or two until the noise of chatter abates].

Okay, if you've got your pictures, I want you to put in some movements and some sounds. Okay? Five minutes to do that.

The teacher turns to watch one particular group who are working on establishing their three frozen pictures and moving between them.

T: So, you're still working on your sounds and movement? … Transitions as well. You could try doing a transition in role …

T: Five! … We're going to be seeing them in two minutes. Actually, let's rehearse them. Into positions! Three, two, one, freeze! Freeze!

All groups run through their three images, practising moving between them.

The teacher returns to watching the group she's just been talking to.

One student mimes offering another some food.

S: Eat, my child.

S: No! Don't eat, or else you'll never be able to return.

T: Transitions. What are the different transitions?

S: Slow motion, fast motion.

S: You can use in-role transition.

T: 30 seconds!

Class organizes themselves into an audience whilst the first group to show takes up position in the performing space. The teacher draws attention back to the 'learning question' that she puts up again on the board.

T: So, what we're going to do … 'Can I create a piece of drama that retells a section of a myth?' … What did they show and how are they showing? What drama techniques are they using? I could ask any person.

GROUP 1 SHOW

FP (frozen picture) 1: Different figures are shown at low level, bending, kneeling and looking around at different levels, with their arms raised. One student bends down, making a gesture as if plucking the 'flowers' represented by other students.

S: I like picking pretty flowers.

FP 2: They shift position, showing discomfort and wonder, postures that depict a loss of balance, puzzled and frightened expressions on their faces.

Ss: Wow!

FP 3: Most of the group perform a strange, arrhythmic, dance, bodies askew, stamping their feet, arranged in a semi-circle around focusing on one student, centre-stage, in a semi-crouch, who looks up with a fearful expression.

S [crouching]: What's happening?!?

T: What did you like?

S: I liked the effect. They did duh, duh, duh [she kicks her heels against the floor]

T: What did they do?

S: Used their feet.
S: I liked the drunken effect with the earthquake.
T: What was the 'drunken effect'?
S: I don't know the word for it. It was like an earthquake – they stamped their feet
T: I think it was nice the way they used their bodies as flowers …
S: [having found the 'right' term] Physical theatre!
T: Physical theatre, that's right.

Analysis – talk about drama and the development of concepts

Varieties of talk, you will recall, their relation to dramatic activity and the possible connections of these varieties of talk to teaching and learning are the subjects of inquiry here. In the opening section, students synoptically recount the narrative that is at the core of their work in the previous lesson. On the board, the 'learning question' points to and frames the content and forms of drama they will be involved in through the lesson. The first student is so brief in her account of 'what blue was' that a second student adds that in the explanation that in the 'world' they had come from 'everything was grey'. It is perhaps because they have had a shared experience of the drama the previous week and they are aware that the teacher will know what they have done that their narratives appear so attenuated. The explanation and recount are nonetheless sufficient. Interspersed in this first section of talk are key terms signalling their involvement and understanding of the concepts of drama and its contents: 'spontaneous improvisation', a technical term setting their activity within drama's disciplinary boundaries, with 'cautionary tale' and 'weird kind of story' reaching towards the generic content of the drama. The teacher does not refute or modify these terms, but states simply that they were creating their 'own myth', so instating a key concept for the lesson, and providing an elaboration on the functions of myth, how they explain things. In just this brief section, it is apparent how the teacher and students are engaged in dialog that elaborates and underlines key concepts.

Next the teacher establishes another mode of working, framed by a particular term and concept in her head that she invites the students to guess at – not 'spontaneous improvisation', as before, but 'in role', guessed correctly by another student. Adopting the role of 'Demeter' in this section enables the teacher to shift the dramatic frame to move the talk to another level, to initiate the drama and draw in the students. It is simply done, the role allowing the teacher to introduce the narrative of Persephone in the Underworld in a different form of storytelling. The role enables her to shift the narrative into first person, encouraging engagement and participation. Her speech culminates with a question: 'Were any of you there?', inviting the students into the 'balloon' world of the imagination. The first student picks up the immediate cue and concurs that, yes, they were picking flowers, daisies to be precise, but another student appears to recognize the scenario and provides an essential link to the story of Persephone, as the ground cracks open and a 'disgusting' demon appears. Such 'tuning into' (see Barrs and Cork, 2001) the story is something that the teacher expects, or hopes for, at least, and it enables her to name the 'demon' as 'Hades, King of the Underworld'. The 'balloon' of make-believe inflates some more, drawing in the students within its boundaries, as they suggest that the strong figures of Hercules or Zeus might save the day for Persephone. Some of them know the story and are pleased to mobilise and share this knowledge with others. So that she is sure that everyone is clear, the teacher then tells the story again, this time in the third person. Although clearly a leading figure, the teacher has now established the lesson as a collective and shared experience – she is hoping to encourage an ensemble approach to learning in drama (see Neelands, 2009).

The excerpts of talk during the phase of the lesson when students are devising their three frozen pictures, depicting their allotted section of the story, sees a shift into other forms of talk. Here, the talk is mostly and directly transactional, i.e. intended to get things done, and is almost inseparable from the physical activity that the students are engaged in – it would be difficult to comprehend without the 'staged movements' I have inserted in square brackets. It is fragmented and its tenor and modality is largely in the imperative mode. They are aware that, working in this way, physical action alone has to connect with and communicate to an audience and so their postures and gestures take on heightened, emblematic or iconic qualities. At the same time, the technical concept of 'transition' is introduced, concerned with how they will move smoothly and dramatically from one tableau to another. Later, with the intervention of the teacher in one group's devising, teacher and students consider the varieties of 'transition' and, again, are concerned with technical aspects of drama. One student hits upon the notion of transitions that sustain their dramatic roles, again, so that the 'balloon' of make-believe is not punctured by awkwardness. The concept of transition, here, perhaps crosses the divide between live drama and that which is recorded and edited on video and film.

In the last section of transcript, students return to a search for terminology, i.e. terms adequate to describe, label and evaluate the drama they have just watched. How can they describe the 'earthquake effect' demonstrated by this group? The first attempt is onomato-poeic, accompanied by a physical demonstration, and the second, the 'drunken effect', a resort to metaphor, drawn from everyday discourse. Finally, the teacher's comment – 'I think it was nice the way they used their bodies' – serves as a prompt and signpost to the term a particular student is searching for, 'physical theatre'.

Drama, talk and learning

There are many ways to come at describing varieties of talk connected with doing drama, as there are different ways to analyze its functions. It would be possible, for example, to do an analysis that works at Perera's levels of word order and word choice, a finer linguistic analysis drawing from descriptive and analytical grammars such as Halliday's functional grammar (Halliday, 1985). Or to do conversation analysis (Have, 2007) or a finer-grained analysis of turn-taking between teacher and student and student to student, looking at how classroom talk can be articulated more strongly with learning processes (Edwards and Mercer, 1987). What is apparent in the extracts above is how talk in drama, interactions between teacher and students and students one to another, serves a variety of functions in learning, and moreover that this learning is socially predicated. The learning of terminology, either the genres of courtroom discourse, or the genre particular to drama lessons, is not an end in itself. Genres of language connected with dramatic action allow *conceptual* movement in and around imaginary worlds that are collectively and *actively* constructed in a social context.

At the beginning of the twentieth century, the Russian psychologist Vygotsky wrote powerfully about the relationship between action, language (spoken and written) and learning, and how learning relates to the development of thinking, feeling and acting in the world (Vygotsky, 1986). For Vygotsky, play is key in children's learning and development. He characterizes play as imagination in and through action which, as a child grows and develops, gradually becomes internalized and part of internal mental activity (Vygotsky, 1978). Furthermore, broadening out from individual to cultural development, Vygotsky identifies a relationship between play and art, that there is '*a psychological kinship between art and play*' (emphasis in original, 1971, p. 257). Drama, particularly unscripted, improvised drama, is particularly effective as a developmental activity. Drama is characterized by him as a *syncretic* mode of creativity in that word, action, thinking and feeling are united in dramatic activity and thus … 'The staging of drama provides the pretext and material for the most diverse forms of creativity on the part of children' (Vygotsky, 1967/2004, p. 71).

At the center of interest here, however, is how talk in drama relates to learning and development. For Vygotsky, as for Piaget (Piaget, 1978), concepts are developed in relation to language development. Words do not simply carry concepts as a jug carries water, but concepts develop and mature over time and through repeated usage in social interaction in particular cultural contexts. In both extracts it is possible to see how students are experimenting with language and developing particular concepts. In the first extract, the students are rehearsing and experimenting with formal, legalistic language. It is the imagined context of the courtroom that provides a context for them to inhabit language associated with the roles of judge and lawyer. In the second extract, students can be seen to be grappling with the concepts concerned with mythical forms of narrative as they relate to human thinking and cultural life. At the same time, crucially they are developing their understanding and control of the concepts of drama and how they relate to specific forms of action. Crucial to their learning in both examples is the social situation of learning that drama provides which allows for the intervention of the teacher and their peers, in which others modify and contribute to understanding and the ability to take action. The term that Vygotsky used for the potential for learning and development through the involvement of others is usually translated as the 'zone of proximal development', or ZPD, which he defined as the 'discrepancy between a child's actual mental age and the level she reaches solving problems with the assistance of others' (1986, p. 187).

Talk in drama, then, draws on student experience, enhanced by teaching expertise and directed through interaction with teachers and others, within or about the imaginary world of drama. Fuelled by everyday realities of social and cultural life, through its union of action (including speech, gesture and so forth), thinking and feeling, drama also feeds from and feeds into what Helen Nicholson refers to as 'social imagination' creating alternative worlds that belong to a 'social imaginary' (2005, pp. 74–9). Writing about drama within English shortly after the inception of the National Curriculum in England, Jonothan Neelands conceptualized drama as 'imagined experience' (1992). 'Experience' here refers to the thoughts and feelings of individuals, experienced and shared through participation in everyday social life. It is lived, face-to-face experience, or it is mediated experience that comes via literature, television, film and now, newer digital media which constitute contemporary culture.

Inquiry into talk in drama – histories and currencies

It might have not escaped notice that, for the most part, I have doggedly stuck to the term *talk* and have mostly avoided *speaking and listening*. To be anecdotal for a moment, a colleague who had returned to the UK from Canada to find the National Curriculum in place commented, 'Speaking and listening? What's wrong with talk?' The point here is that the coupling of speaking and listening is a relatively new way of talking about talk in classrooms. One reason for the separation of talk into the speaking and listening is to make a kind of an economy of curriculum for the purposes of assessment. It tends to reify and ossify something that is a process and part of the effects of this is to delimit thinking. Whilst I do not want to overemphasize Orwellian tendencies in Nationalcurriculumspeak, where I started on this investigation of talk in drama was with the notion of thinking teachers who are willing to inquire into their own practise and realize in students' voices their material presence. On this view, teachers and students are seen as creative agents, who work together, each contributing to others' learning and development. In order to see things, albeit in small chink-like segments, one has to maintain an inquiring attitude. What raises the coupling and elevation of 'speaking and listening' over talk is a sense of how these terms and concepts come into being through history.

Conclusion

Coming towards the end of this chapter, therefore, I want to raise some sense of the history of inquiring into talk, however briefly. Whilst I was still just about a school student in the 1970s, researching and valuing talk became a key part of schooling beyond English and drama lessons. The publication of what has come to be known as the Bullock Report (DES [Department of Education and Science], 1975) instigated a move to look at language, including talk, across the whole school curriculum. Many schools established staff committees to look at and promote language policies, largely because Bullock and his colleagues established the importance of language and learning. Indeed, a chapter in this report was entitled 'Language and Learning', largely authored by James Britton, who, a few years earlier, had published a book of the same title, drawing on Vygotsky and Piaget (1970/92). Britton was part of a cohort of teachers, academics and advisors who collaborated in all kinds of ways on various projects to research language and learning (e.g. Barnes, 1976; Barnes et al., 1990). Around the same time, Harold Rosen and colleagues initiated a series of conferences on 'Language in Inner City Classrooms', which again had teachers, academics and advisors working together over a period of years. Out of this came several projects: one volume that remains etched in my memory came out of such a collaboration between teachers and academics researching talk in one particular south London girls' school entitled *Becoming Our Own Experts* (The Talk Workshop Group, 1975). One chapter, particularly pertinent here, is an analysis of the language repertoire of one student, Jennifer, normally a rather challenging young woman, who performed a mostly improvised but rather brilliant play called 'Brixton Blues' that was recorded on videotape. Later, in the 1980s, a National Oracy Project was established, which continued until the National Curriculum was well instated in schooling (see Howe and Johnson, in Brindley, 1994). All of these cited texts still have something to offer inquiring teachers of today, including research perspectives and methods as well as theoretical insights into the value of talk, not just in drama but also across the curriculum.

Finally, it is worth saying something about current perspectives and resources for researching into talk in drama, its range and its value in teaching and learning. One source is a chapter I wrote recently based on a survey of available research into drama and language learning (Franks, 2010). In the recent past, Andy Kempe has produced a book and journal articles on talk in drama, both improvised and scripted (Kempe, 2003; Kempe and Holroyd, 2004). In this work, Kempe makes clear arguments, based on evidence and drawing on the work of sociologist Pierre Bourdieu (Bourdieu, 1992), on ways in which drama can provide the context for extending language repertoires and giving students access to the 'cultural capital' of 'standard' forms of spoken English. Sections of a report into surveys conducted by Harland and colleagues in the 1990s give a good sense of the benefits of students engaging in drama, including language development and so these too are worth a look (Harland, 2000).

References

Bakhtin, M. M. (1986). 'The Problem of Speech Genres' (V. W. McGee, trans.). In C. H. Emerson, M (ed.), *Speech Genres and Other Late Essays*. Austin: University of Texas Press, pp. 60–102.

Barnes, D. (1976). *From Communication to Curriculum*. London: Penguin.

Barnes, D., Britton, J. N. and Torbe, M. (1990). *Language, the Learner and the School*, 4th edn. Portsmouth, NH: Boynton/ Cook.

Barrs, M. and Cork, V. (2001). *The Reader in the Writer: The Links Between the Study of Literature and Writing Development at Key Stage 2*. London: Center for Language in Primary Education.

Boal, A. (1995). *The Rainbow of Desire: The Boal Method of Theatre and Therapy*. London: Routledge.

Bolton, G. (1984). *Drama as Education*. London: Longman.

Bourdieu, P. (1992). *Language and Symbolic Power*. Oxford: Polity Press.

Brecht, B. (1978). *Brecht on Theatre: The Development of an Aesthetic*. New York: Hill and Wang; London: Eyre Methuen.

Brindley, S. (1994). *Teaching English*. London: Routledge/OU.

Britton, J. (1970/1992). *Language and Learning: [Importance of Speech in Children's Development]* ([New] edn). London: Penguin.

DES (1975). *A Language for Life [The Bullock Report]*. London.

Edwards, D. and Mercer, N. (1987). *Common Knowledge: The Development of Understanding in the Classroom*. London: Methuen.

Franks, A. (2010). 'Drama in Teaching and Learning Language and Literacy'. In D. Wyse, R. Andrews and J. Hoffman (eds), *The Routledge International Handbook of English, Language and Literacy Teaching,* Abingdon, Oxon: Routledge, pp. 242–53.

Halliday, M. A. K. (1978). *Language as Social Semiotic: The Social Interpretation of Language and Meaning*. London: Edward Arnold.

—(1985). *An Introduction to Functional Grammar*. London: Edward Arnold.

Harland, J. (2000). *Arts Education in Secondary Schools: Effects and Effectiveness*. Slough: National Foundation for Educational Research.

Have, P. T. (2007). *Doing Conversation Analysis: A Practical Guide*, 2nd edn. London: Sage.

Hodge, R. and Kress, G. (1993). *Social Semiotics*. Ithaca, NY: Cornell University Press.

Howe, A. (1994). 'Perspectives on Oracy'. In S. Brindley (1994), *Teaching English*. Abingdon: Routledge and Open University, pp. 43–54.

Jewitt, C. and Kress, G. R. (2003). *Multimodal Literacy*. New York; Oxford: Peter Lang.

Johnson, J. (1994). 'The National Oracy Project'. In S. Brindley (1994), *Teaching English*. Abingdon: Routledge and Open University, pp. 33–42.

Kempe, A. (2003). 'The role of drama in the teaching of speaking and listening as the basis for social capital'. *Research in Drama Education, 8*(1), 65–78.

Kempe, A., and Holroyd, J. (2004). *Speaking, Listening and Drama*. London: David Fulton.

Kress, G. (2001). *Multimodal Teaching and Learning: The Rhetorics of the Science Classroom*. London: Continuum.

—(2003). *Literacy in the New Media Age*. London: Routledge.

Kress, G. R., and van Leeuwen, T. (2001). *Multimodal Discourse: The Modes and Media of Contemporary Communication*. London: Arnold.

Neelands, J. (1992). *Learning Through Imagined Experience: The Role of Drama in the National Curriculum*. London: Hodder & Stoughton.

—(2009). 'Acting together: Ensemble as a democratic process in art and life'. *Research in Drama Education: The Journal of Applied Theatre and Performance, 14*(2), 173.

Nicholson, H. (2005). *Applied Drama: The Gift of Theatre*. Basingstoke: Palgrave Macmillan.

Perera, K. (1984). *Children's Writing and Reading: Analysing Classroom Language*. Oxford: Blackwell.

Piaget, J. (1978). *The Development of Thought: Equilibration of Cognitive Structures* (A. Rosin, trans.). Oxford: Blackwell.

The Talk Workshop Group (1975). *Becoming Our Own Experts: The Vauxhall Papers*. London (Orchard Primary School, Well St., E.1): Talk Workshop Group.

Vološinov, V. N. (1986). *Marxism and the Philosophy of Language*. Cambridge, Mass.: Harvard UP.

Vygotsky, L. S. (1967/2004). 'Imagination and creativity in childhood'. *Journal of Russian and East European Pschology, 42*(1), 7–97.

—(1971). *The Psychology of Art*. Cambridge, MA; London: M.I.T. Press.

—(1978). 'The Role of Play in Development'. In M. Cole (ed.), *Mind in Society: The Development of Higher Psychological Processes*. Cambridge.; London: Harvard University Press, pp. 92–104.

—(1986). *Thought and Language*, rev. edn. Cambridge.: MIT Press.

The Importance of Oracy 12

Simon Gibbons

Chapter Outline

Oracy should be the foundation on which effective classroom practise is constructed, whatever the subject being taught. Enhancing students' talking and listening skills from the very earliest age is fundamental in enabling them to develop as skilled users, interpreters and analyzers of language. The links between the development of oral language and the development of thinking underline how critical it is that children have every opportunity to expand their capacities as speakers and listeners. Talk is also fundamentally a social activity; through their interaction with others, children make sense of their own place in the world and interpret and internalize the cultures and societies with which they engage.

English, it seems to me – whatever one's view of the subject – is primarily concerned with language in all its forms. It is a subject that aims to enable students to make meaning themselves, and make meaning from what they hear, see and read. As students strive to make meaning, talk is the most powerful tool at their disposal. Thus oracy deserves to be at the heart of the English curriculum.

Oracy in English: A historical perspective

Oracy, defined as the ability to use and understand spoken language, is a term often used synonymously with the phrase 'speaking and listening', or simply 'talk'. It is probably safe to assert that most English teachers share the view that good speaking and listening work is essential in the classroom and critical to the development of students as powerful and articulate thinkers, talkers, readers and writers.

The centrality of oral work to the successful English classroom is, of course, nothing new. The Newbolt Report (Departmental Committee of the Board of Education, 1921), still viewed by many as the first seminal report on the teaching of English in England, made clear in its recommendations that speaking and listening were fundamental to English, stressing not only the importance of oral language as the foundation for proficiency in writing, but also making it clear that students' own dialects ought not to be suppressed in any attempt to impose standard English.

Despite the recommendations of Newbolt, however, for many, advocating oral work in English is associated with the advances made by the so-called 'progressive' English educators from the post-war period, particularly in London. The work of the London Association for the Teaching of English (LATE) is important here. This group – a network of teachers and academics founded in 1947 – sought to develop a new model of English in the wake of the Butler Act, which made secondary-aged schooling statutory in England, and in the context of the rise of comprehensive schooling. Critical to their work was the idea that oral language and speaking and listening ought to be the foundation on which good teaching and learning is constructed, calling it of 'utmost importance' in their document *The Aims of English Teaching*, which was a manifesto for the subject prepared for the British Council to send to schools overseas (LATE, 1956). The work of LATE (see Gibbons, 2013) was central to the development of London English, a paradigm for the subject also termed 'English as Language' that has, at times somewhat simplistically, been seen as in opposition to the more traditional English as Literature or Cambridge English model (Ball, 1985, 1987; Ball, Kenny and Gardiner, 1990; Sawyer, 2004). Developing what became known as London English was not a reaction to existing paradigms for the subject, rather it was driven by the proactive desire to create a model for the subject that would satisfy the needs of all children in a new age of statutory secondary-age schooling (see Gibbons, 2008, 2009a, 2009b).

Central to the ideas of LATE, and subsequently to the National Association for the Teaching of English (NATE), formed in 1963 and which quickly adopted many of LATE's guiding principles, was the link between spoken language and experience, and the importance of allowing children to speak to order and make sense of their experience of the world. This was ultimately bound up in a larger notion of a model of English as 'personal growth', given full outline in Dixon's *Growth through English* (1967). Dixon's work, the result of the 1966 Dartmouth Seminar where 40 teachers of English from the US and the UK met for a period of four weeks to debate the subject, is essentially an articulation of London English.

Dixon's ideas were informed by colleagues at Walworth School in South London, including Leslie Stratta and Simon Clements. Together Clements, Dixon and Stratta published *Reflections* (1963), a seminal text book (with accompanying teachers' guide) that was based on the Walworth fourth-form English syllabus, and as such was a practical exposition of this new English. Whether termed London English, English as Language or growth English, it is a model for the subject that has maintained its currency amongst English teachers across the globe, particularly in the United Kingdom, North America, Australia and New Zealand (see, for example, Goodwyn and Findlay, 1999; Marshall, 2000; Reid, 2003).

Key scholars in English teaching were James Britton and Harold Rosen, though it was their colleague in the national association, Andrew Wilkinson, who first coined the term 'oracy'. Harold Rosen was particularly interested in the importance of allowing children to use their own language and dialect, an interest driven by his concern with the educational experience of working-class children in particular, which was evident in much of his work as an English teacher (Gibbons, 2009c). Britton was more explicitly concerned with the links between language development and the development of thinking and it was he who played a significant role in harnessing the ideas of Vygotsky to provide a strong theoretical framework to support the promotion of classrooms rich in talk (Britton, 1987). Vygotsky's work – in the form of two translated texts, *Thought and Language* (1986) and *Mind in Society* (1978) – only really became widely available in the West in the mid-1960s, but his theories about the links between language development and concept development and the social construction of knowledge were quickly harnessed by Britton to underpin what he, and others, deemed to be common sense from their work with, and observations of, children. Put simply this was the idea that children *learned* through talk; it was not simply a language mode used to communicate understanding. Britton's ideas, most clearly presented in *Language and Learning* (1970) were influential in the status given to oracy in the Bullock Report (Department for Education and Science, 1975). Britton was a member of the committee responsible for this report, and the chapter on 'Language Across the Curriculum' makes clear the importance of small-group talk. The importance of talk across the curriculum had in fact been made explicit in *Language, the Learner and the School* (Barnes, Britton and Rosen, 1969). Britton's arguments about the importance of speaking and listening, an importance given weighty backing by the ideas of Vygotsky, are most plainly set out in his article 'Vygotsky's contribution to pedagogical theory' in which he makes the powerful assertion that 'If speech in childhood lays the foundations for a lifetime of thinking how can we continue to prize a silent classroom?' (Britton, 1987, p. 25).

Britton's work was important in the setting up of a UK National Oracy Project in 1986 and this ground-breaking work preceded the official sanctioning of speaking and listening as central to the English curriculum in the first version of the National Curriculum for English (Department for Education and Science, 1989). Subsequent rewrites of the curriculum retained speaking and listening as one of the language modes in English and this was reinforced by the significant percentage of marks given at the examination at 16, the General

Certficate of Secondary Education (GCSE) for teachers' assessment of talk. Drafts for new programs of study in English in 2013 have marginalized the importance of talk for learning, but the fact that this has provoked much disquiet among both primary and secondary practitioners perhaps underlines the fact that it is the case for most teachers that oracy should be central to curriculum development.

Oracy in English

The best English classrooms are rich in talk, and speaking and listening can take many forms and fulfill many purposes. Oracy is often intrinsically linked to other language modes: students spend much time in class discussion of literature and other texts to show their reading comprehension and skills of analysis, and talk will often precede and follow writing. At the presentational end of the scale, enactment of scripted drama and poetry recital – currently undergoing something of a renaissance – are perhaps examples of the most formal uses of spoken language. Some may argue in such uses of talk, spoken language is – to all intents and purposes – divorced from thought (when discussing the intersection of thought and language, Vygotsky, for example, suggested that recitation was an example of non-intellectual speech (Vygotsky, 1986)). At the less formal end of the spectrum is the kind of oracy that goes on when students work in groups to discuss a topic, issue or problem. Here spoken language perhaps is most closely linked to the development of understanding, as in the best examples it might be said that on such occasions students are using talk to think aloud.

In England, since its introduction in 1989, the National Curriculum for English has included explicit requirements for students' speaking and listening. Originally a separate program of study, the 2008 rewrite of the curriculum included sections on talk in the 'Key Processes', 'Range and Content' and 'Curriculum Opportunities' sections (Department for Children, Schools and Families, 2008). Within 'Key Processes' are the skills students are expected to develop, including adapting to different audiences, contributing to group talk and taking on different roles. 'Range and Content' specifies types of activity – formal debates, pair and group discussion, performance of script – and 'Curriculum Opportunities' indicates specific tasks that students might undertake, for example participating in workshops with actors to discuss the impact of spoken performance.

Twenty years' teaching and observing English lessons in secondary schools has shown me that the two most dominant uses of talk in the classroom are whole-class discussion and interaction and small-group oral work. Thus, the rest of this chapter will focus on some of the key issues associated with these practises and also consider some of the problems associated with ideas about progression in speaking and listening. The question of progression is perhaps more troublesome in this area than it is when considering issues around students' development in reading and writing, if only due to the ephemeral nature of much classroom talk.

Whole-class oral work

I struggle to remember a lesson, English or otherwise, that I have either taught or observed that has not involved some element of whole-class oral work. From the teacher introducing the topic or task at the lesson's outset and fielding questions, to the sharing of ideas and conclusions at a lesson plenary, the practise of one teacher engaging thirty students in talk seems a commonsense way to communicate ideas and pool information.

Whole class oral work was emphasized in England in the 1990s and early 2000s by the government-backed National Literacy Strategy and Framework for English. These non-statutory but heavily recommended initiatives were central to the New Labor administration's focus on raising standards, with what was termed 'whole class interactive teaching' featuring as 'a central component of the . . . . Strategy at both primary and secondary level' (Coles, 2005, p. 114). 'Whole class interactive teaching' purported to promote traditional whole-class talk in a new, more interactional way, but to what extent it was effective has been questioned. Viewing the video training material that supported teachers in developing this kind of work, Coles observed that what actually happened:

> More often than not relies upon whole-class question and answer episodes, where the teacher maintains tight control over apportioning (unequal) speaking rights and pupils' responses are usually limited in scope. It is a model of teaching which presupposes classes consisting of well motivated, co-operative pupils, who share similar cultural experiences. It perpetuates the idea that only teachers ask questions; that teachers control the transference of a prescribed bank of knowledge; and that the prime purpose of pupil talk is in order to check that this transference has taken place.
>
> (Coles, 2005, p. 115)

Coles' view is that the supposedly new interactive whole-class teaching was merely replicating the traditional problems associated with whole-class talk, that it too is teacher dominated and often characterized by what is known as the IRF structure – where the teacher Initiates (probably through a question), a student Responds (with an answer) and the teacher then offers follow-up with Feedback to the student. Clearly such forms of interaction do have a role to play, but they have been subject to criticism on a number of fronts. For example, as suggested in the research leading to the publication of *Language, the Learner and the School* (Barnes, Britton and Rosen, 1969), such classroom interaction can revolve around closed questions, where teachers are not looking to invite thought but simply looking for students to give right or wrong answers. While there may be times when this is important, perhaps worse are the pseudo-open questions, where teachers apparently encourage thinking on the part of the class and invite a range of possible answers, but it becomes clear that there is, in effect, an answer in the teacher's head that the students grope for, or are led towards. Another key problem associated with traditional teacher-led whole-class discussion is how to ensure that students listen to one another – often in such talk there is a tendency for teachers to 'revoice' what are considered to be helpful answers from the class, thus reinforcing the idea that the teacher's voice is the authoritative one and so the only one that students really need to listen to.

There has been relatively recent work on whole-class talk (for example, QCA, 2003) that has suggested ways in which such interaction might genuinely be used to develop thinking in students, and actively encourage listening and engagement. Though having a long tradition, one strand of this work might be seen to re-emerge strongly from the growing body of work on assessment for learning. It is most easy to see the starting point for this work in the publication of *Inside the Black Box* in 1998 (Black and William), and most notably within this work the emphasis on the improvement of teachers' use of questions during class talk. A general principle from this work might be that in most cases a question is probably only worth asking if thinking is demanded. In such cases, it is only right that students are given thinking time before being expected to answer, or perhaps encouraged to rehearse their thinking or answers through brief collaboration with a talk partner. If the culture of classroom discussion can be developed in this way, then the teacher could expect that all students should be able to contribute to class talk. (Good examples of the ways in which teachers have developed their practise in whole class talk can be found in *Assessment for Learning: Putting it into Practise* (Black et al., 2005)).

Small-group oral work

Small-group speaking and listening work is perhaps the most common practise in many English classrooms, indeed it could be said that if one walked into a classroom the presence of students sitting in fours chatting in an animated fashion might be the strongest clue that it is an English classroom. Whether it be the discussion of a poem or a section from a novel, the analysis of a newspaper article, or the consideration of a topic for debate, many English teachers see small groups as the obvious way to structure lessons. Group talk often acts as a precursor to some more formal event – a presentation or performance – but this should not obscure the fact that what is actually important is the group talk itself. The kind of talk that goes on in these types of session is what Mercer calls 'exploratory talk', a term that dates back at least as far as the Bullock Report. For Mercer exploratory talk is that:

> in which partners engage critically but constructively with each other's ideas. Relevant information is offered for joint consideration … It is an effective way of using language to think. The process of education should ensure that every child is aware of its value and able to use it effectively. However, observational research evidence suggests that very little of it naturally occurs in classrooms when children work together in groups.
>
> (Mercer, 2000, p. 98)

Planning for progression in speaking and listening

When thinking about enabling students to make progress as speakers and listeners working in the kinds of small-group activities that are central to many English lessons, it is always worth starting from Mercer's observation that productive group talk behavior is learned rather than instinctive. It is not simply a case of setting up interesting topics for discussion, and then perhaps assuming that increasing the complexity of the topic will engender increased sophistication in speaking and listening. Rather one needs to begin from the position of thinking about how to engender productive talk behaviors, and use this as the starting point for developing different models of group talk that will stretch and challenge students in different ways.

To some, discussion can feel 'natural', but for anyone who has set up an interesting group activity only to see it flounder as students quickly go off task, argue or simply opt out, the need to induct students into talk is only too obvious. It is common to set up tasks, for example role plays, where students are forced into productive talk behaviors, and then allow them to consciously reflect upon these behaviors in order to make explicit what it is that good speakers and listeners do – and this should include non-verbal aspects of productive talk behavior. In fairness to the National Literacy initiatives, such activities were included as part of teacher training material. There can be a feeling that some contexts present particular difficulties for establishing good oral work; Valerie Coultas' book *Constructive Talk in Challenging Classrooms: Strategies for Behaviour Management and Talk-based Tasks* (2006) may be a helpful resource to any teachers who consider their working environment presents particular problems for the development of oracy.

Varying size and composition of small groups, using techniques such as jigsawing, snowballing and rainbowing, and introducing increasingly sophisticated and more challenging topics and issues for discussion can promote progress as students face new contexts within which they develop their oral skills.

Whether speaking and listening takes place in whole classes or in small groups, Vygotsky's theory supports the importance of the teacher in ensuring that students make progress in their use of speech, and so ultimately in their capacity for thought. If we can assume that the teacher in the classroom is the most able user of language, then the careful modelling of language – in the introduction of vocabulary, the demonstration of key rhetorical devices associated with different speech genres, the phrasing of questions – is critical in introducing students to ways of using language effectively. In fact, whereas to the uninformed eye (or ear) the teacher's involvement in whole-class dialogic discussion, or her interventions in a small-group discussion, might make her seem less influential in comparison to the traditional model of teacher-led oral work, the opposite should be true. Certainly this is the case when teachers are acutely aware of their role in such discussions and of the links between language, thought and learning. Mercer found that 'a program of carefully designed teacher-led and group-based activities enables children not only to become better at talking and working together but also at solving problems alone' (2003, p. 76).

Monitoring and assessing progression in speaking and listening

In an age and culture of accountability, it is impossible to avoid questions of assessment and monitoring. We may set up activities and plan lessons that are designed to challenge students and enable them to make progress in their speaking and listening skills, but the problem often with talk is that – at the end of any given activity – there may be nothing concrete to assess. This is particularly the case when it comes to small-group work that is designed to develop ideas and thinking and where there may not be a direct product, and where it may be a challenge to accurately observe and assess the contributions of particular individuals in the group context. Clearly where there is some sort of formal talk product – the performance of a drama, the reading of a poem, a monolog, speech or presentation – then assessment is made much simpler for the teacher. It can even be the case that a group presentation can reveal the strength of the input to the presentation of a particular individual – though this need not necessarily be the case. An obvious way to monitor progress of individual students when more informal whole-class or small-group talk is happening is to keep notes in a markbook. Particular students' significant contributions to whole-class or small-group talk can be noted – and it can be useful to plan before a lesson a particular group of students who will be observed. Thus over the course of a few weeks or a half term comments on all students within a class can be collected. If a permanent record is required of a formal talk activity, then it is always possible to record students' work – this is ever more easy with voice recorders on phones and tablets. Such recordings could be used to moderate progress and assessment across an English department.

Policy decisions on the future of assessment of speaking and listening make this next section difficult. At the time of writing, it is held likely that speaking and listening will not be an assessed part of the English National Curriculum or examinations. In the past, much thinking about assessing speaking and listening was based on the 'levels' – descriptions of progress enshrined in the National Curriculum. While this has been the official position, there is a question as to what extent the National Curriculum levels are in fact helpful in describing progress in oracy. The levels themselves are imprecise, and though the best-fit descriptions have their strengths in that they offer an overall impression of how a student may perform, rather than suggesting a rigid checklist of features, the difference in wording between two levels is to some extent ambiguous. Students at level 6, for example 'adapt their talk to the demands of different contexts, purposes and audiences with increasing confidence', while those at level 7, the next level up and so presumably performing more skilfully, 'are confident in matching their talk to the demands of different contexts, including those that are unfamiliar' (QCA, 2010, p. 16). Aside from the addition of the unfamiliar contexts, there seems little to distinguish the descriptions. The 'fuzziness' of the levels is certainly one reason that they have been called into question in the most recent review of the National Curriculum. One problem of the 'fuzziness' in terms of speaking and listening in particular is that increasingly policymakers call into question teachers' assessments.

For those wanting to look at alternative models to describe what progress in speaking and listening might look like, the material provided by The Communication Trust may prove useful. A collaboration of voluntary and community organizations, The Communication Trust aims to support those who work with children to develop the speech and communication skills of young people. They have a particular concern for those children with specific communication needs, but their series of publications entitled *Universally Speaking* are an attempt to describe what progress in speaking and listening looks like from the early years through to eighteen. The two publications that relate specifically to the primary and secondary phase include descriptions of what young people should be able to do in their communication skills at certain ages in categories such as 'Vocabulary', 'Sentence structure and narrative' and 'Social Interaction'. In addition they provide checklists (appropriate for teachers) as to features of speech to look for at certain ages, and suggestions to help support the development of speaking and listening skills. As such, this material may not only help teachers identify students who may have specific difficulties, but also provide a useful supportive resource in monitoring and assessing the progress of students across the class. Certainly the material from The Communication Trust seems to provide much more concrete information on age-related talk and listening behavior than the general level descriptors of the National Curriculum.

The future for speaking and listening in the curriculum

It is somewhat disheartening to find that current indications suggest that impending curriculum policy in the UK will significantly downplay the importance of speaking and listening in the classroom. This is particularly depressing in the context of the report of the expert panel who were charged with the task of reviewing and making recommendations for the new National Curriculum in England. However, in a more promising move, the report dedicated its final chapter to 'Oral Language and its Development within the National Curriculum' (Department for Education, 2011). The chapter referenced both the seminal Bullock Report of 1975 and the work of the National Oracy Project in reaffirming what all good English teachers – indeed all good teachers whatever their discipline – know: the development of oracy in children is of critical importance to their cognitive development and their progress in learning. The report called for effective oral work to be embedded across the curriculum, not simply buried in a Speaking and Listening attainment target in English. The report also pointed to the work of The Communication Trust in its recommendation that a more robust model for progress in speaking and listening ought to be presented in the curriculum. In addition, the report noted the challenge that embedding good oral work across the curriculum would present and thus acknowledged the need for effective teacher education and development.

Despite the recommendations of the Expert Group, policymakers in England have apparently failed to appreciate the importance of oracy. The direction of travel of the National Curriculum in England is one that threatens to bypass oracy altogether; the dangers of this, given what we know, are clear. Children's development and achievement in the subject will suffer if those responsible for curriculum fail to pay more than lip service to talk.

Conclusions

Despite the apparent direction of public policy in the field in England, the strong research evidence that exists about the importance of oracy and its place at the very heart of students' learning and development should ensure that good speaking and listening work continues to thrive in English classrooms. However, if the official curriculum climate provides little support for teachers who advocate talk and group work, or worse still appears to marginalize or be hostile towards such practise, there is an increased onus on teachers to make the arguments to protect their practise. Thus the work of those such as James Britton, Douglas Barnes and Harold Rosen, the advances made by the National Oracy Project, and the theoretical underpinning should be at teachers' hands. In a hostile climate there is also even greater pressure on teachers to be able to articulate how the speaking and listening activities they undertake with students in classrooms enable the students to develop and progress as not only speakers and listeners, but as readers, writers and thinkers too. And, in an age of accountability, a model for monitoring, assessing and recording progress in these areas becomes of crucial importance.

References

Ball, S. (1985). 'English for the English Since 1906'. In Goodson, I. (ed.), *Social Histories of the Secondary Curriculum*. Sussex: Falmer Press.

—(1987). 'English teaching, the state and forms of literacy. Research on mother tongue Education'. In Kroon, S. and Sturm, J. (eds), *An International Perspective: Papers of the Second International Symposium of the International Mother Tongue*. Enshde: International Mother Tongue Education Network.

Ball, S., Kenny, A., and Gardiner, D. (1990). 'Literacy Politics and the Teaching of English'. In Goodson, I. and Medway, P. (eds), *Bringing English to Order*. Sussex: Falmer Press.

Barnes, D., Britton, J. and Rosen, H. (1969). *Language, the Learner and the School*. Harmondsworth: Penguin.

Black, P. and Wiliam, D. (1998). *Inside the Black Box: Raising Standards through Classroom Assessment*. London: GL Assessment.

Black, P., Harrison, C., Lee, C., Marshall, B. and Wiliam, D. (2003). *Assessment for Learning: Putting it into Practice*. Maidenhead: Open University Press.

Britton, J. (1970). *Language and Learning*. Harmondsworth: Penguin.

—(1987). 'Vygotsky's contribution to pedagogical theory'. In *English in Education, 21*(3), 22–6.

Clements, S., Dixon, J. and Stratta, L. (1963). *Reflections*. Oxford: Oxford University Press.

Coles, J. (2005). 'Strategic voices? Problems in developing oracy through "interactive whole-class teaching"'. *Changing English,* 12:1, 113–23.

Coultas, V. (2006). *Constructive Talk in Challenging Classrooms: Strategies for Behaviour Management and Talk-based Tasks*. London: Routledge.

Department for Children, Schools and Families (2008). *English in the National Curriculum*. London: The Stationery Office.

Department for Education (2011). *The Framework for the National Curriculum. A Report by the Expert Panel for the National Curriculum review*. London: Department for Education.

Department for Education and Science (1975). *A Language for Life (The Bullock Report)*. London: HMSO.

—(1989). *English in the National Curriculum*. London: HMSO.

Departmental Committee of the Board of Education (1921). *The Teaching of English in England (The Newbolt Report)*. London: HM Stationery Office.

Dixon, J (1967). *Growth through English*. London: Penguin.

Edwards, D. (2003). 'Purposes and Characteristics of Whole-class Dialog'. In *New Perspectives on Spoken English in the Classroom*. London: QCA.

Gibbons, S (2008). 'How L.A.T.E. it was, how L.A.T.E'. *English in Education*, 42(2), 118–30.

—(2009a). 'Back to the future – a case study in changing curriculum and assessment: the story of the London Association for the Teaching of English's alternative 'O' level English language paper'. *English in Education*, 43(1), 19–31.

—(2009b). 'Lessons from the past?' *English Teaching-Practice and Critique*, 8(1), 64–75.

—(2009c). '"To know the world of the school and change it" An exploration of Harold Rosen's contribution to the early work of the London Association for the Teaching of English'. *Changing English An International Journal of English Teaching*, 16(1), 93–101.

—(2013). *The London Association for the Teaching of English, 1947-67: A History*. London: Trentham/IoE Press.

Goodwyn, A. and Findlay, K. (1999). 'The Cox models revisited: English teachers' views of their subject and the National Curriculum'. *English in Education*, 33(2), 19–31.

LATE (1956). *The Aims of English Teaching: A Pamphlet Prepared for British Council Study Boxes to be used in India*. LATE Archive, London Institute of Education Library.

Marshall, B. (2000). 'A rough guide to English Teachers'. *English in Education,* 34(1), 24–41.

Mercer, N. (2000). *Words and Minds: How we Use Language to Think Together*. London: Routledge.

—(2003). '"The Educational Value of "Dialogic Talk" in "Whole-Class Dialogue"'. In *New Perspectives on Spoken English in the Classroom*. London: QCA, pp. 73–6.

QCA (Qualifications and Curriculum Authority, UK) (2003). *New Perspectives on Spoken English in the Classroom*. London: QCA.

—(2010). *The National Curriculum: Level Descriptors for Subjects*. Coventry: QCA.

Reid, R. (2003). 'The Persistent Pedagogy of "Growth"'. In B. Doecke, D. Homer and H. Nixon (eds), *English Teachers at Work: Narratives, Counter Narratives and Arguments*. Kent Town: Wakefield Press.

The Communication Trust. *Universally Speaking* – The ages and stages of children's communication development from 5 to 11, http://www.thecommunicationtrust.org.uk/media/7412/universally_speaking_5-11_final.pdf [accessed 26 January 2013].

—*Universally Speaking* – The ages and stages of young people's communication development from 11 to 18, http://www.thecommunicationtrust.org.uk/media/7817/universally_speaking_11-18_final.pdf [accessed 26 January 2013].

Vygotsky, L. (1978). *Mind in Society*. Cambridge, MA: Harvard University Press.

—(1986). *Thought and Language*. Cambridge, MA: MIT Press.

13 Dialogism and Technology

Carl Hendrick

Chapter Outline

In 2003 QCA (Qualifications and Curriculum Authority, UK) amended its guidance on speaking and listening to include dialogic teaching, an event that on the surface would which appear to signal a rapid acceptance of the tenets of dialogism into British state education. However, in many instances at the heart of government, policy on education is the very antithesis of meaningful dialog. For Robin Alexander (2008) the dynamic of dialogism is not only an imperative methodological framework for students but something that should be adopted by policymakers themselves as a means of creating and attenuating viable strategies:

> For in a centralising culture policy is legitimated by compliance rather than argument and the mantra 'evidence-based-policy' all too often means its opposite – that policy is devised first and its authors then look around, selectively, for evidence to justify it.
>
> (2008, p. 8)

For education policymakers the nascent power of Web 2.0 and its explosive technological affordances would present a whole new set of problems which would ultimately subvert and radically question traditional notions of educational research. The central issue has been the very rapid shift from a largely technologically monologic culture to a technologically dialogic culture and the frameworks within which policy could be implemented. Indeed the very frames of reference are often being eroded as fast as they are erected. The tipping point was the proliferation of information at a rate never before seen in human history, and its subsequent exponential trajectory. Internet usage has gone from approximately 260 million users in 2000 to 1.4 billion users in 2012. More alarmingly, children now have almost unrestricted access to the internet with the ubiquity of mobile devices. A recent survey (Childwise, 2011) showed that six out of ten children aged 7–16 have a mobile phone that can access the internet (61 percent), rising to three in four among 11–16s (77 percent).

However, in all too many classrooms the exchange between pupil and teacher is still a fixed dynamic of 'specific finalization' (Bakhtin, 1986). One of the most common inter-actions between teacher and student is still the IRE or 'initiation–response–evaluation' (Mehan, 1979), in which a teacher asks a question which is responded to by the pupil and then evaluated by the teacher, who had a pre-ordained answer. This dynamic is highly limiting (Cadzen, 1988/2001) and often disadvantages the majority of pupils as the trans-action can only occur between the teacher and one student. Indeed, the process is often used as a means of controlling a class and giving the semblance of 'covering' content or knowledge (Pressley and McCormick, 2007), while actually what is really occurring is a low-level and often tacit engagement with content. Many surveys support the view that the dominant mode of classroom talk is still the closed questioning of the IRE method (Galton, Simon and Croll, 1980; Nystrand and Gamoran, 1991). In addressing the question 'What ways of talking do children most commonly encounter in classrooms?' Lefstein and Snell argue that 'the dominant pattern of classroom discourse is problematically monologic' (Lefstein, 2011, p. 161). Indeed three decades of research would seem to corroborate this point (Cazden, 2001; Edwards and Westgate, 1994).

A further criticism is that students are rendered powerless in their own learning as they answer questions that they had no process in creating (Bowers and Flinders, 1990). From a dialogic perspective, this process is particularly negative as it compounds the notion that knowledge is something to be received from an authoritative figure as opposed to working with existing material to construct new knowledge through alternative dialogic frameworks (Pressley and McCormick, 2007). Within a very short space of time, the affordances of new internet technologies have allowed teachers to truly give students a new arena for learning, to enter a dialogic space where the limitations of the classroom could be not only arrested but radically reconfigured.

Using Google docs with a group of year 10 students I created an online forum where the aim was to allow them to transcend the temporal and spatial boundaries of the traditional classroom and enter into a 'dynamic process constituted through the interaction of past experience, ongoing involvement, and yet-to-be-accomplished goals' (Brown and Renshaw, 2006). The central idea was to get them to pay more attention to what other students were writing and to use the knowledge gained from that as a means of informing their own progress.

Writing tasks were set weekly in a series of topics where I provided the primary resources used in the classroom, a series of secondary resources such as wider reading and essays that allowed lesser/higher ability ranges to access the task and then a series of instructions which stipulated that I wanted qualitative analysis of their peers work in the form of bullet points such as:

- Something I do not understand
- Something I thought was highly effective
- Something that could be written better
- Something that could be expanded upon
- A word or phrase I can now adopt into my semantic field
- Three questions (arising from three contextual videos surrounding the task).

What was interesting was that the more-confident students in terms of classroom oral discourse held back initially and the less-vocal students in terms of the chronotope of the classroom posted their work first. An additional factor was the voices of students asking the type of questions that they would never normally ask in class such as:

At this point I would clarify the task:

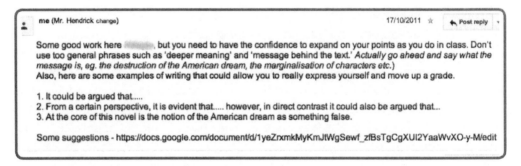

What was particularly effective about this was that students were now able to see one or two attempts at the task, *but also* some detailed formative feedback from the teacher.

Quite spontaneously, this seemed to elicit a similar type of constructive feedback from other students:

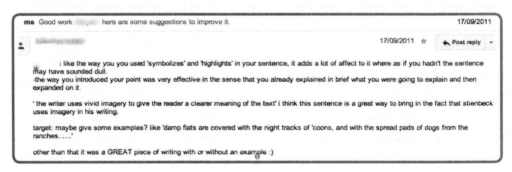

What is notable about this piece of feedback is that the student draws upon a polyphony of voices to frame her response. For example, in lauding her peer's use of words such as 'symbolizes' and 'highlights' she notes that it 'adds a lot of effect to it where as if you hadn't the sentence may have sounded dull'. Although clumsily phrased, I think that it is nonetheless heartfelt, and that for this student, the use of these analytical words by her peer elevates their work to a level beyond that which she might have achieved in the monlogic chronotopic space of many traditional classroom landscapes.

However in the next paragraph she praises her peer for the fact that she 'explained in brief what you were going to explain and then expanded on it'. This of course, is very much the voice of many an English teacher and their injunction to use P.E.E (point–evidence–explain) and indicates, I think, an awareness by this student of the fact that she is not just writing this for her peer but that there is a wider audience comprising her English teacher and possibly her parents.

An additional unforeseen aspect of this forum was the level of altruism between peers. Again this is something that is rarely displayed in the class or rather is not given a vehicle to be displayed within the all-too-often monologic dynamic of the aforementioned traditional classroom.

I like way you used really good vocabulary.
Such as 'vivid, linguistic& sinister'
This definitely creates a picture to me that you know exactly what your talking about.
 I definitely agree with ⬛⬛⬛ expand your work.
Make sure you analyse every single section, suck out all your GREAT IDEASSS!!!   Until you have nothing more to suck out.
But superb work definitely an A.
well done!

https://docs.google.com/document/d/1853uPfFcilQbMs1nr_g6-cnQ096nlPQZODhr

Although welcome, this kind of feedback can often be reductive and not formative in any way with students posting simple comments such as 'well done!' or even awarding wayward grades.

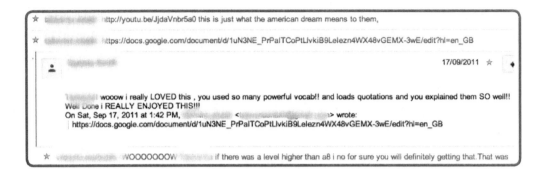

This dynamic of near-boundless interaction made actual by technology is defined by Clay Shirky as a 'cognitive surplus' (Shirky, 2010), whereby greater and greater pools of talent linked by a similar interest are now able to work together through technology regardless of geographical location.

Another very positive result was the linking of abstract ideas and contexts through media such as YouTube videos. One student comments on the interconnectivity inherent within the task, which then allowed me to encourage the student to further investigate the subject matter by exploring another aspect of the task.

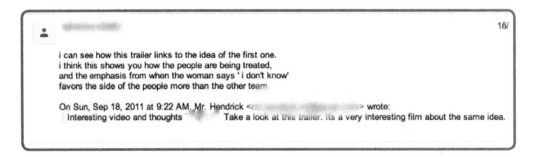

Through the affordances of technology, the means by which pupils address these types of activities has changed beyond all recognition from that which the curriculum makers originally envisaged. Pupils now not just construct meaning from an engagement with the original texts, but often have a polyphony of voices in the form of instant messaging from their peers (often from pupils outside their own class and ability range), an ongoing *dialogue* from student online forums, and in many cases through email contact with their teacher. The question then becomes how do we assess progress against such a radically different backdrop from that which the original framework of assessment was set?

Perhaps the problem lies with the fact that traditional notions of 'progress' in a truly dialogic English classroom are something that by their very nature resist classification and measurement. In the Bakhtinian sense they are very much 'unfinalizable'. A common illustration of this is when a group of pupils begin a certain task, such as the current (at the time of writing) AO2 focus on language (How does the author use language to show …), and then through a dialogic interchange (which can often include 'voices' and 'utterances' from beyond the range of their peers in the form of online interaction) the same group arrives at a radically different conclusion to other groups on even what the limits of the original task were, but which nonetheless indicates a high level of engagement, creativity and collaborative critical thought. At this point, pupils are usually expected to write their thoughts down, but often they are instructed to do so within the confines of a narrow set of parameters, within which they can 'progress' from a D to a C, measured, of course, by what they have written. Trying to catalog this type of learning within that set of parameters is all too often asynchronous with the spirit of the original dialogic enquiry.

An additional issue arising from this binary opposition between knowledge transmission and knowledge creation is to what extent are teachers involved in the actual production of knowledge? And when the situation arises where pupils need to acquire 'prior knowledge' in order to complete a task, how does the teacher facilitate that?

What technology has done for the secondary English classroom has been to not only reaffirm but vigorously reassert constructivist and social constructivist pedagogies, which put forward the notion that the intrinsic epistemological site of a poem, play or newspaper article is socially constructed, as opposed to something merely transmitted. With the advent of Web 2.0 technologies this reassertion has gathered momentum as knowledge has become democratized and available at the click of a button. Whereas students could previously have been subjected to a monologic presentation of social and historical 'facts' pertaining to a specific topic, those same students can now harness technology to construct, collate, modify and attenuate information to create a far richer tapestry of learning. The central question then becomes (perhaps more implicitly than explicitly) to what extent should teachers 'teach' when all the information, and the means by which to construct knowledge is now freely available?

The concomitant shift in terms of the traditional teacher within the new technological age then is one from 'arbiter of knowledge' to 'facilitator of learning'. This seismic shift in pedagogical dynamic has not divided teachers along the lines of age, but rather along the lines of technical proficiency and ambition, with many older teachers showing the kind of patience and ambition required to master new technological literacies. The current trend is certainly one that 'valorizes the virtual' (Goodfellow and Lea, 2007) but this has often has the effect of polarizing discourse on technology and creating a reductive 'either/or' mindset among many English teachers.

For Robin Alexander, there is however a clear disjunction to be made between the 'hands-off facilitator' (Alexander, 2008) and the more traditional teacher who merely tells or 'transmits' knowledge. Alexander bridges this gap to a certain extent by suggesting a model of 'learning to a specific cultural purpose' through a specific type of classroom intervention, a new approach that demands 'both pupil engagement and teacher intervention'. The principal vehicle, he argues, through which not only can pupils engage but teachers can affect or 'intervene' is talk. Alexander then highlights Daniel's recent work on activity theory which warns against classroom talk as being mere 'interaction' that can end up being 'narrowly conceived and bounded by the immediacy of the learning task in hand'. Too often, speaking and listening tasks can become perfunctory tasks where pupils will adopt roles imposed upon them (as in the Lacanian notion of language speaking itself) in terms of the both 'character' of the specific task and their 'character' as pupils within a largely monologic classroom, as opposed to the limitless possibilities of a dialogic engagement with the wider world as facilitated through technology.

This notion of 'purposeful' interventionist teaching within the techno-dialogic classroom landscape is an area that warrants much investigation and is of particular importance to classrooms where the dynamic is not conducive to a positive common goal. Key to this is the fact that children do not just merely 'discover' certain things through talk and interaction. Furthermore, the imperative of effective intervention within the dialogical framework is made more and more important by the fact that pupil success in the contemporary English classroom (and there are many ways to define success in a classroom but I am referring specifically to the creation and attainment of knowledge, not merely the memorization information) is largely defined by the relationship between teacher and pupil. Technology has augmented this dynamic in a very effective way through the use of online class groups, pupil–teacher contact through email and even class Twitter feeds.

Alexander goes on to point out that from the 1980s theories on teaching and learning radically shifted from the Piaget model of the child as a 'lone scientist' who develops through stimulating materials, to a model where the child learns through a dialogic engagement not just with the teacher and their immediate peers but also through 'conversations' with wider culture. This paradigmatic shift occurred chiefly through the development of theories from writers such as Vygotsky and later Bakhtinian dialogism. This notion of a 'wider conversation' and an ongoing dialog with wider culture has become a more pressing necessitation through the initial prevalence of the internet in the mid-1990s and then later the comprehensiveness of Web 2.0 technology with the now ubiquitous 'write-back' functionality. The 'texts' of wider culture are now in a constant dialogic exchange through the affordances of these new technological contingencies. Instead of digesting a news story as one might have done 15 years ago by reading it in a monologic exchange, people are now more likely to read the comment section and even often engage in dialog themselves with not only the author but a polyphony of voices from a now radically stratified community base. The 'meaning' then of such a text resides not in the original authoritative voice of the author, but in the polyphony of voices surrounding it. Social networking sites take these ideas further and can propel and 'restate' ideas back into the community through Twitter and Facebook, resulting in a situation where the attenuation of knowledge or 'meaning' is in a constant state of dialogic flux. The seeds of this de-construction of the 'author' figure as can be traced back to French post-structuralist thinkers such as Roland Barthes (1977):

> We know now that a text is not a line of words releasing a single 'theological' meaning (the 'message' of the Author-God) but a multi-dimensional space in which a variety of writings, none of them original, blend and clash. [. . .] Once the Author is removed, the claim to decipher a text becomes quite futile. To give a text an Author is to impose a limit on that text, to furnish it with a final signified, to close the writing.

Recent developments in technological contingency make positions such as these seem almost prophetic despite the fact that post-structuralists such as Barthes could have had no knowledge of the myriad of possibilities and technological affordances that the advent of the internet could offer.

Despite this paradigmatic shift in the location of 'meaning' and the ensuing technological growth, as mentioned earlier there still persists in Britain, and especially among policymakers, the retrograde notion that knowledge is something merely to be 'transmitted' to the pupils through a series of lessons where pupils digest information and are assessed through a series of standardized tests which are then aggregated nationally. This then gives rise to a wider debate about the democratization of knowledge and an often reductive and divisive debate between libertarian and conservative ideologies, a debate that, despite the protestations of many conservative commentators, often results in reactionary decision making. The ultimate example of this in schools today is the fact that most local authorities have created firewalls to control school (pupil) access to sites such as YouTube and Twitter and the plenitude of information and dialogic possibilities they contain, as opposed to setting out a framework to creatively deal with how that information is accessed and knowledge created

If English teachers and policymakers are to truly embrace the central tenets of dialogism within this new technological landscape, there needs to be a radical shift from viewing students as mere passive consumers of knowledge to active producers of knowledge within a rapidly changing technological world. For Scardamalia and Bereiter (2006) this paradigmatic shift represents not only a change in traditional ideological trajectories but also

> an attempt to refashion education in a fundamental way, so that it becomes a coherent effort to initiate students into a knowledge creating culture. Accordingly, it involves students not only developing knowledge-building competencies but also coming to see themselves and their work as part of the civilization-wide effort to advance knowledge frontiers. In this context, the Internet becomes more than a desktop library and a rapid mail-delivery system. It becomes the first realistic means for students to connect with civilization-wide knowledge building and to make their classroom work a part of it.

So how exactly should educators and policymakers create the conditions in which pupils can become creators of knowledge as opposed to mere passive consumers of it against the backdrop of rapid technological change? It is perhaps helpful here to look at how Bakhtin defines notions of self and other. For Bakhtin, the notion of a 'center' in relation to the subject is highly problematic. Michael Holquist (2002) writes:

It is important from the outset, then, that 'center' in Bakhtin's thought be understood for what it is: a relative rather than an absolute term, and, as such, one with no claim to absolute privilege, least of all one with transcendent ambitions.

For both the student and the teacher of English the concept of a 'relative Other' is vital in creating a truly dialogizing dynamic in two key respects, which I will define here as two main precepts:

1. There can be no 'fixed' meaning of any text or artwork.
2. The logocentric roles of pupil and teacher are themselves interchangeable.

First, in more traditional pedagogical discourse there is an absolute Other in the form of a definitive 'meaning' of a novel or poem for example. This meaning is then transmitted from teacher to pupil in the form of information which the pupil then 'digests' into what we can loosely term as knowledge. The relative attainment of any given pupil is then measured by their ability to regurgitate this information in a standardized test or essay. There is a very clear delineation then between self and Other (consciousness and 'meaning') in this dynamic that results in an apparent transcendent union in the form of a nominal synthesis. In dialogism, this transaction is radically subverted:

In dialogism, the very capacity to have consciousness is based on otherness. This otherness is not merely a dialectical alienation on its way to a sublation that will endow it with a unifying identity in higher consciousness. On the contrary: in dialogism consciousness is otherness. More accurately, it is the differential relation between a center and all that is not that center. (Holquist, 2002, p. 17)

Undoubtedly, technology provides the dialogizing infrastructure from which knowledge can be created through this disjunction between 'center and all that is not center'. In the English classroom then, true dialogic interchange can be said to reside in the liminal spaces *between* self and other. A very important aspect of Bakhtinian dialogism is the notion that there can be no privileged entity, no one position can have priority over another. Meaning is something always in transit, never arriving at any one location. Secondly, the relational interplay between pupil and teacher in a dialogic classroom assumes a more fluid dynamic. For example, instead of having the teacher ask questions which are then answered 'correctly' by a pupil, what might occur is an ongoing dialog where the pupil and teacher ask questions not of each other but of the text itself and possible interpretations of it. An example of a logocentric exchange with a fixed meaning might look like this:

> Example 1
>
> Teacher: 'What does the white flower in this poem symbolize?'
> Pupil: 'Purity.'
> Teacher 'Correct.'

Here, not only are teacher and pupil roles fixed but the relation to subject and meaning is at once static and final. For Bakhtin true dialogic expression is 'unfinalizable, always incomplete, and productive of further chains of responses: meaning is never closed and always oriented toward the future'. That is to say a final meaning cannot be truly arrived at in this closed way. In direct contrast, a dialogic exchange might look like this:

> Example 2
>
> Teacher: 'What could the white flower in this poem symbolize?'
> Pupil: 'Could it symbolize purity?'
> Teacher: 'Whose purity?'
> Pupil: 'Could it be the purity of the "central character"?'
> Teacher: 'Possibly, or could it be the purity of the author herself?'
> Pupil: 'It could be … or could it be that she is making a comment of a lack of purity within society itself?'
> Teacher: Can you find any more evidence from the text that might support that view?

In this example, although the teacher is facilitating the discussion, there are no clearly defined roles, both teacher and pupil are elucidating meaning by asking questions of each other and never quite arriving at a fixed meaning. It is also evident that in this exchange, a far higher level of engagement with the text is present where a more hermeneutic exploration takes place rather than a simple 'X = Y' conclusion. However, a further extension of this trajectory expedited through technology gives rise to an even greater dialogic possibility. Bakhtin (1984, p. 143) writes:

> Every level of expression from live conversational dialog to complex cultural expression in other genres and art works is an ongoing chain or network of statements and responses, repetitions and quotations, in which new statements presuppose earlier statements and anticipate future responses.

Example 3

In groups, pupils could be set a task of finding out various biographical pieces of information on the life of a particular poet and the factors that influenced the writing of a poem. From there, they could collaboratively sketch out a timeline of events that correlate with the events in the poem. In addition to this, another group of pupils could collapse all the words in the poem and evaluate the poem from a structuralist perspective. But perhaps the most powerful tool that technology affords pupils in this situation is the ability to transcend temporal and spatial parameters. By creating an online message board, or a virtual stick-note board, the teacher could create an arena where not only can pupils continue to construct meaning in a collaborative sense, but they can also review and peer-assess every other piece of work by every other pupil in the class (indeed in their year group if properly facilitated) and then bring in that learning to the next lesson to build on again. The work of Brown and Renshaw (2006) illustrates the possibilities of Bakhtin's dialogic principle within the traditional classroom when used to reorient traditional teacher/student roles via classroom positioning and a reorganization of temporal boundaries:

> The chronotope provides a way of viewing students participation in the classroom as becoming a situated, dynamic process constituted through the interaction of past experience, ongoing involvement and yet-to-be-accomplished goals.

However, the legitimacy of chronotopic application within the classroom dynamic has become hugely augmented by technology. How many more dialogs can students enter into through sitting in different groups as opposed to the near infinite number of dialogs available online?

A key facet to this shift in procedural dynamic is an emphasis on play, but play within the context of a framework of almost infinite informational regress. Thomas and Seely Brown define play as 'the tension between the rules of the game and the freedom to act within those rules' (2011, p. 18.) In order to maximize the effectiveness of play, it needs to be supplemented with questioning and creativity. An additional example of this new culture of engagement is the hitherto previously monologically seemingly impenetrable wall of Shakespeare and where meaning resides in relation to his work. Even in what might traditionally be termed a dialogic classroom, children learning about Shakespeare, for example, might have previously had a starter about what they know about a certain aspect of Shakespeare's life or a particular play. They then might have some teacher input followed by some group work where they are tentatively led towards a predefined learning objective whereby they would experience a plenary consolidating their knowledge. The lesson is broadly what Ofsted might term 'outstanding' if delivered in a certain way, under the four-part lesson rubric.

However within a post-Web 2.0 dialogic classroom pupils might again research a multitude of different historical and scholarly aspects of Shakespeare's life and arrive at a (aggregate) composite picture that is never quite 'closed' and that asks even more questions of the student, they then might use Google Maps to explore Stratford-upon-Avon or the Globe theater, they might then use interactive timeline software to collaboratively collate this information using multimodal forms such as text, video, images and speech. They might then create a revision mind-map of this work which would create a dialog with future versions of themselves and others.

A second major aspect is the creation of authentic (virtual) situations where students are aware of an audience other than their teacher. By giving students an arena where it is not simply their teacher reading their work but their peers, parents and the wider online community, they learn very rapidly to craft their work more carefully and be more attentive to its final result. This is perhaps best illustrated in the way students interact online today where every post and comment is recorded. Mercer et al. (2007) write that:

> In the 1990s, classroom-based observational research by ourselves and other colleagues, revealed that much of the interaction taking place was not of any educational value.

In all too many situations, students see group work as an opportunity to chat about other issues, or to let stronger students lead, or even to contribute nothing at all. The problem here is one of accountability. Mercer et al. (2007) continues:

> [In reference to exploratory talk] students should be encouraged in such discussions to make all relevant knowledge publicly accountable.

This notion of 'all relevant knowledge' being 'publicly accountable' is given a new and perhaps radical possibility through the technological affordances of online collaboration. A simple Google document can be shared with an entire class during or outside a lesson, whereby pupils are directly accountable for what they write. Equally significant is what pupils don't write in a virtual space. When pupils are given a task whereby they are asked to, say, write down an introductory sentence or paragraph to a proposed essay, what is often observed is a completely different dynamic to classroom discussion. The more orally confident pupils will often write nothing until other pupils have written something down. They will wait, staring at their screens and then when five or so examples have been written, only then will they write something. The fact that their work is 'publicly accountable' transforms the task and its learning possibilities, most notably in the exponential learning through peer assessment.

Technology offers the opportunity for dialogic interaction to happen outside the confines of the classroom, without the actual presence of another person and, more radically, without the need for simultaneity. The affordances of new technology in the form of online forums, message boards and other Web 2.0 software allow the learner to transcend temporal and spatial parameters and engage with others who they would never otherwise engage with. An everyday example of this is when a message is posted in an online forum and is read, engaged with and replied to weeks, months maybe even years after the original topic was posted and yet the comment is still 'publically accountable' and continues in an ongoing chain of dialog long after the utterance was formed. Furthermore, being able to place vital bits of information that scaffold learning in an online space further asks the question of what exactly the role of the teacher is today. What this dynamic effectively does is subvert the traditional classroom and provide what is commonly referred to now as the 'flipped classroom' model, a term coined by J. Wesley Baker in 2000 which refers to the notion of pupils creating and consuming knowledge that would previously have been transmitted by the teacher in the classroom primarily through the use of short instructional videos which then leaves classroom time available to the application of that knowledge in groups and further exploration. In this arena, the teacher very much conforms to Alexander's model of the 'hands off facilitator'.

Over the next 20 years the traditional problems facing English teachers, of low literacy and getting students to read will be usurped by the more complex problem of trying to marry these boundless worlds of information and knowledge afforded by technology with the traditional structures of discipline that will make the best use of them. Now more than ever, Bakhtin's notion that the locus of an objective 'truth' does not reside in the individual but rather in the collective has never been more pertinent:

> Truth is not born nor is it to be found inside the head of an individual person, it is born between people collectively searching for truth, in the process of their dialogic interaction. (Bakhtin, 1984, p. 110)

The bald truth is that, as Marc Prensky (2001) points out, 'Our students have changed radically. Today's students are no longer the people our educational system was designed to teach'. Until relatively recently, technology had not afforded the opportunity for effective dialogic teaching and learning (Wegerif, 1996, 1997). Although the Smartboard and the ubiquitous PowerPoint became mainstays in contemporary classrooms, their affordances were primarily monologic. They essentially did what the blackboard did but in a brighter, more vibrant way. Today the affordances of technology can provide the type of processing power that took up whole floors of the MIT building in the 1970s and now place that same technology in the pocket of every child at a fraction of the cost, and this dynamic is increasingly exponentially. However, in too many cases, there is at present a singular failure of imagination and ambition to harness this technology to facilitate a truly dialogic interaction.

At third level, technological integration as a means of dialogic interaction is at a far higher level with many prestigious universities now offering whole courses online. The emphasis is very much on social interaction and connectivity as a means of constructing meaning. Robin Goodfellow and Mary Lea (2007, p. 6) refer to nascent technologies as 'sites of practice in which activity and meaning-making are shaped by the social relations derived from the wider social and institutional setting within which educational interaction is played out'. So if Universities can get it right why is it that the primary and secondary sectors cannot? Too often pupils are instructed to use outmoded forms of technology such as PowerPoint to present a summary of a novel or poem.

Conclusion

The challenge then for the dialogic English classroom of the future is not the traditional one of how to provide content, but rather how to provide the best conditions in which students cannot just be passive consumers of knowledge but active co-creators of it and to curate and develop that same content (now in a state of constant fluid dialogic exchange) collectively and creatively, in order to maximize their own knowledge and understanding.

References

Alexander, Robin (2008). 'Towards dialogic teaching', *Dialogos*, 4th edn (15 March 2008).

Baker, J. Wesley (2000). 'The "Classroom Flip": Using Web Course Management Tools to Become the Guide by the Side.' Selected Papers from the 11th International Conference on College Teaching and Learning (11th, Jacksonville, Florida, 12–15 April 2000).

Bakhtin, M. M. (1984). *Problems of Dostoevsky's Poetics*. Caryl Emerson (ed. and trans.). Minneapolis: University of Minnesota Press.

—1986. 'The Problem of Speech Genres.' *Speech Genres and Other Late Essays*, pp. 76–7. Vern W. McGee (trans.), Caryl Emerson and Michael Holquist (eds). Austin: University of Texas Press.

Barthes, Roland (1977). *The Death of the Author, Image-Music-Text*, S. Heath (trans.). New York: Hill and Wang, pp. 142–8.

Bowers, C. A. and Flinders, D. (1990). *Responsive Teaching: An Ecological Approach to Classroom Patterns of Language, Culture, and Thought*. New York: Teachers College Press.

Brown, R. and Renshaw, P. (2006). 'Positioning students as actors and authors: a chronotopic analysis of collaborative learning activities'. In *Mind, Culture and Activity*, Vol. 13(3), (1984). pp. 247–59.

Cazden, C. B. [1988] (2001). *Classroom Discourse: The Language of Teaching and Learning*, 2nd edn. Portsmouth, NH: Heinemann.

Edwards, A. D. and Westgate, D. P. G. (1994). *Investigating Classroom Talk*, 2nd edn. Lewes: Falmer Press.

Galton, M., Simon, B. and Croll, P. (1980). *Inside the Primary Classroom*. London: Routledge and Kegan Paul.

Goodfellow, Robin and Lea, Mary (2007). *Challenging E-Learning in the University: a Literacies Perspective (Society for Research into Higher Education)*. Maidenhead and New York: McGraw Hill: Open University Press.

Holquist, Michael [1990] (2002). *Dialogism: Bakhtin and His World*, 2nd edn. London: Routledge.

Lefstein, A. and J. Snell (in press). 'Classroom Discourse: The Promise and Complexity of Dialogic Practice.' In S. Ellis, E. McCartney and J. Bourne (eds). *Insight and Impact: Applied Linguistics and the Primary School*. Cambridge: Cambridge University Press.

Mehan, H. (1979). *Learning lessons: Social Organization in the Classroom*. Cambridge: Harvard University Press.

Mercer, N., Dawes, L., Sams, C. and Fernandez, M. (2007). 'Computers, Literacy and Thinking together'. In A. Adams and S. Brindley (eds), *Teaching Secondary English with ICT*. Maidenhead: Open University Press, pp. 3–4.

Nystrand, M. and Gamoran, A. (1991). 'Instructional discourse, student engagement, and literature achievement.' *Research in the Teaching of English, 25*(3), 261–90.

Prensky, Mark (2001). 'Digital natives, digital immigrants Part 2: Do they really think differently?'. *On the Horizon*, Vol. 9, No. 6, pp. 1–6.

Pressley, M. and McCormick, C. B. (2007). *Child and Adolescent Development for Educators*. New York: Guildford Press.

Scardamalia, M. and Bereiter, C. (2006). 'Knowledge Building: Theory, Pedagogy, and Technology'. In K. Sawyer (ed.), *Cambridge Handbook of the Learning Sciences* (pp. 97–118). New York: Cambridge University Press.

Shirky, Clay (2010). *Cognitive Surplus: Creativity and Generosity in a Connected Age*. London: Penguin. pp. 1–3.

Thomas, Douglas and Seely Brown, John (2011). *A New Culture of Learning: Cultivating the Imagination for a World of Constant Change*. Amazon: CreateSpace.

Wegerif, R. (1996). 'Collaborative learning and directive software', *Journal of Computer Assisted Learning, 12*: 22–32.

—(1997). 'Factors Affecting the Quality of Children's Talk at Computers', in R. Wegerif and P. Scrimshaw (eds), *Computers and Talk in the Primary Classroom*. Clevedon: Multilingual Matters.

Wegerif, R. and Scrimshaw, P. (eds) (1997) *Computers and Talk in the Primary Classroom*. Clevedon: Multilingual Matters.

Web: CHILDWISE – Monitor Survey 2011–12 – Press Release – 10 January 2012 (accessed June 2012).

Part 5
CONCLUSION

Progress in English

14

Bethan Marshall

Chapter Outline

English has been beset by problems as to what it means to be good at the subject. Students get better at talking, reading and writing from five to 18 and beyond but how they do it is much more controversial. Long have people argued as to what proficiency means and this chapter is no exception. It takes a point of view that some will disagree with. In it I will argue that English is essentially an arts subject – that someone good at English learns to use the language imaginatively, but with purpose, and that in doing so they perceive how others have used it too. The stages of progress, however, are fuzzy and vague.

This contrasts, in some ways, with two theories that have come to the fore in English teaching – genre theory, or systemic functional linguistics, which has been particularly influential in Australia, and 'grammar for writing', which has come to prominence in the UK. And it is with these two theories that this chapter will first look at before considering English as an art. It must be said also that I will look at genre theory and 'grammar for writing' from a UK perspective and this is particularly so of genre theory because it has developed slightly differently in the UK, concentrating more on literary genres rather than the linguistic.

Other theories have been influential too, especially critical literacy, but like English as an arts subject this has not set out a deliverable means of progression. In contrast both genre theory and 'grammar for writing' were established to help less advantaged children access English, in particular written English. Both argued that for many English was just a matter of writing more and getting better but that for some the mechanics of English was important in gaining fluency. So both focused attention on the details of the language – how it was formed and worked.

The teaching of grammar was not new. The formalities and so-called rules of grammar had been taught since the introduction of English, but this formalism went out of fashion in the late sixties and early seventies. Part of the problem was that it was a very prescriptive approach to grammar and was taught separately from anything else. Pupils learned the parts of speech and did clause analysis but this was in no way related to how they, or other people, wrote. Arid exercises were plowed through but little was said about how it might improve their writing. And so, certainly in the UK, this formal teaching of the rules of grammar was largely abandoned. If it was discussed it was done largely in the context of what a child had written.

Replacing it was the idea of 'Growth through English' (Dixon, 1967), which came to prominence after the influential International Federation of Teachers of English (IFTE) Dartmouth conference, held in the USA in 1967. John Dixon was a UK academic but his view of English was accepted by most of those who attended the conference. His view was a curious mixture of a student increasing in maturity in general and improving the quality of their English in particular. Growth, essentially, came about through exposure to life and then writing about it. The work of James Britton (1974) was significant, too. Influenced by the Russian psychologist Vygotsky (1978a, b) Britton argued that children learn through the language they use. English teaching became vital, then, in the development of children because it was essentially a subject about language – about thought, speech and written expression.

The nature of progress was, however, ill defined. In the early eighties a new type of rigor was coming into English teaching and the ad hockery that had characterized the growth through English model was questioned. If English teachers could not explain how their pupils developed, except in vague terms, then this was no good. 'Grammar for writing' and genre studies came into this gap. They both attempted to explain how and why children got better.

Grammar for writing

As early as 1987, and The Kingman Report (DES and WO, 1988), grammar of a different kind to the rigid model that had existed previously, was attempting to make a comeback. The Kingman Report, published in England and Wales, established that grammar was an essential part of English teaching and said that teachers should have some knowledge of it if they were going to teach the subject. Set up, as a result of this, was Language in the National Curriculum, a vast network of advisors who worked on projects with serving teachers which eventually made their way into a report called by the same title (Carter, 1991).

The report, however, never saw the light of day. It took grammar descriptively and analyzed how people spoke and used language. It was aided, in England, by the publication of first the Cox Report (DES and WO, 1989) and then the National Curriculum for English (DES and WO, 1990). Professor Brian Cox, the chair of the committee, had also served on Kingman and his curriculum demanded that children had a knowledge about language but not a rule book. The then Conservative government disagreed and wanted a return to the more traditional values they believed grammar embodied. They equated written standard English with standards of behavior (see for example Tebbit, cited in Graddol et al., 1991, and Rae, cited in ibid.).

It took a Labour government, however, to formally introduce the phenomena we now call 'grammar for writing'. This was not the same as the conservative wish for grammatical rules to be introduced, nor the grammar suggested by the Kingman Report, it was more a way of helping all children come to terms with the basics of the language. First introduced in the literacy hour in England's primary schools in 1998, and in the secondary sector in 2001, it was felt that children needed the so-called fundamentals of language before they could proceed with writing in general. A systematic program, through the literacy hour, was established so that they could be taught. Language was parcelled up and served out in neat packages throughout a child's primary education and much of it was then repeated when they got to secondary school.

The literacy framework was in part based on the premise that teaching grammar explicitly would improve the quality of children's written work and in so doing help them in later life. As David Blunkett, then Secretary of State for Education wrote on the cover of the literacy framework, 'All our children deserve to leave school equipped to enter a fulfilling adult life. If children do not master the basic skills of literacy and numeracy they will be seriously disadvantaged later' (DfEE, 1998).

It was taken up with some enthusiasm, particularly in the primary sector. Even in secondary schools it was not dismissed, because it appeared to have a certain rigor, which had been lacking before. It provided an explanation, or schemata, for how pupils improved. Texts were analyzed for the use of verbs and adjectives. Teaching was introduced on parts of speech and clause analysis in the hope that evidence of use would be found in pupils' writing.

Pupils given the literacy hour, in England, have now reached 16. If we look at Jane, who was identified as being reasonably good at English, and compare her work written in the last year of primary school and then four years later, at the end of her fourth year in high school, we can see distinct progression.

Age 10

Andy was the new kid in school. He'd just moved here from Lakewood elementary. He'd just started but he'd noticed that something was funny about this new town. They all walk around in straight lines and never look anywhere except at what's directly infront of them. They are always busy and never stop working. The weirdest thing of all is they never seemed to sleep.

Andy felt strange and uncomfortable. He didn't know how to act around these people because they seemed so unatural!

Age 15

> The little house had been built seventy or eighty years ago, on the main street of what had been a village miles outside the town; now the town had crept up on all sides. Initially there had only been one floor, but at some point along the way an extra room had been added above the kitchen. On a clear day from a window in the upstairs room you could still see the mountains to the southwest. It was here that Aicha liked to sit, where she would run her fingers over her beads as she considered how greatly her life had changed since her son had brought her to the town to live with him. Somewhere behind the mountains amongst the forest of trees was the valley where she had passed her life. She didn't expect to see it again.

Jane's writing, on the surface, does show some evidence of the effects of 'grammar for writing'. To begin with, at 10, Jane is inconsistent in the tenses she uses, shifting from the past tense into the present half way through the description she is writing. Almost all her sentences, too, begin with a main noun, the subject of the sentence – 'Andy', 'he' and 'they'. Yet at the age of 15 her tenses are consistent and she has a variety of beginnings. Pupils are asked to alter the way they start sentences for effect and to vary sentence length and both of these she does. She also uses a variety of punctuation – the comma, inconsistently, the full stop and the semi-colon, and her paragraphs are longer too.

There is the use of the subordinate clause as well, 'It was here that Aicha liked to sit, where she would . . . ' and 'Somewhere behind the mountains amongst the forest of trees was the valley where she had passed her life'. She misses the commas in the second sentence but there is a sophistication in the way she describes where the valley where her village was 'behind the mountains amongst a forest of trees'.

And this is where the arguments for grammar begin to have problems. Her use of punctuation is faulty but her vocabulary is not. The valley was not only behind mountains it was 'amongst' a 'forest of trees'. The use of the word 'amongst' has a slightly old-fashioned feel, like that of Aicha, which is compounded by the spelling out of the forest – 'of trees'. She ends with a short sentence but the important thing about it is that it works within the prose. It has a slightly plaintive, melancholic air, one of regret. Something more then, than simply the grammar, is at work. There is a lexical density about the passage that plays on the mind of the audience who is reading it and it is Jane's ability to do this, more than the grammatical details, some of which she does not do, that make the paragraph work.

In 1999 the Qualifications and Curriculum Authority in England commissioned Deborah Myhill to research into the effectiveness of grammar for writing. Published under the title *Improving Writing at Key Stage 3 and 4*, Myhill examined the work of pupils in the secondary sector and found a greater complexity of grammatical usage in the candidates who were deemed better at English than those who were not. The work concludes with a section entitled 'Implications for Teaching', much of which revolves around explicit teaching of grammatical features at word, sentence and text level.

But also in *Improving Writing at Key Stage 3 and 4,* Myhill admits that the 'reader–writer relationship' was the usual 'strength of the piece' (QCA, 1999, p. 23). In other words giving, for example, 'varies sentence length' as a criterion for a good piece only works if something other the grammar is applied in interpreting it. The pupil must have a good ear for language, a sense of prosody, as the extracts from Jane's writing show.

More recent studies have also cast doubt over the efficacy of grammar teaching for improving writing. One major literature review, looking at all the research done in the past 30 years or so, was carried out into whether or not the explicit teaching of grammar helped improve the quality of pupils' writing (EPPI, Andrews, 2004, and Andrews et al., 2006). While they found that it is probably worth teaching for its own sake, as part of knowledge about how language works, they concluded that teaching grammar in itself does nothing to improve writing. It gave pupils an elaborate metalanguage for describing a text but did not help them write it in any way.

Genre theory

'Grammar for writing', however, was not the only source of for improving pupils' work. Another major influence, as we have seen, was that of genre theory and this gave pupils a new but different metalanguage. Genre theory came into being through the work of Michael Halliday (1994) and Jim Martin (1992) in the early 1980s in Australia, with systemic functional linguistics and was developed by people such as Cope and Kalantzis (1993). Halliday and Martin felt that while many pupils progressed well in English, a minority did not, particularly children who were in some way disadvantaged. At first, genre theory was aimed specifically at these pupils. Again they had a linguistic source for their suggestions as to how they might progress in English. They identified specific genres in school writing, which they broke down into linguistic components, which could then be taught.

Genre theory shares much in common with assessment for learning practises. It required that teachers always made explicit the criteria by which they were writing, to the pupils. The specific components of any piece of writing were always analyzed and made clear. This later became a key component of the AfL technique (Black et al., 2003). Genre theory, however, became much more widespread than the initial pilot and a degree more complex too. It looked beyond simple types of school writing to all writing in general and in particular the relationship between the genre and the society, that defined it. Clare Wyatt Smith defines it thus:

> In particular, the model explores systematically how the structure of language enables people to achieve their communication purposes in social contexts. From this position, learning the genres of one's culture is a necessary part of becoming a successful participant in the culture.
>
> (Morgan and Wyatt-Smith, 2000, p. 127)

Genre theory also took hold in England and became part of the literacy strategy too, particularly at secondary level. It gave pupils a way of describing what they were doing – again it gave a metalanguage. If we look once again at Jane, our candidate who was exposed to the literacy strategy from the beginning of schooling, we can see the influence of genre theory, applied this time to literature (which as we have seen was much more typical in England than it was in Australia). Both pieces of writing fall into a specific genre. Though it is not immediately apparent the first piece of writing was written for suspense, the second – revenge.

The second was also written having read the short story 'The Vendetta' by Guy de Maupassant (1903), which concerns a mother avenging her son's death. In the previous year Jane had done much work on this particular genre of story. She had filled in many charts, identified key characters, thought about plot devices, all dealing with suspense and revenge. What we see in this short story is in a way the fruition of that work.

In the opening paragraph we see her setting the scene. In a curious way the passage also reflects Maupassant's style of writing. Although it is by no means the same, the slightly old-fashioned, almost elegiac form echoes the stark prose style of the Maupassant translation, which she read. While Maupassant's short story is Mediterranean, hers, because of the name, has a Middle-Eastern feel. But both these reflect Wyatt-Smith's strictures on what should be included in genre theory. She has reflected the style and context of the story.

Yet it goes beyond this. If we compare the story to that which she wrote when she was ten, we find a similar, if less sophisticated, attempt to produce the same effect – a starkness in the feel of what she is writing. As a ten-year-old, Jane has a kind of journalistic precision in the way in which she conveys the information. Although the passages are very different in some respects, there is nevertheless a voice that appears in the ten-year-old's work. It is possible, then, that she wrote like Maupassant subconsciously, or even coincidentally, rather than consciously to create an effect. And here we find a difficulty with genre theory. Some of the writing that pupils do may not be a deliberate attempt to imitate the genre.

There may be another problem too. In the first piece of writing, Jane was given no help whatsoever in what she wrote. She was simply asked to write a story that was slightly scary and would make people want to read on. At that point she had not encountered suspenseful writing formally in school at all. She took about 15 minutes to complete the task. The result is something like a cross between *The Midwich Cuckoos* (Wyndham, 1957) and *The Stepford Wives* (Levin, 1975/2004), the characters walking around like automata. What Jane appears to have been able to do, intuitively, is enter a kind of imaginative space that enables her to see the people involved and then convey this in an albeit simple form. This is the skill she possesses, not a mastery of the conventions of this type of writing. Even the familiar baldness of the opening phrase, 'Andy was the new kid in school' works perhaps because it is something of a cliché.

Genre theory has come under scrutiny as well. To begin with, the number of genre has increased exponentially. Whereas at the beginning there were just a few types of writing that pupils encountered during the course of their school career, the number now has risen considerably. But it is the way it is taught that has also been criticized. Much of genre theory is taught using writing frames which can be restrictive, a gap-filling exercise that prompts little thought, discussion or imagination (see Fones, 2001). Lists of what the genres consist of can make writing a dull almost mechanistic exercise where pupils try to fulfill the requirements of the list but are in no way asked to be creative. And this too defeats the purpose of writing. While arguing vociferously for genre theory, the writers Christie and Misson argue 'Good writers in fact often play with the genre' (1998, p. 11). In other words good writers do something else other than repeat the rules of the genre.

Moreover it has been argued that genre has become what it was never intended to be: a knowledge-based model of learning (see Wyatt-Smith and Murphy, 2001). What becomes important is knowing what a particular style of writing consists of: like 'grammar for writing', the terminology becomes the thing that is significant.

English and the art of language

If 'grammar for writing' and genre theory, which apparently chartered progression in a very organized, systematic manner, have come into question, what then do we replace them with? This is where the language as an art form comes in. One way of describing the improvements made in Jane's work is that she has developed artistry – that amorphous quality that is ill defined and hard to quantify. In a way this is not unlike the Growth through English model but even that model had at its heart language development. Children improved in English through using the language they spoke.

Peter Abbs, who in the eighties classified English teachers, saw such teachers as the 'socio linguist school'. Instead he argued that we should see 'English not as a literary-critical discipline, but as a literary-expressive discipline within the wider epistemic community of the arts' (Abbs, 1982, p. 33). Abbs' view of English and art, despite calling it 'progressive', ends up as rather elitist, but the idea of seeing English in this way is a good one. Both 'grammar for writing' and genre theory tend to eliminate the aesthetic when considering a piece of work, concentrating instead on the how something is written rather than what is written, the means rather than the meaning.

If we take one last look at Jane's writing we can see that concentrating on the meaning of writing rather than the means makes a huge difference to how we see what might be going on. As a ten-year-old she muddled her tenses, got them confused so that she started writing in the present tense when she should have been writing in the past. If, however, we do not examine her work from a grammatical perspective, we see that it is possible that she became so involved in what she was writing that it became immediate, as if it were actually happening there and then. The flaw, if we can call it that, lies not so much in how it was written but in what she was writing. Remediation would not involve correcting the tenses per se, merely reminding her that all events, however real, took place in the past.

The act of writing becomes so much more than fulfilling certain rules of grammar or genre. It becomes about having something to say. John Dewey, who wrote extensively on progressive education and work within the arts in particular, wrote 'There is all the difference in the world between having to say something and having something to say' (Dewey, 1899, p. 67). And this, in some respects, becomes the essential difference between these two modes of progression in English, 'grammar for writing' and genre, and English as a language art. English, as a language art is about conveying or interpreting meaning. People progress and get better but not according to a neat road map that can be chartered and mapped out, or written up in a government document.

Elliot Eisner, writing in 2002 in *The Arts and the Creation of Mind*, grappled with what it meant to create art. In it he writes 'The linguistic act is the product of a linguistic imagination. The attitude required to use language of this kind is one that eludes the limiting constraints of literalism in perception and allows one to enter work emotionally' (Eisner, 2002, p. 88). And this is what Jane has done. She has entered into the world of the imagination and recreated that world in words. The fact that she is more proficient at this at 15 than she is at ten does not mean that something else is going on; it just means that she has got better at expressing what she wants to say. There is an art to writing, which defies the rules.

For Eisner, art is about 'judgement in the absence of rules. Indeed, if there were rules for making such choices, judgement would not be necessary' (ibid., p. 77). He goes on to write 'Work in the arts, unlike many other rule-governed forms of performance, always leaves the door open to choice, and choice in this domain depends upon a sense of rightness' (ibid., p. 77). His notion of judgment and also the sense of rightness depend upon an appreciation of the aesthetic and of artistry. 'Artistry', for Eisner, consists in having an idea worth expressing, the imaginative ability needed to conceive of how, the technical skills needed to work effectively with some material [in English the medium being words], and the sensibilities needed to make the delicate adjustments that will give the forms the moving qualities that the best of them possess (ibid., p. 81).

When creating a piece of work in English, therefore, what becomes crucial is the message you are trying to convey – the meaning of the text – and then choosing how you are going to produce it. It means that 'grammar for writing' and genre theory have a place but a subsidiary one. Rather than having a neat order of progression in English, one builds up a repertoire. Implicit within the term is the sense of a body of knowledge acquired through exposure, experimentation and practise. It connotes technique, artistry and interpretation but not an order in which they should be acquired. Above all it means that in English, judgment is practised and this is where criticism comes in.

We teach novels, plays, poetry and film for numerous reasons. We might teach a poem or a play for pleasure but also because we wish to see the language the writers use to describe the world they are in. We could teach a novel partly because the writer is worth reading in their own right, and partly because in so doing we can see how other people have used imagery to create effect. We may look at films to discuss how they impact on us as an audience or to consider theories of narrative. We study adverts because we want to see how people make us want to buy a product or text messages because we want to know how people are changing modes of communication. And in so doing we gain judgment. We learn of people's opinions about plays, their point of view on a text they have studied and all the time their judgment is called into question, challenged by those around them in the class. Each time our views on the novel, the poem the film are refined and we are able to talk about them with increased sophistication.

But English as a language art has not only this practical effect that helps us progress, it enhances our standing within arts education in general. Eisner wrote,

> Work in the arts is not only a way of creating performances and products; it is a way of creating our lives by expanding our consciousness, shaping our dispositions, satisfying our quest for meaning, establishing contact with others and sharing a culture. (Eisner, 2002, p. 3)

Like Dewey, this is not an elitist view of culture. In fact Dewey was very keen that culture and aesthetics should not become elitist terms. He saw, 'The continuity of the aesthetic experience with the normal process of living' (Dewey, 1934/2005, p. 9). While slightly oversimplifying his position, Dewey believed that art arose out of a person's ability to shape the experiences they had, to give them or to perceive 'pattern and structure'. ·

In this respect he saw art as entirely about our ability to see things aesthetically, as about 'interaction between a live creature and some aspect of the world' (Dewey, 1934/2005, p. 45). But he saw more. Art, he claimed was also about people producing or creating works of art. For him artistry interwove these two elements: the ability to appreciate something as an audience and the ability to create or produce an artifact. The artist, then, is a person who can stand within an experience and outside it simultaneously. In so doing they have a dual perspective which enables them to position themselves as both as the audience and creator at the same time. 'To be truly artistic,' Dewey wrote, 'a work must be aesthetic – that is framed for enjoyed receptive perception' (ibid. p. 49).

In their book *The Reader in the Writer* (2002), Myra Barrs and Valerie Cook found something similar. Working with children of primary school age they noted that pupils read books and used them in their writing but not in any systematic way. In other words they did not follow the rules of any particular genre but rather played with ideas and expression to create new effects. Moreover reading books helped them have a sense that they were writing for someone. It gave them a sense of audience, that what they wrote was 'framed for enjoyed receptive perception' (ibid., p. 49).

Conclusion

It seems in some ways unsatisfactory to say that people progress in English in a haphazard manner, particularly if one is writing about the subject, but if one thinks about it for more than a short while it becomes true. We do not progress in English in an orderly way. It is slightly chaotic. That does not mean, however, that we should teach the subject any old how and our pupils will improve. There is a method. To begin with we should tell people why they are studying English, constantly, and in that context expose them to the full repertoire that the subject offers. Grammar plays its part and so does studying genre but they have their place. In the end English is about art.

References

Abbs, P. (1982). *English Within the Arts: A radical alternative for English and the Arts in the curriculum*. London, Hodder and Stoughton.

Andrews, R. (2004). *The Effect of Grammar Teaching (Syntax) in English on 5–6 Year Olds' Accuracy and Quality in Written Composition*. London: EPPI.

Andrews, R., Torgerson, C., Beverton, S., Freeman, A., Locke, T., Low, G., Robinson, A. and Zhu, D. (2006). 'The effect of grammar teaching on writing development.' *British Educational Research Journal, 32*(1), 39–55.

Black, P. J., Harrison, C., Lee, C., Marshall, B. and Wiliam, D. (2003). *Assessment for Learning: Putting It into Practise*. Buckingham: Open University Press.

Carter, R. (ed.) (1991). *Language in the National Curriculum: The LINC reader*. London: Hodder and Stoughton.

Christie, F. and Misson, R. (1998). 'Framing the Issues in Literacy Education.' In F. Christie and R. Misson (eds), *Literacy and Schooling*. London: Routledge.

Cope, B. and Kalantzis, M. (1993). *The Powers of Literacy: A genre approach to teaching writing*. Pittsburgh: University of Pittsburgh Press.

DES and WO (1988). *A Report of the Committee of Inquiry into the Teaching of English* [The Kingman Report]. London: HMSO.

—(1989). *English for Ages 5–16* [The Cox Report]. London: HMSO.

—(1990). *English in the National Curriculum*. London: HMSO.

DfEE (1998). *The National Literacy Strategy*. London: HMSO.

—(2001). *KS3 Literacy Framework*. London: HMSO.

Dewey, J. (1899). *The School and Society, Being Three Lectures by John Dewey*. Chicago: University of Chicago Press.

—(1934/2005). *Art as Experience*. New York: Perigree.

Dixon, J. (1975). *Growth Through English*. Oxford: Oxford University Press.

Eisner, Eliot (2002). *The Arts and the Creation of Mind*. New Haven: Yale University Press.

Fones, D. (2001). 'Blocking them in to Free Them to Act: Using Writing Frames to Shape Boys' responses to Literature in the Secondary School.' *English in Education, 35*(3).

Graddol, D., Maybin J., Mercer, N. and Swann, J. (eds) (1991). *Talk and Learning 5–16: An In-service Pack on Oracy for Teachers*. Milton Keynes: Open University Press.

Halliday, M. (1994). *Functional Grammar*. London: Edward Arnold.

Levin, I. (1975/2004). *The Stepford Wives*. London: HarperCollins.

Martin, J. (1992). *English Text: System and structure*. Philadelphia: John Benjamin.

de Maupassant, G. (1903). *The Complete Short Stories of Guy de Maupassant*. London: W. J. Black.

Morgan, W. and Wyatt-Smith, C. (2000). 'Improper Accountability: Towards a theory of critical literacy and assessment.' *Assessment in Education, 7* (1).

QCA (1999). *Improving Writing at Key Stage 3 and 4*. London: QCA Publications.

Vygotsky, L. (1978a). *Mind in Society*. Cambridge, MA: MIT Press.

—(1978b). *Thought and Language*. Cambridge, MA: MIT Press.

Wyatt-Smith, C. and Murphy, J. (2001). 'What counts as writing assessment? An Australian move to mainstream critical literacy.' *English and Education*, 35(1) 12–32.

Wyndham, J. (1957). *The Midwich Cuckoos*. London: Penguin.

Index

Page references in italics denote a figure